JIM BUTCHER'S

The DRESDEN FILES

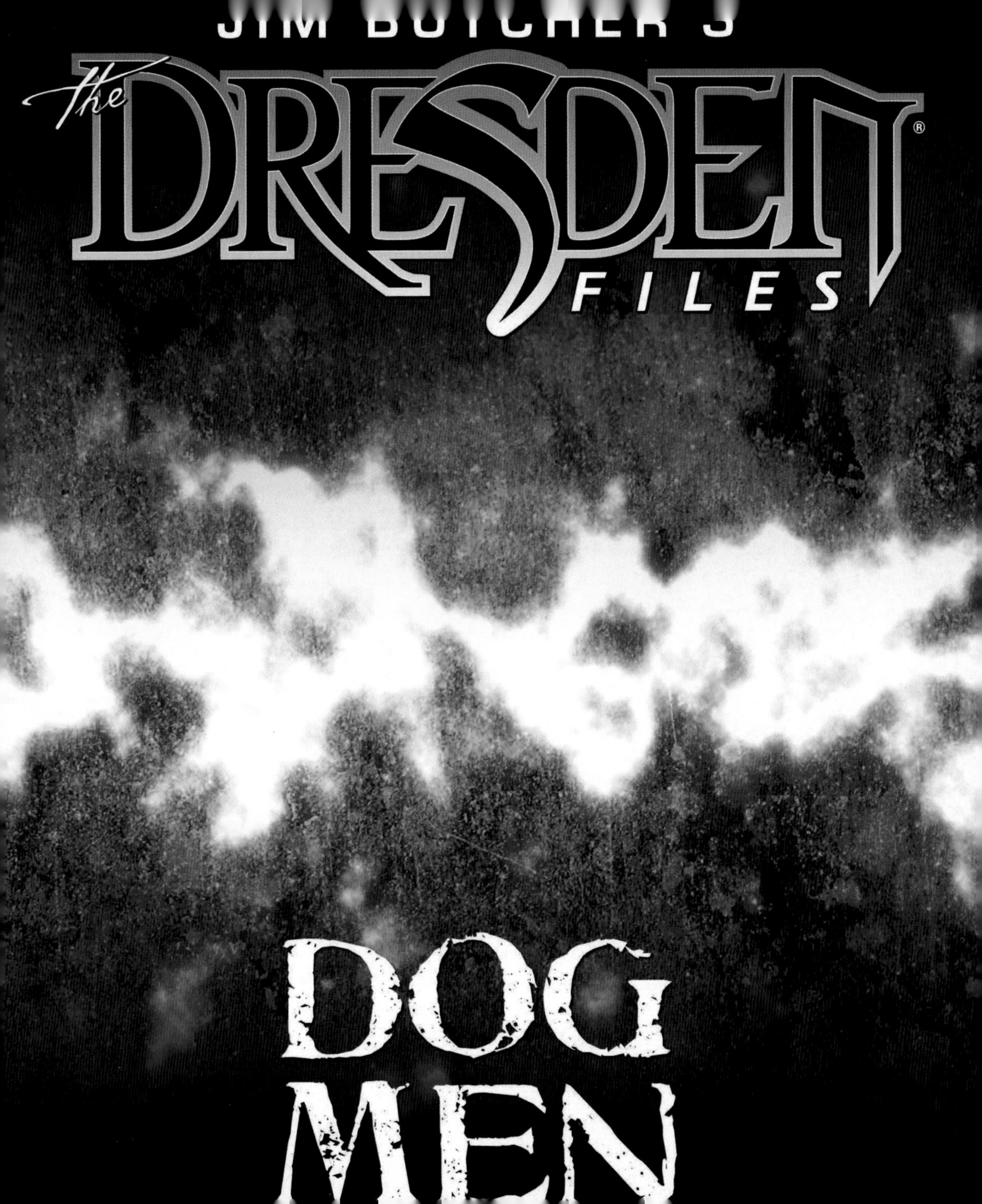

DOG MEN

DOG
MEN

It's been a rough few months for Chicago's only wizard for hire.

For Harry Dresden, putting his life on the line against the likes of the Red Court of Vampires and crazed demigods comes with the territory. But what he cannot abide - and what is taking a greater and greater toll on his psyche -- is the suffering his enemies inflict on the innocent. Especially those he cares for most. He's seen a lot of horror lately, the kind that can make a man feel powerless. When that happens, anger and guilt take root, growing like a cancer.

That's a dangerous state of being for a wizard, and a figure of great power has taken notice...

written by **MARK POWERS**

art by **DIEGO GALINDO**

colors by **MOHAN**

letters by **TOM NAPOLITANO**

collection cover by **DIEGO GALINDO**

edits by **ANTHONY MARQUES**

collection design by **GEOFF HARKINS**

thematic consultants: **PRISCILLA SPENCER, PAMELA ALEXANDER, MICHAEL ASHLEIGH FINN & FRED HICKS**

DYNAMITE®

Nick Barrucci, CEO / Publisher
Juan Collado, President /COO

Online at www.**DYNAMITE**.com | On Facebook /Dynamitecomics
On Instagram /Dynamitecomics | On Tumblr dynamitecomics.tumblr.com
On Twitter @dynamitecomics | On YouTube /Dynamitecomics

STANDARD EDITION ISBN-13: 978-1-5241-0544-0

PEFC Certified
Printed on paper from
sustainably managed

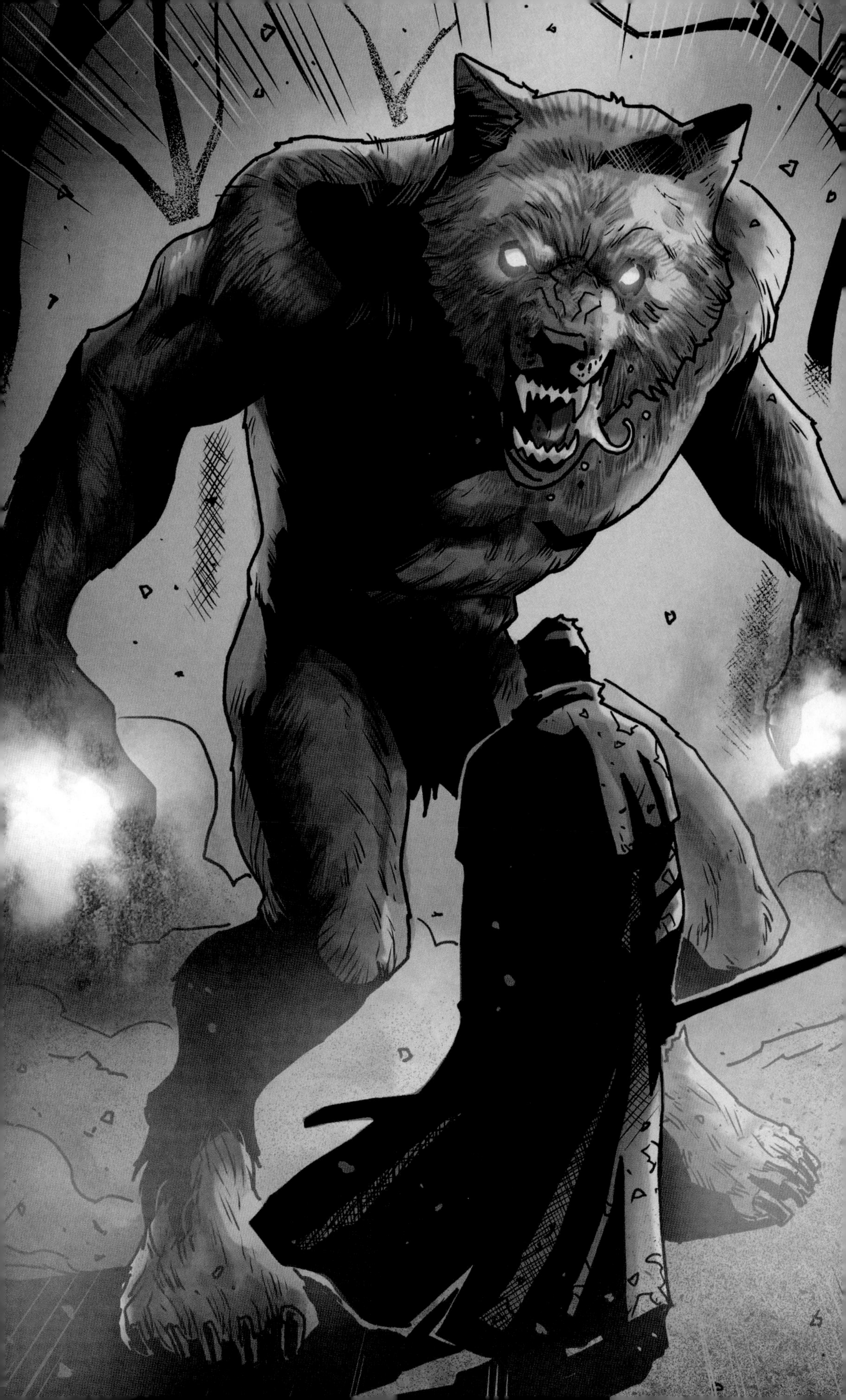

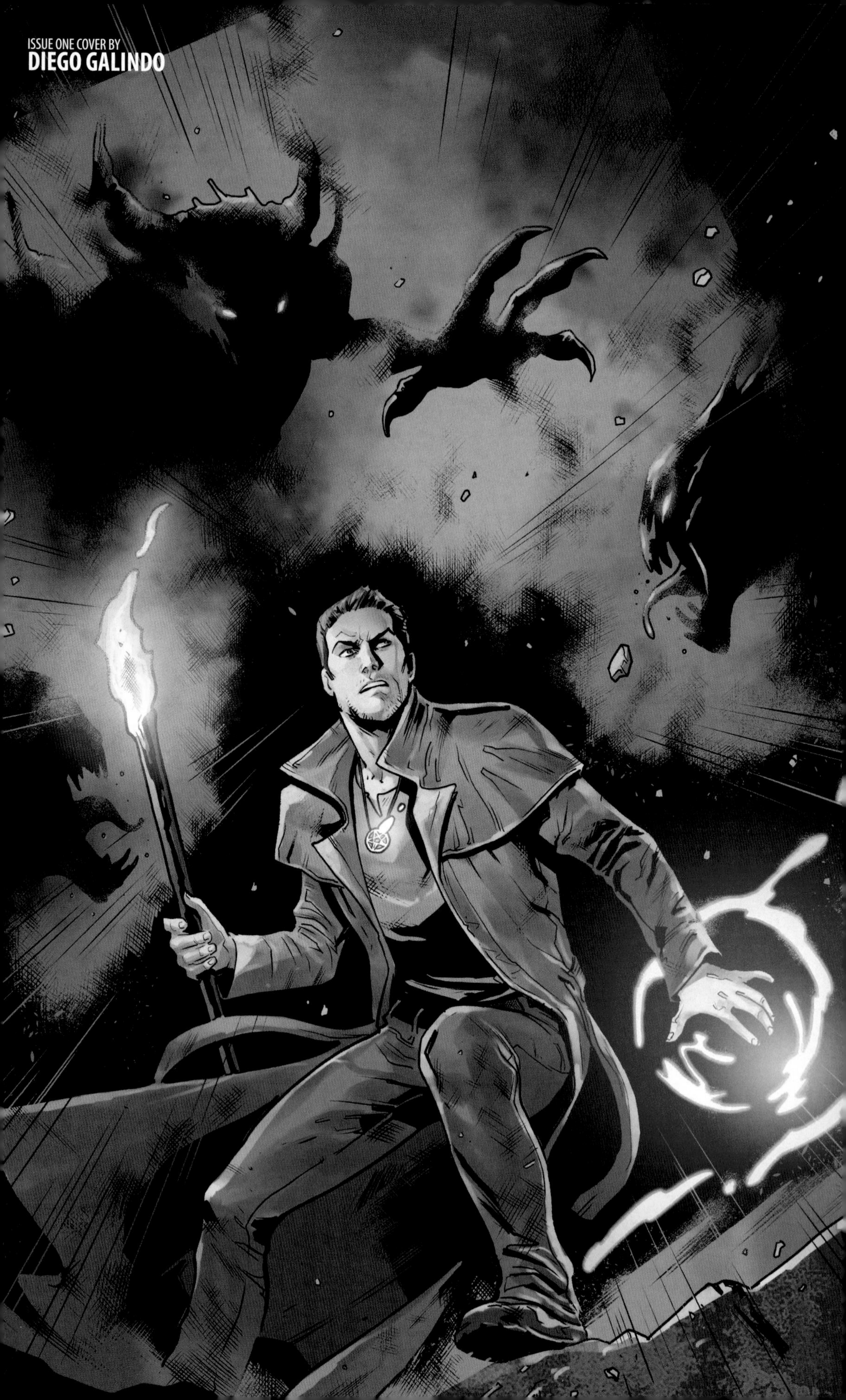

ISSUE ONE COVER BY
DIEGO GALINDO

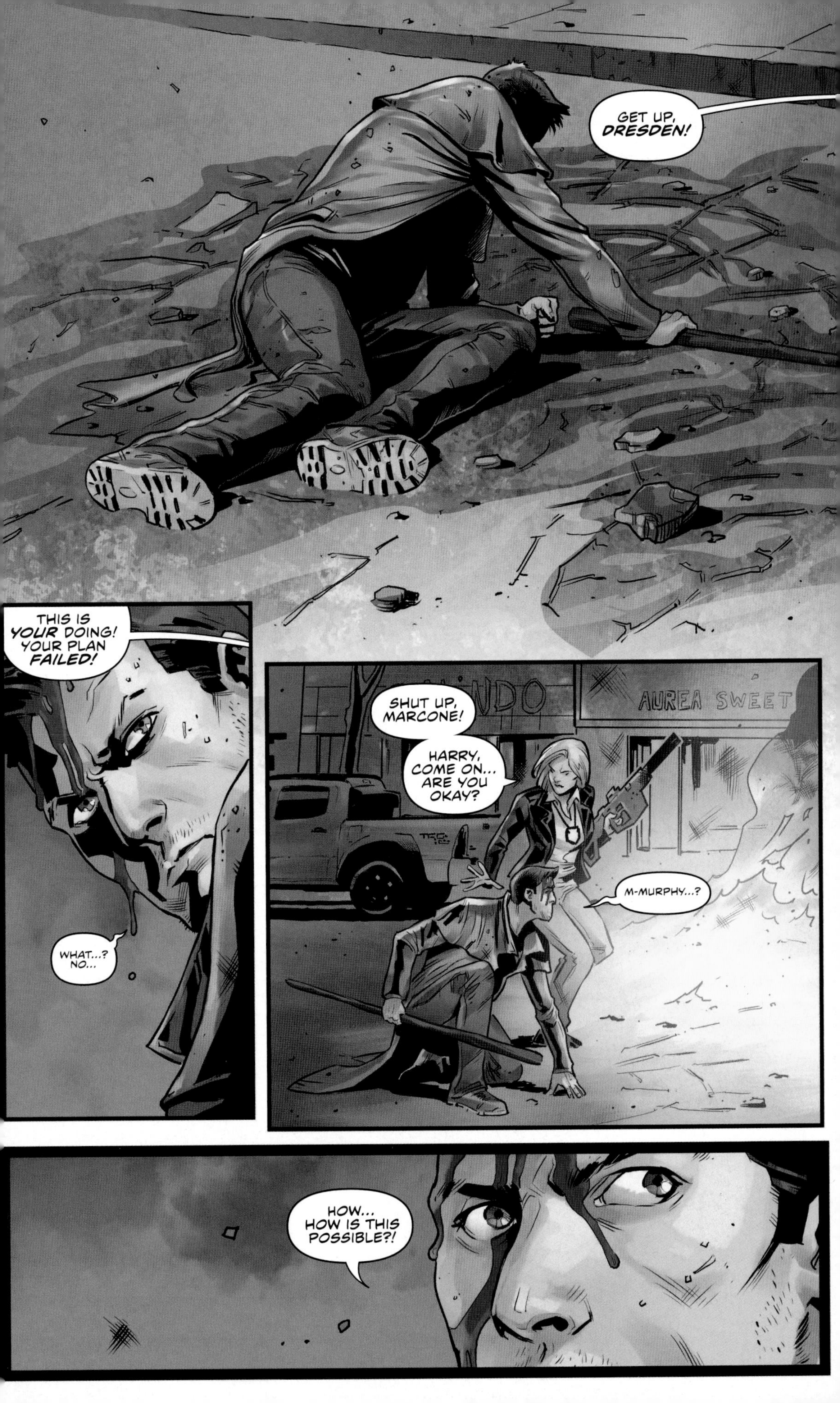

GET UP, DRESDEN!
THIS IS YOUR DOING! YOUR PLAN FAILED!
WHAT...? NO...
NDO
AUREA SWEET
SHUT UP, MARCONE!
HARRY, COME ON... ARE YOU OKAY?
M-MURPHY...?
HOW... HOW IS THIS POSSIBLE?!

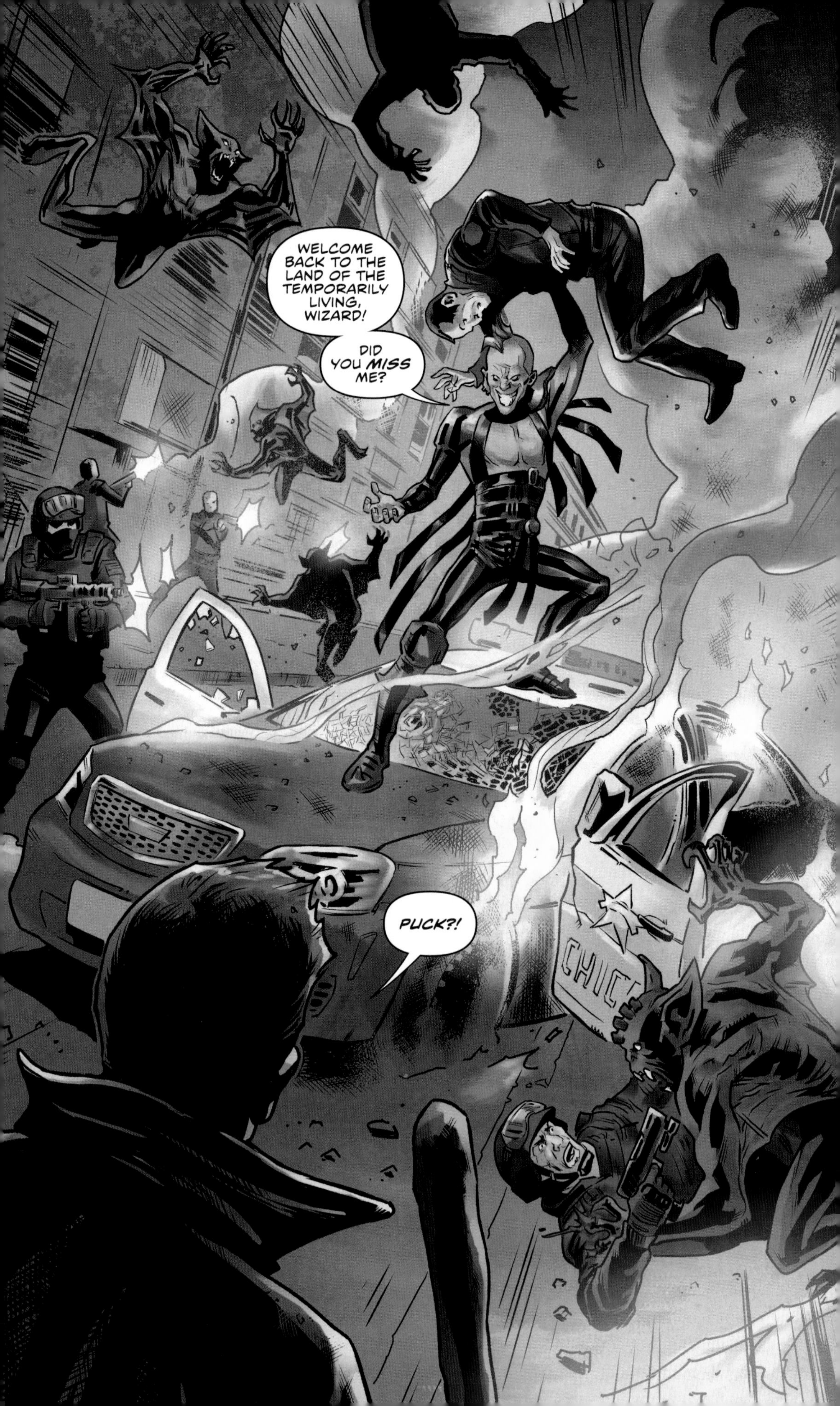
WELCOME BACK TO THE LAND OF THE TEMPORARILY LIVING, WIZARD!
DID YOU MISS ME?
PUCK?!
CHIC

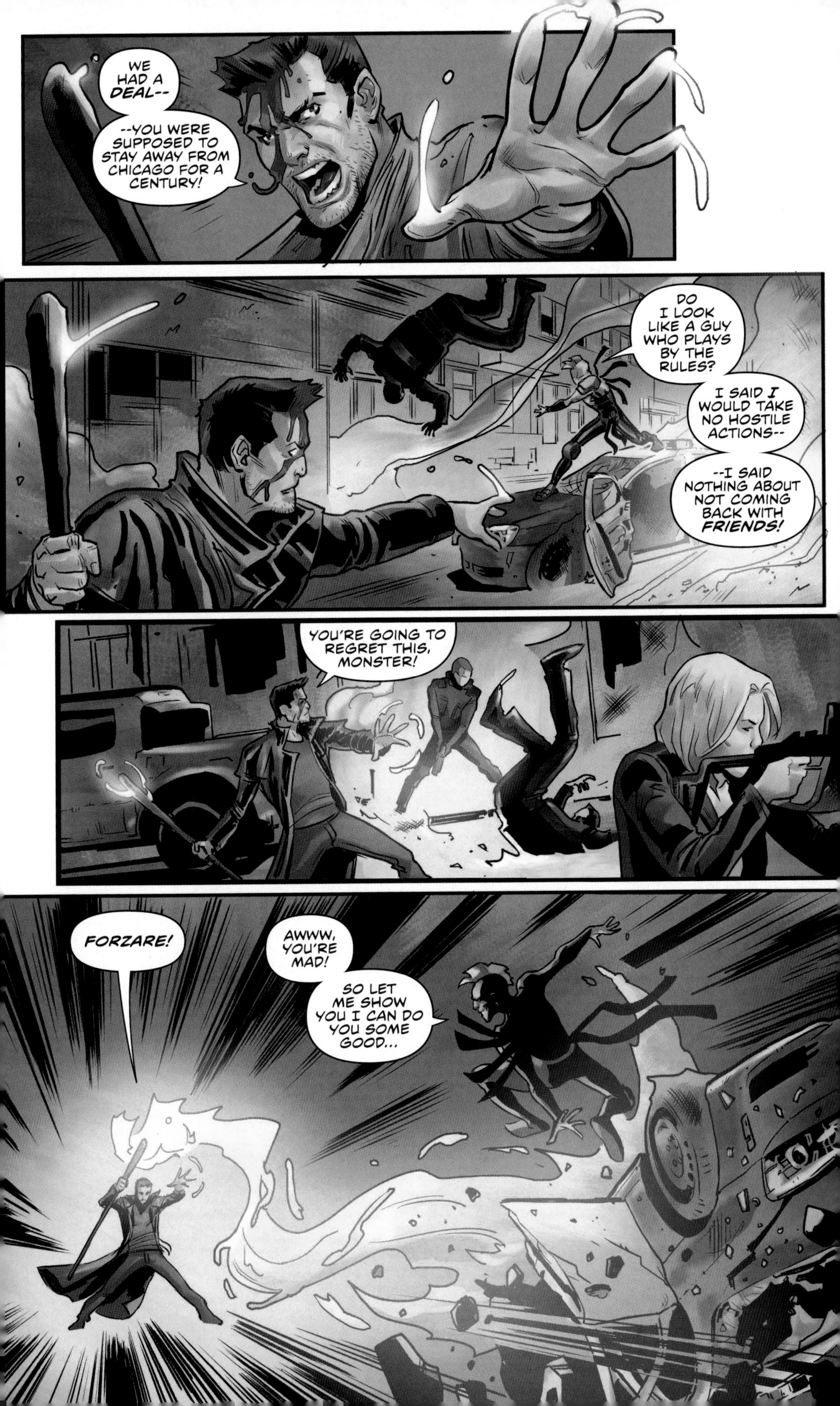

WE HAD A DEAL--
--YOU WERE SUPPOSED TO STAY AWAY FROM CHICAGO FOR A CENTURY!
DO I LOOK LIKE A GUY WHO PLAYS BY THE RULES?
I SAID I WOULD TAKE NO HOSTILE ACTIONS--
--I SAID NOTHING ABOUT NOT COMING BACK WITH FRIENDS!
YOU'RE GOING TO REGRET THIS, MONSTER!
FORZARE!
AWWW, YOU'RE MAD!
SO LET ME SHOW YOU I CAN DO YOU SOME GOOD...

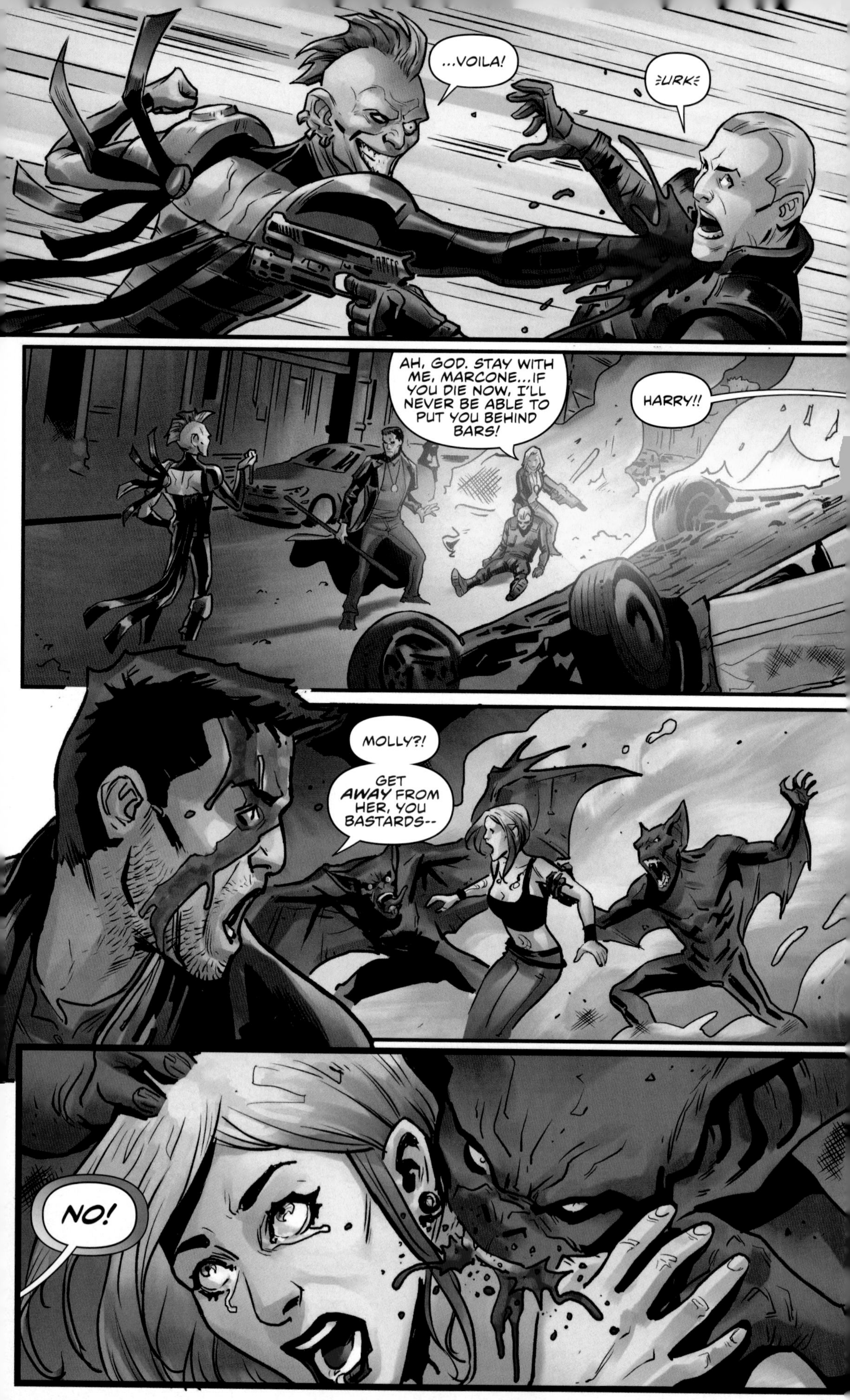
...VOILA!
URK
AH, GOD. STAY WITH ME, MARCONE...IF YOU DIE NOW, I'LL NEVER BE ABLE TO PUT YOU BEHIND BARS!
HARRY!!
MOLLY?!
GET *AWAY* FROM HER, YOU BASTARDS--
NO!

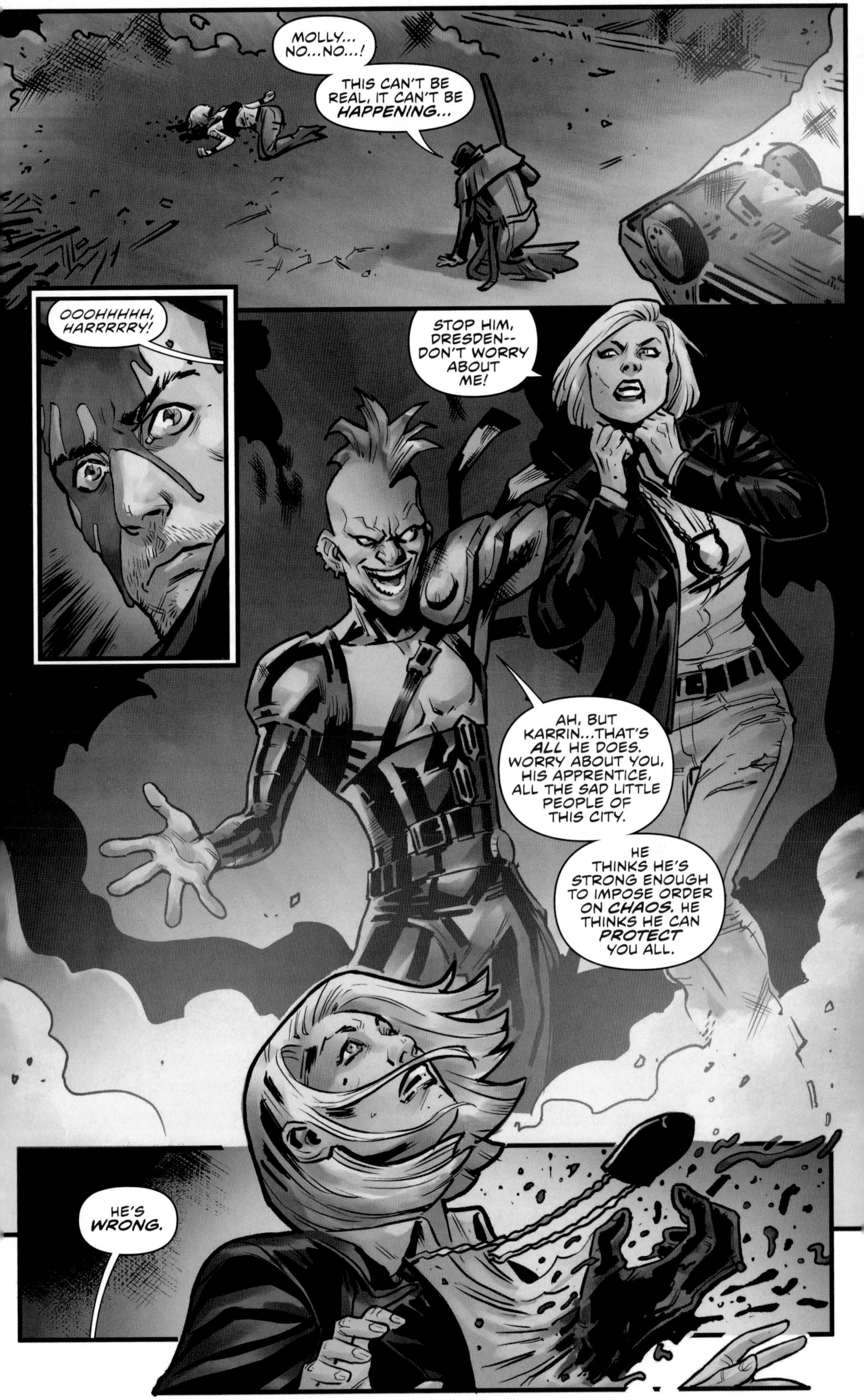
MOLLY... NO...NO...!
THIS CAN'T BE REAL, IT CAN'T BE HAPPENING...
OOOHHHHH, HARRRRRY!
STOP HIM, DRESDEN-- DON'T WORRY ABOUT ME!
AH, BUT KARRIN...THAT'S ALL HE DOES. WORRY ABOUT YOU, HIS APPRENTICE, ALL THE SAD LITTLE PEOPLE OF THIS CITY.
HE THINKS HE'S STRONG ENOUGH TO IMPOSE ORDER ON CHAOS. HE THINKS HE CAN PROTECT YOU ALL.
HE'S WRONG.

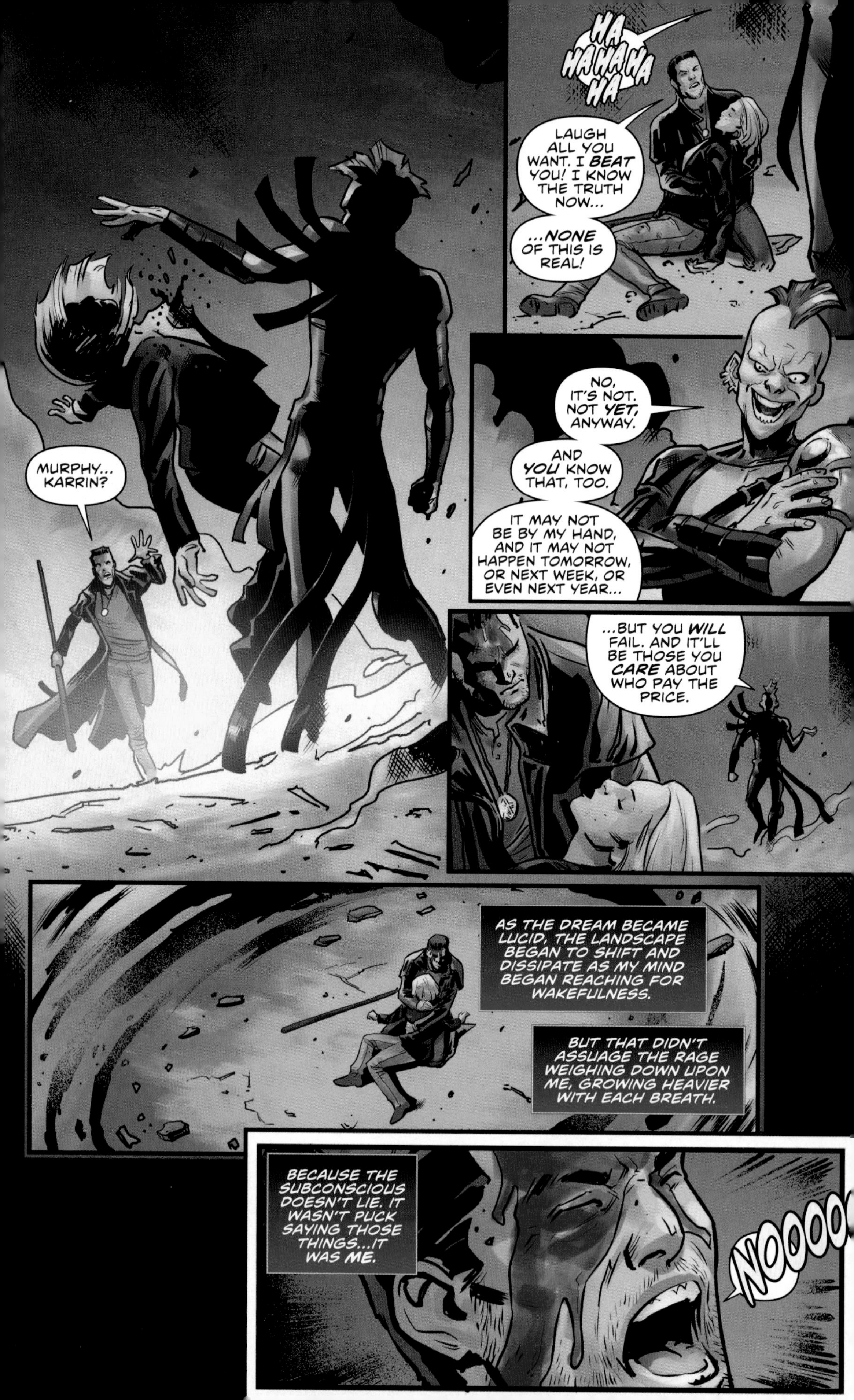
MURPHY... KARRIN?
HA HA HA HA HA HA
LAUGH ALL YOU WANT. I BEAT YOU! I KNOW THE TRUTH NOW...
...NONE OF THIS IS REAL!
NO, IT'S NOT. NOT YET, ANYWAY.
AND YOU KNOW THAT, TOO.
IT MAY NOT BE BY MY HAND, AND IT MAY NOT HAPPEN TOMORROW, OR NEXT WEEK, OR EVEN NEXT YEAR...
...BUT YOU WILL FAIL. AND IT'LL BE THOSE YOU CARE ABOUT WHO PAY THE PRICE.
AS THE DREAM BECAME LUCID, THE LANDSCAPE BEGAN TO SHIFT AND DISSIPATE AS MY MIND BEGAN REACHING FOR WAKEFULNESS.
BUT THAT DIDN'T ASSUAGE THE RAGE WEIGHING DOWN UPON ME, GROWING HEAVIER WITH EACH BREATH.
BECAUSE THE SUBCONSCIOUS DOESN'T LIE. IT WASN'T PUCK SAYING THOSE THINGS...IT WAS ME.
NOOOO

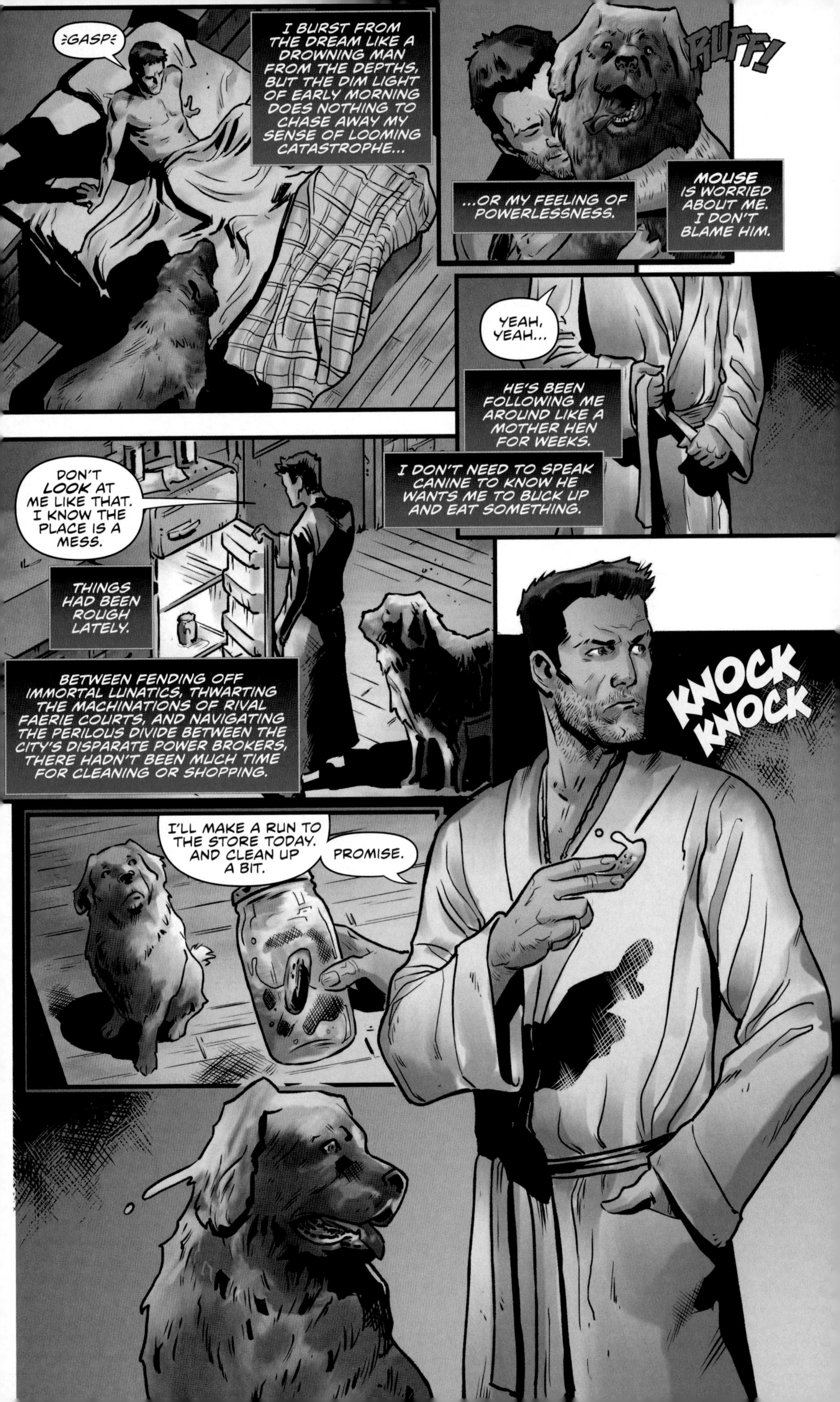

GASP
I BURST FROM THE DREAM LIKE A DROWNING MAN FROM THE DEPTHS, BUT THE DIM LIGHT OF EARLY MORNING DOES NOTHING TO CHASE AWAY MY SENSE OF LOOMING CATASTROPHE...
RUFF!
...OR MY FEELING OF POWERLESSNESS.
MOUSE IS WORRIED ABOUT ME. I DON'T BLAME HIM.
YEAH, YEAH...
HE'S BEEN FOLLOWING ME AROUND LIKE A MOTHER HEN FOR WEEKS.
I DON'T NEED TO SPEAK CANINE TO KNOW HE WANTS ME TO BUCK UP AND EAT SOMETHING.
DON'T LOOK AT ME LIKE THAT. I KNOW THE PLACE IS A MESS.
THINGS HAD BEEN ROUGH LATELY.
BETWEEN FENDING OFF IMMORTAL LUNATICS, THWARTING THE MACHINATIONS OF RIVAL FAERIE COURTS, AND NAVIGATING THE PERILOUS DIVIDE BETWEEN THE CITY'S DISPARATE POWER BROKERS, THERE HADN'T BEEN MUCH TIME FOR CLEANING OR SHOPPING.
KNOCK KNOCK
I'LL MAKE A RUN TO THE STORE TODAY. AND CLEAN UP A BIT.
PROMISE.

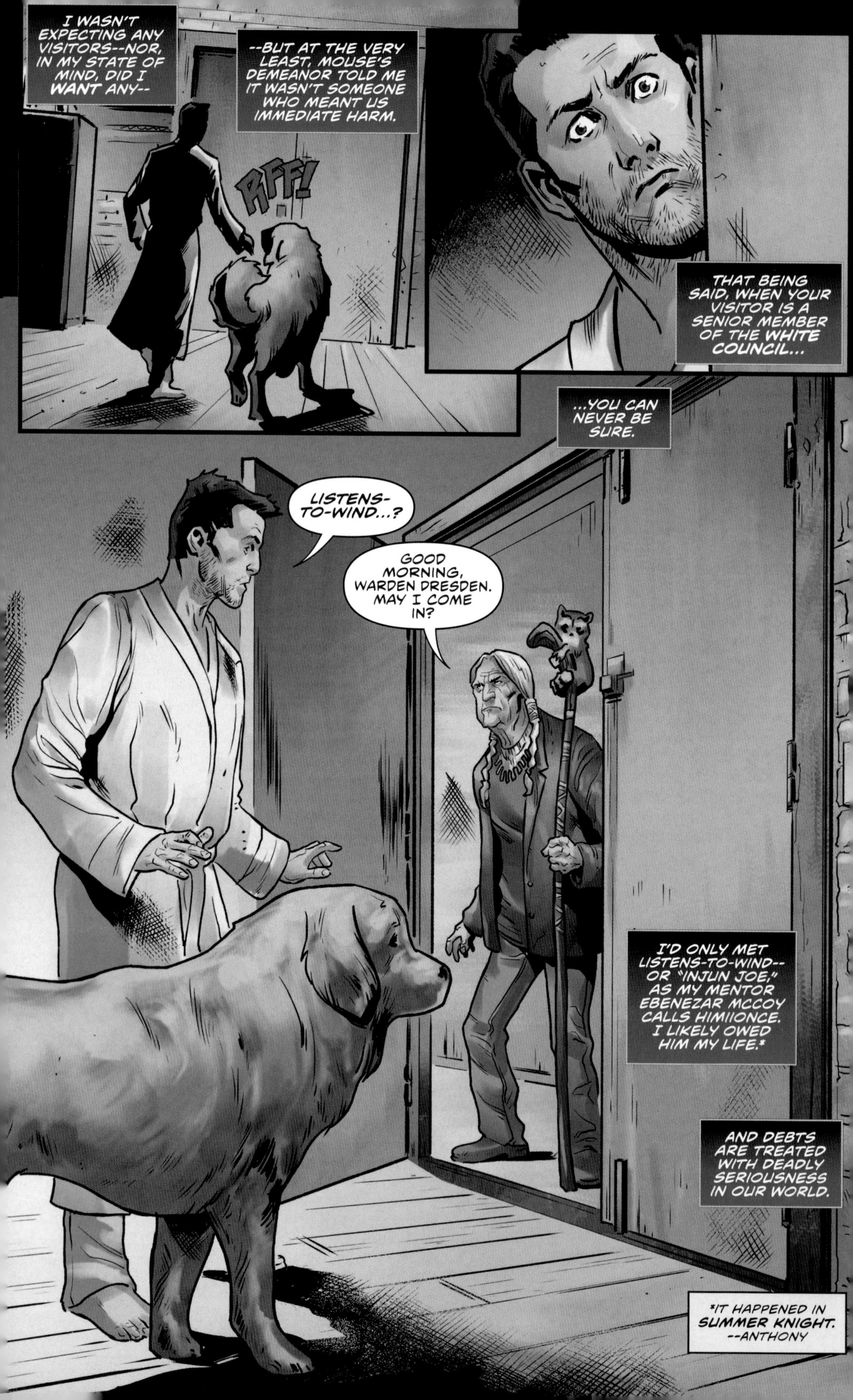
I WASN'T EXPECTING ANY VISITORS--NOR, IN MY STATE OF MIND, DID I **WANT** ANY--
--BUT AT THE VERY LEAST, MOUSE'S DEMEANOR TOLD ME IT WASN'T SOMEONE WHO MEANT US IMMEDIATE HARM.
RFF!
THAT BEING SAID, WHEN YOUR VISITOR IS A SENIOR MEMBER OF THE **WHITE COUNCIL**...
...YOU CAN NEVER BE SURE.
LISTENS-TO-WIND...?
GOOD MORNING, WARDEN DRESDEN. MAY I COME IN?
I'D ONLY MET LISTENS-TO-WIND--OR "INJUN JOE," AS MY MENTOR EBENEZAR MCCOY CALLS HIMIIONCE. I LIKELY OWED HIM MY LIFE.*
AND DEBTS ARE TREATED WITH DEADLY SERIOUSNESS IN OUR WORLD.
*IT HAPPENED IN **SUMMER KNIGHT.** --ANTHONY

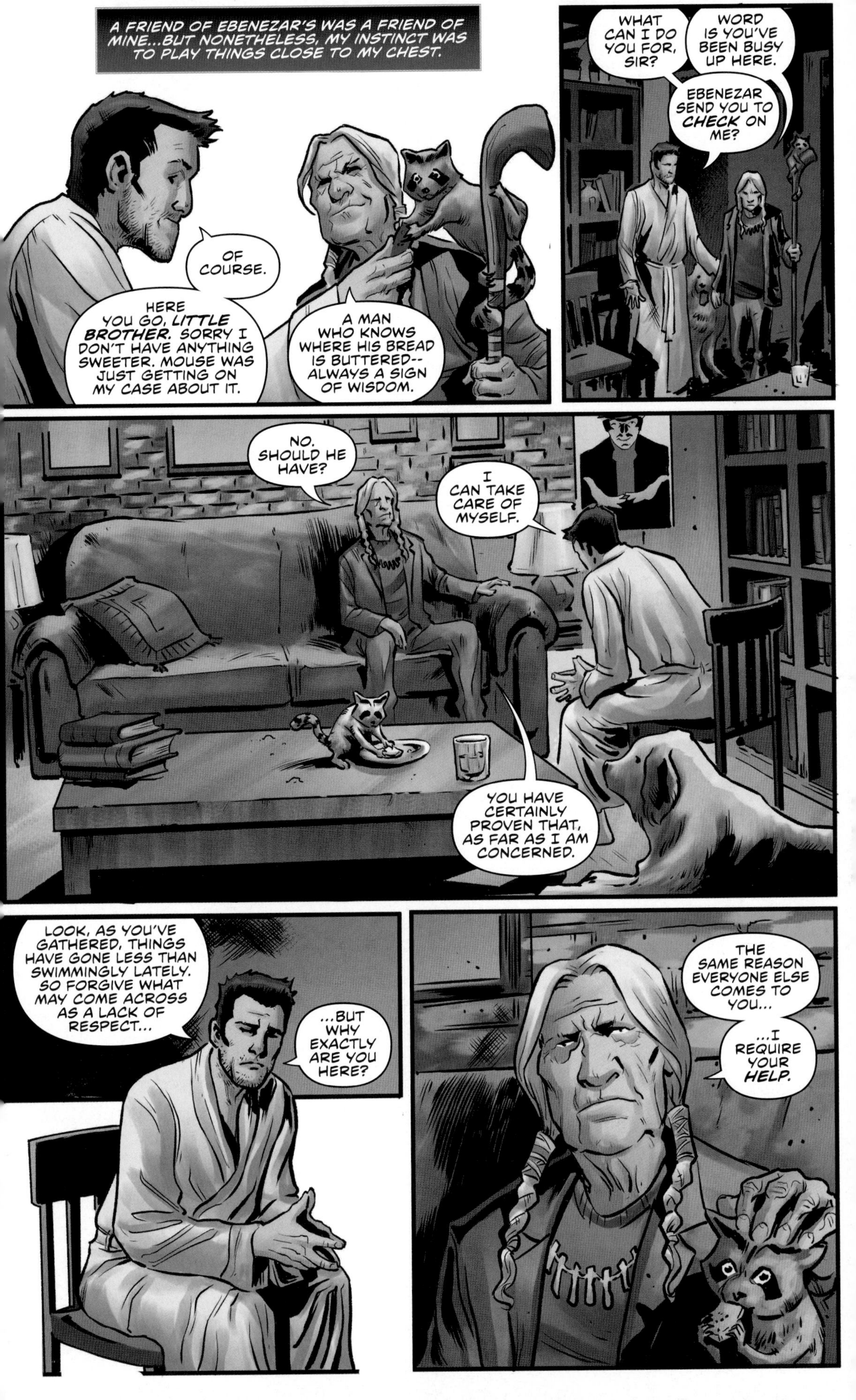
A FRIEND OF EBENEZAR'S WAS A FRIEND OF MINE...BUT NONETHELESS, MY INSTINCT WAS TO PLAY THINGS CLOSE TO MY CHEST.
OF COURSE.
HERE YOU GO, LITTLE BROTHER. SORRY I DON'T HAVE ANYTHING SWEETER. MOUSE WAS JUST GETTING ON MY CASE ABOUT IT.
A MAN WHO KNOWS WHERE HIS BREAD IS BUTTERED-- ALWAYS A SIGN OF WISDOM.
WHAT CAN I DO YOU FOR, SIR?
WORD IS YOU'VE BEEN BUSY UP HERE.
EBENEZAR SEND YOU TO CHECK ON ME?
NO. SHOULD HE HAVE?
I CAN TAKE CARE OF MYSELF.
YOU HAVE CERTAINLY PROVEN THAT, AS FAR AS I AM CONCERNED.
LOOK, AS YOU'VE GATHERED, THINGS HAVE GONE LESS THAN SWIMMINGLY LATELY. SO FORGIVE WHAT MAY COME ACROSS AS A LACK OF RESPECT...
...BUT WHY EXACTLY ARE YOU HERE?
THE SAME REASON EVERYONE ELSE COMES TO YOU...
...I REQUIRE YOUR HELP.

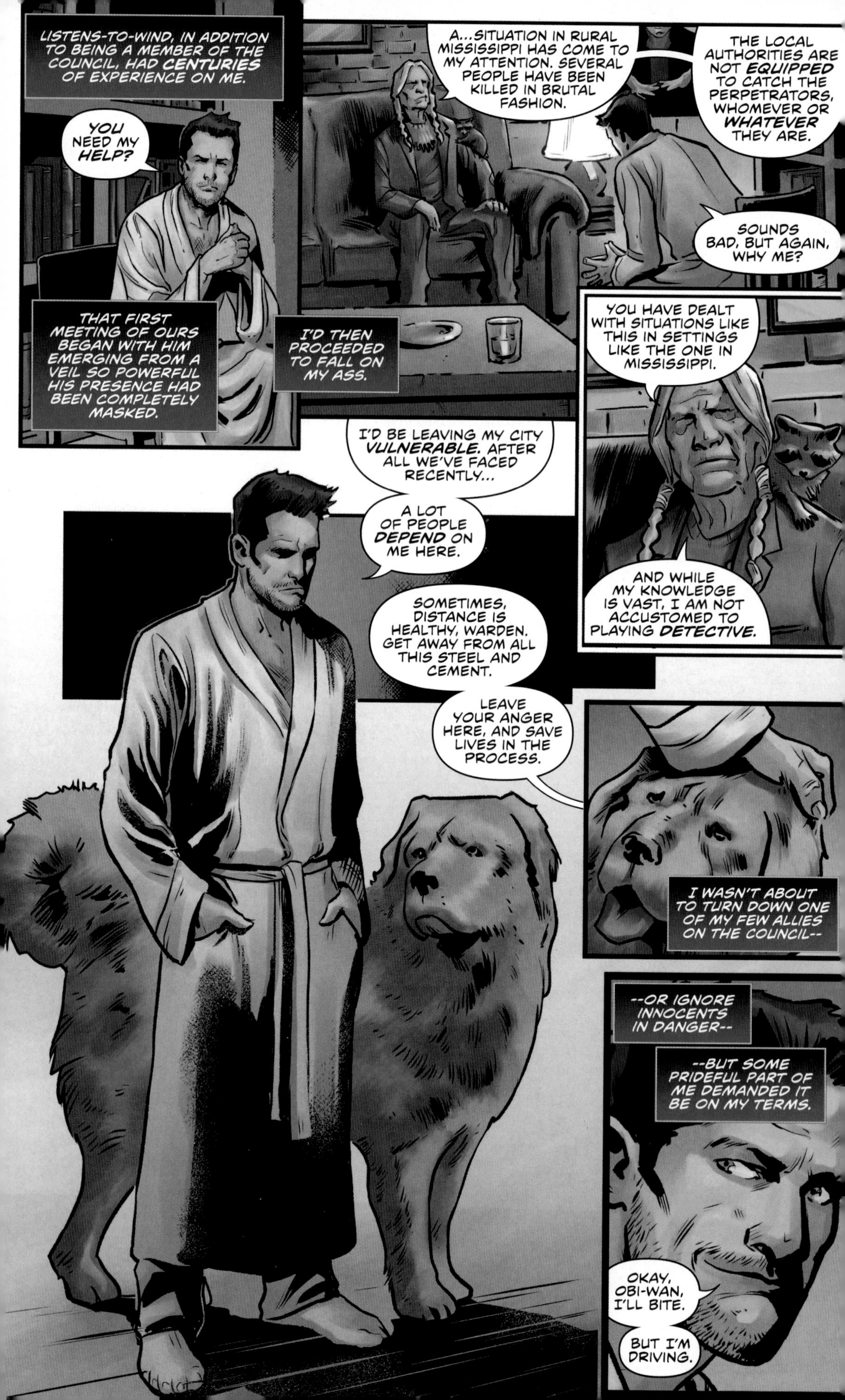
LISTENS-TO-WIND, IN ADDITION TO BEING A MEMBER OF THE COUNCIL, HAD CENTURIES OF EXPERIENCE ON ME.
YOU NEED MY HELP?
THAT FIRST MEETING OF OURS BEGAN WITH HIM EMERGING FROM A VEIL SO POWERFUL HIS PRESENCE HAD BEEN COMPLETELY MASKED.
I'D THEN PROCEEDED TO FALL ON MY ASS.
A...SITUATION IN RURAL MISSISSIPPI HAS COME TO MY ATTENTION. SEVERAL PEOPLE HAVE BEEN KILLED IN BRUTAL FASHION.
THE LOCAL AUTHORITIES ARE NOT EQUIPPED TO CATCH THE PERPETRATORS, WHOMEVER OR WHATEVER THEY ARE.
SOUNDS BAD, BUT AGAIN, WHY ME?
YOU HAVE DEALT WITH SITUATIONS LIKE THIS IN SETTINGS LIKE THE ONE IN MISSISSIPPI.
AND WHILE MY KNOWLEDGE IS VAST, I AM NOT ACCUSTOMED TO PLAYING DETECTIVE.
I'D BE LEAVING MY CITY VULNERABLE. AFTER ALL WE'VE FACED RECENTLY...
A LOT OF PEOPLE DEPEND ON ME HERE.
SOMETIMES, DISTANCE IS HEALTHY, WARDEN. GET AWAY FROM ALL THIS STEEL AND CEMENT.
LEAVE YOUR ANGER HERE, AND SAVE LIVES IN THE PROCESS.
I WASN'T ABOUT TO TURN DOWN ONE OF MY FEW ALLIES ON THE COUNCIL--
--OR IGNORE INNOCENTS IN DANGER--
--BUT SOME PRIDEFUL PART OF ME DEMANDED IT BE ON MY TERMS.
OKAY, OBI-WAN, I'LL BITE.
BUT I'M DRIVING.

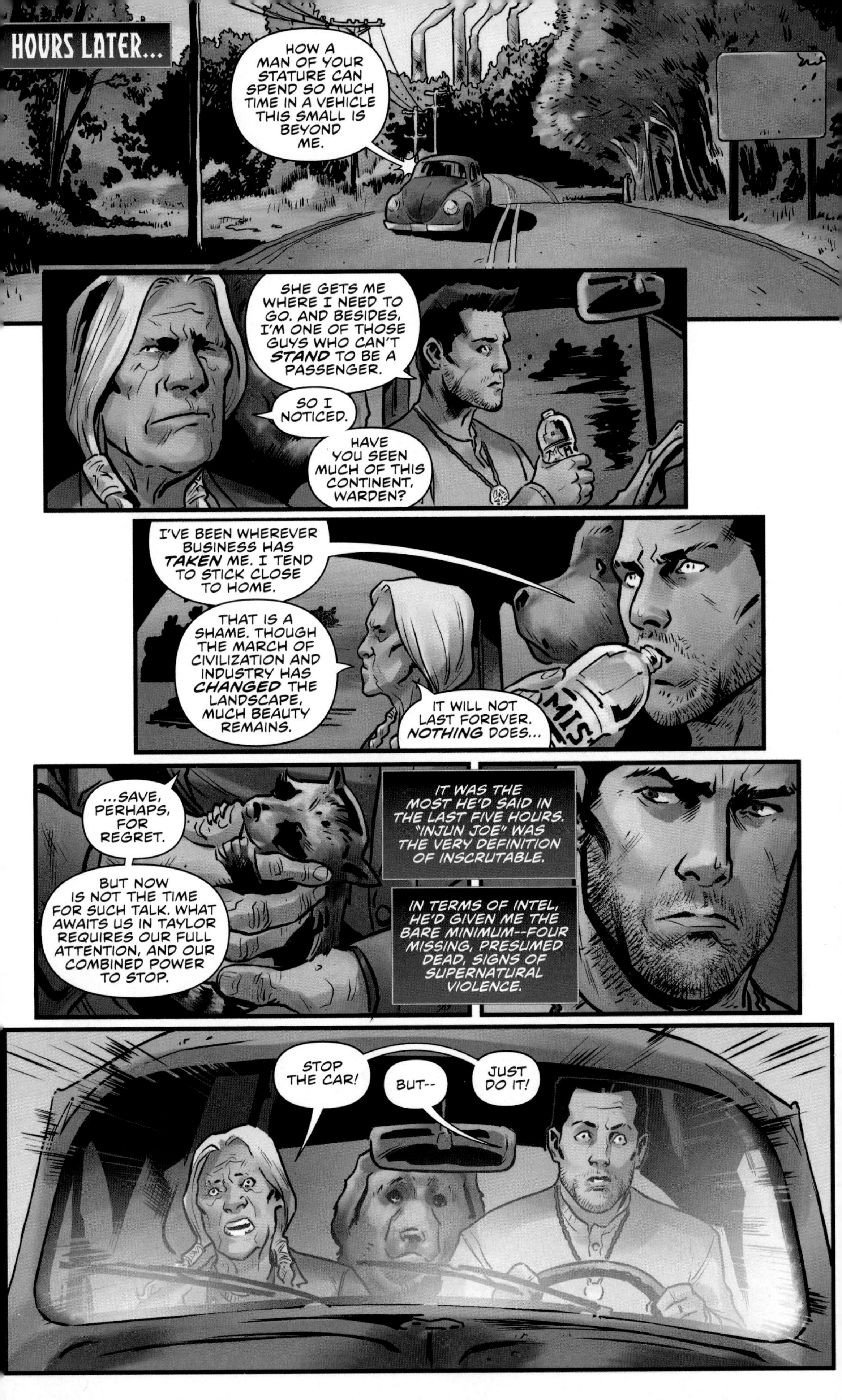
HOURS LATER...
HOW A MAN OF YOUR STATURE CAN SPEND SO MUCH TIME IN A VEHICLE THIS SMALL IS BEYOND ME.
SHE GETS ME WHERE I NEED TO GO. AND BESIDES, I'M ONE OF THOSE GUYS WHO CAN'T *STAND* TO BE A PASSENGER.
SO I NOTICED.
HAVE YOU SEEN MUCH OF THIS CONTINENT, WARDEN?
I'VE BEEN WHEREVER BUSINESS HAS *TAKEN* ME. I TEND TO STICK CLOSE TO HOME.
THAT IS A SHAME. THOUGH THE MARCH OF CIVILIZATION AND INDUSTRY HAS *CHANGED* THE LANDSCAPE, MUCH BEAUTY REMAINS.
IT WILL NOT LAST FOREVER. *NOTHING* DOES...
...SAVE, PERHAPS, FOR REGRET.
BUT NOW IS NOT THE TIME FOR SUCH TALK. WHAT AWAITS US IN TAYLOR REQUIRES OUR FULL ATTENTION, AND OUR COMBINED POWER TO STOP.
IT WAS THE MOST HE'D SAID IN THE LAST FIVE HOURS. "INJUN JOE" WAS THE VERY DEFINITION OF INSCRUTABLE.
IN TERMS OF INTEL, HE'D GIVEN ME THE BARE MINIMUM--FOUR MISSING, PRESUMED DEAD, SIGNS OF SUPERNATURAL VIOLENCE.
STOP THE CAR!
BUT--
JUST DO IT!

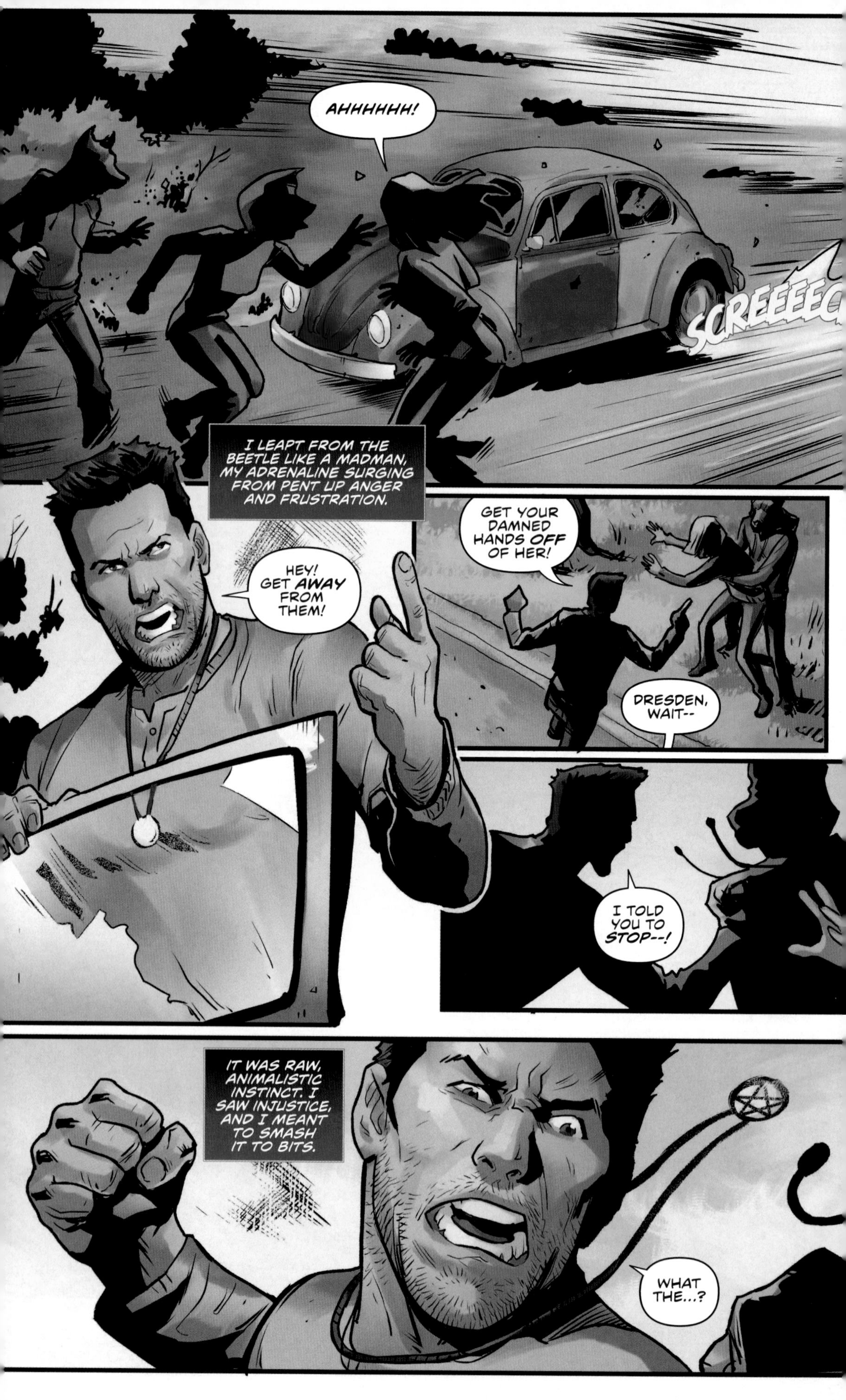
AHHHHHH!
SCREEEEG
I LEAPT FROM THE BEETLE LIKE A MADMAN, MY ADRENALINE SURGING FROM PENT UP ANGER AND FRUSTRATION.
HEY! GET AWAY FROM THEM!
GET YOUR DAMNED HANDS OFF OF HER!
DRESDEN, WAIT--
I TOLD YOU TO STOP--!
IT WAS RAW, ANIMALISTIC INSTINCT. I SAW INJUSTICE, AND I MEANT TO SMASH IT TO BITS.
WHAT THE...?

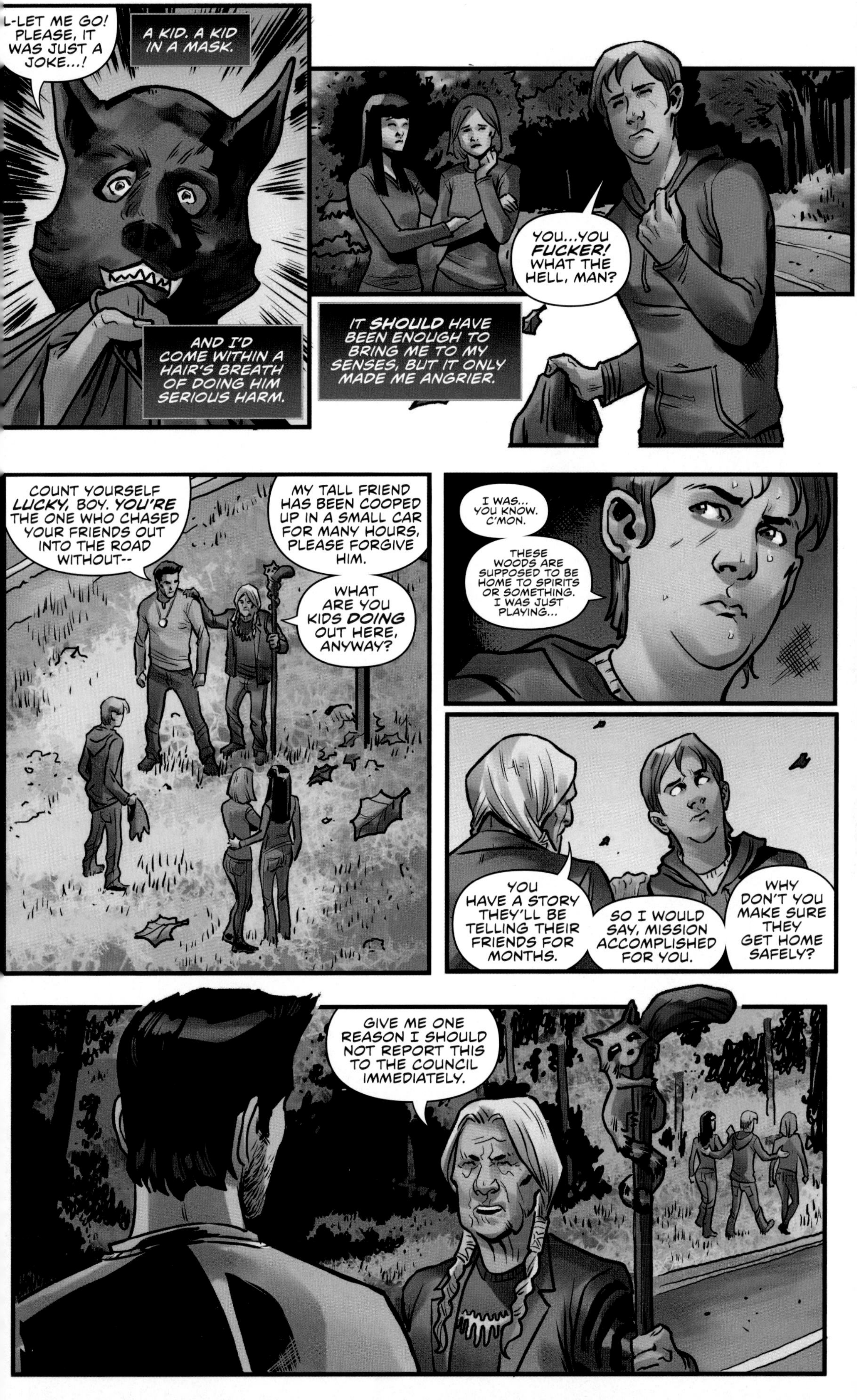
L-LET ME GO! PLEASE, IT WAS JUST A JOKE...!
A KID. A KID IN A MASK.
AND I'D COME WITHIN A HAIR'S BREATH OF DOING HIM SERIOUS HARM.
YOU...YOU FUCKER! WHAT THE HELL, MAN?
IT SHOULD HAVE BEEN ENOUGH TO BRING ME TO MY SENSES, BUT IT ONLY MADE ME ANGRIER.
COUNT YOURSELF LUCKY, BOY. YOU'RE THE ONE WHO CHASED YOUR FRIENDS OUT INTO THE ROAD WITHOUT--
MY TALL FRIEND HAS BEEN COOPED UP IN A SMALL CAR FOR MANY HOURS, PLEASE FORGIVE HIM.
WHAT ARE YOU KIDS DOING OUT HERE, ANYWAY?
I WAS... YOU KNOW. C'MON.
THESE WOODS ARE SUPPOSED TO BE HOME TO SPIRITS OR SOMETHING. I WAS JUST PLAYING...
YOU HAVE A STORY THEY'LL BE TELLING THEIR FRIENDS FOR MONTHS.
SO I WOULD SAY, MISSION ACCOMPLISHED FOR YOU.
WHY DON'T YOU MAKE SURE THEY GET HOME SAFELY?
GIVE ME ONE REASON I SHOULD NOT REPORT THIS TO THE COUNCIL IMMEDIATELY.

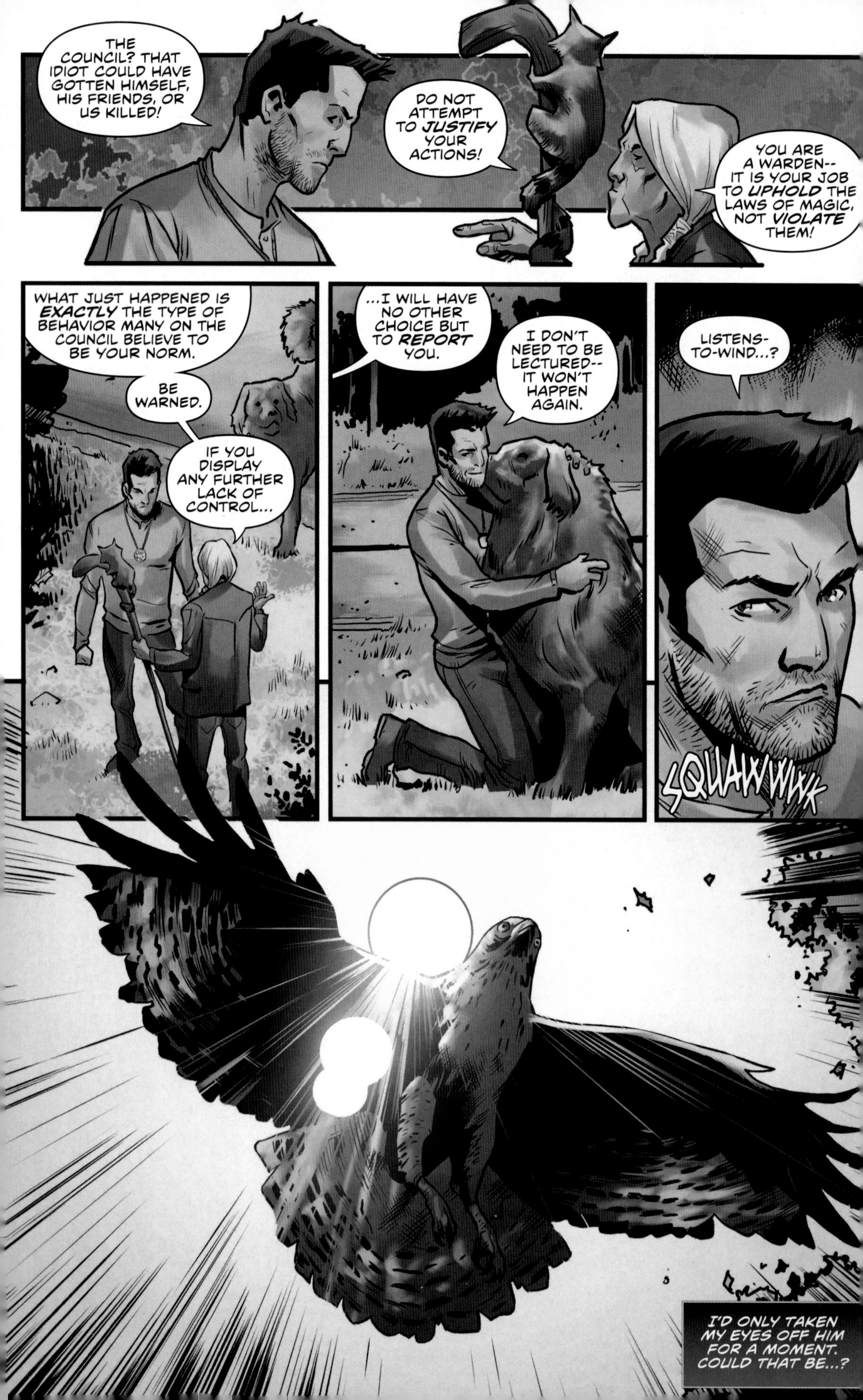
THE COUNCIL? THAT IDIOT COULD HAVE GOTTEN HIMSELF, HIS FRIENDS, OR US KILLED!
DO NOT ATTEMPT TO JUSTIFY YOUR ACTIONS!
YOU ARE A WARDEN-- IT IS YOUR JOB TO UPHOLD THE LAWS OF MAGIC, NOT VIOLATE THEM!
WHAT JUST HAPPENED IS EXACTLY THE TYPE OF BEHAVIOR MANY ON THE COUNCIL BELIEVE TO BE YOUR NORM.
BE WARNED.
IF YOU DISPLAY ANY FURTHER LACK OF CONTROL...
...I WILL HAVE NO OTHER CHOICE BUT TO REPORT YOU.
I DON'T NEED TO BE LECTURED-- IT WON'T HAPPEN AGAIN.
LISTENS-TO-WIND...?
SQUAWWWK
I'D ONLY TAKEN MY EYES OFF HIM FOR A MOMENT. COULD THAT BE...?

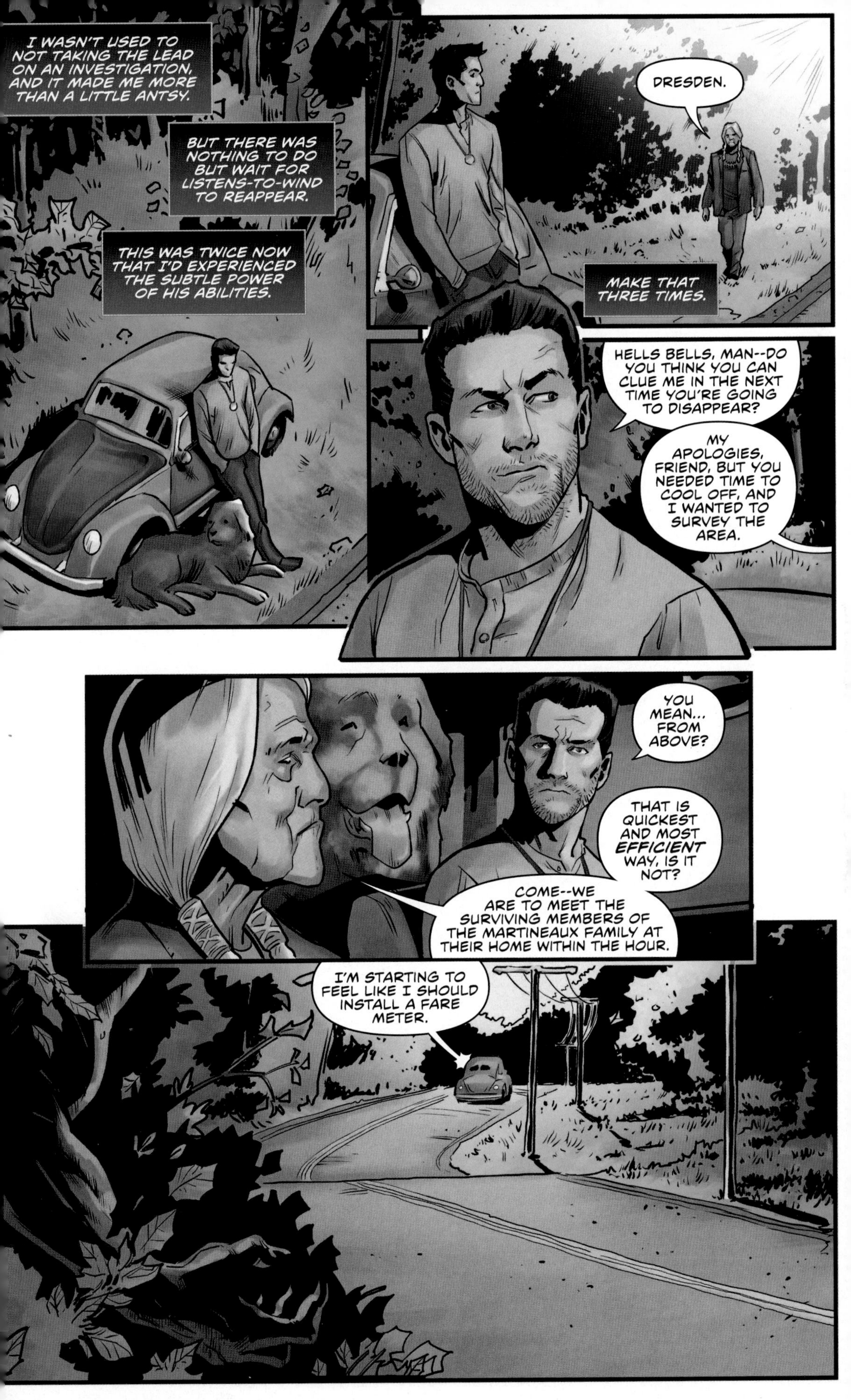
I WASN'T USED TO NOT TAKING THE LEAD ON AN INVESTIGATION, AND IT MADE ME MORE THAN A LITTLE ANTSY.
BUT THERE WAS NOTHING TO DO BUT WAIT FOR LISTENS-TO-WIND TO REAPPEAR.
THIS WAS TWICE NOW THAT I'D EXPERIENCED THE SUBTLE POWER OF HIS ABILITIES.
DRESDEN.
MAKE THAT THREE TIMES.
HELLS BELLS, MAN--DO YOU THINK YOU CAN CLUE ME IN THE NEXT TIME YOU'RE GOING TO DISAPPEAR?
MY APOLOGIES, FRIEND, BUT YOU NEEDED TIME TO COOL OFF, AND I WANTED TO SURVEY THE AREA.
YOU MEAN... FROM ABOVE?
THAT IS QUICKEST AND MOST *EFFICIENT* WAY, IS IT NOT?
COME--WE ARE TO MEET THE SURVIVING MEMBERS OF THE MARTINEAUX FAMILY AT THEIR HOME WITHIN THE HOUR.
I'M STARTING TO FEEL LIKE I SHOULD INSTALL A FARE METER.

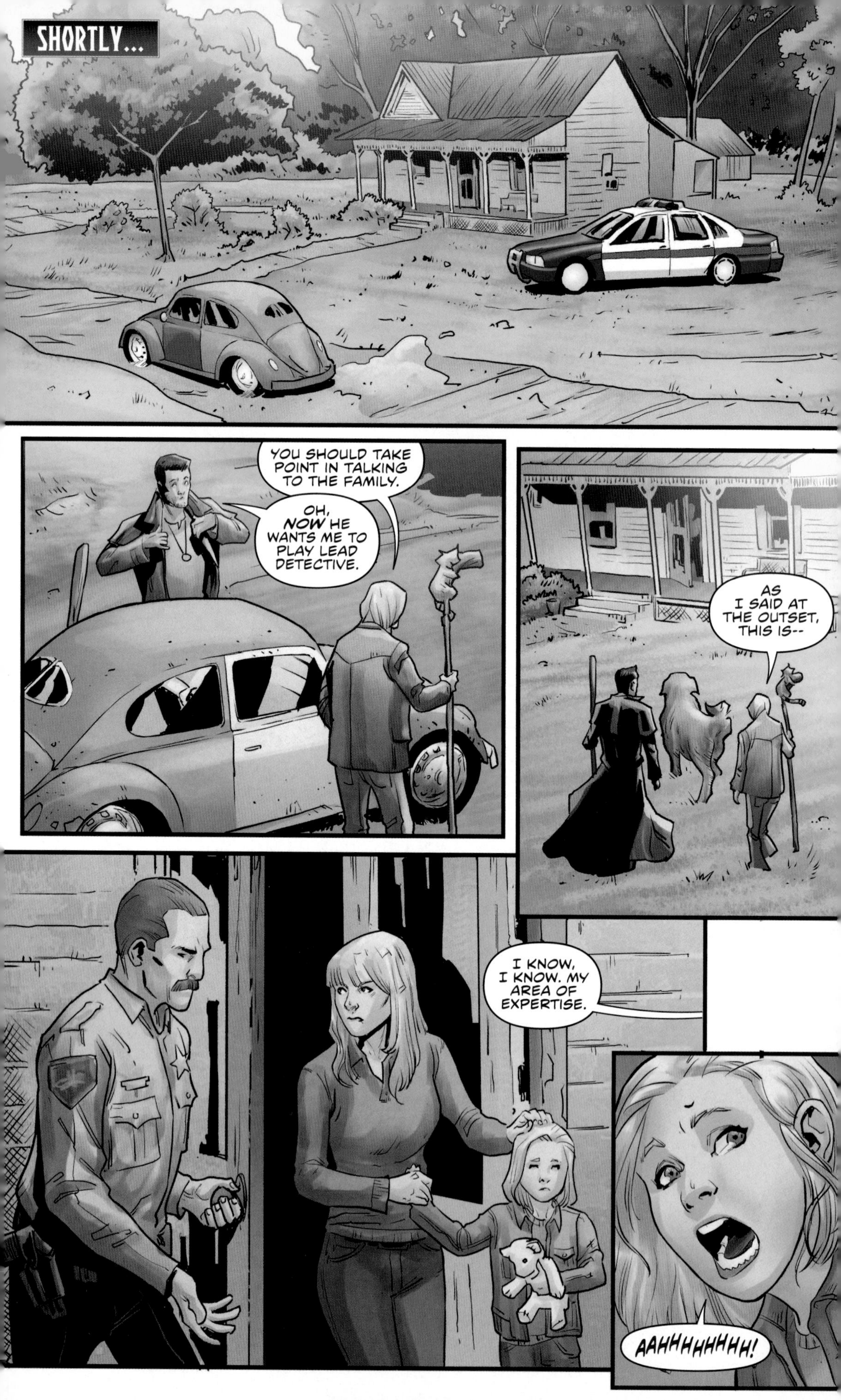
SHORTLY...
YOU SHOULD TAKE POINT IN TALKING TO THE FAMILY.
OH, *NOW* HE WANTS ME TO PLAY LEAD DETECTIVE.
AS I SAID AT THE OUTSET, THIS IS--
I KNOW, I KNOW. MY AREA OF EXPERTISE.
AAHHHHHHHH!

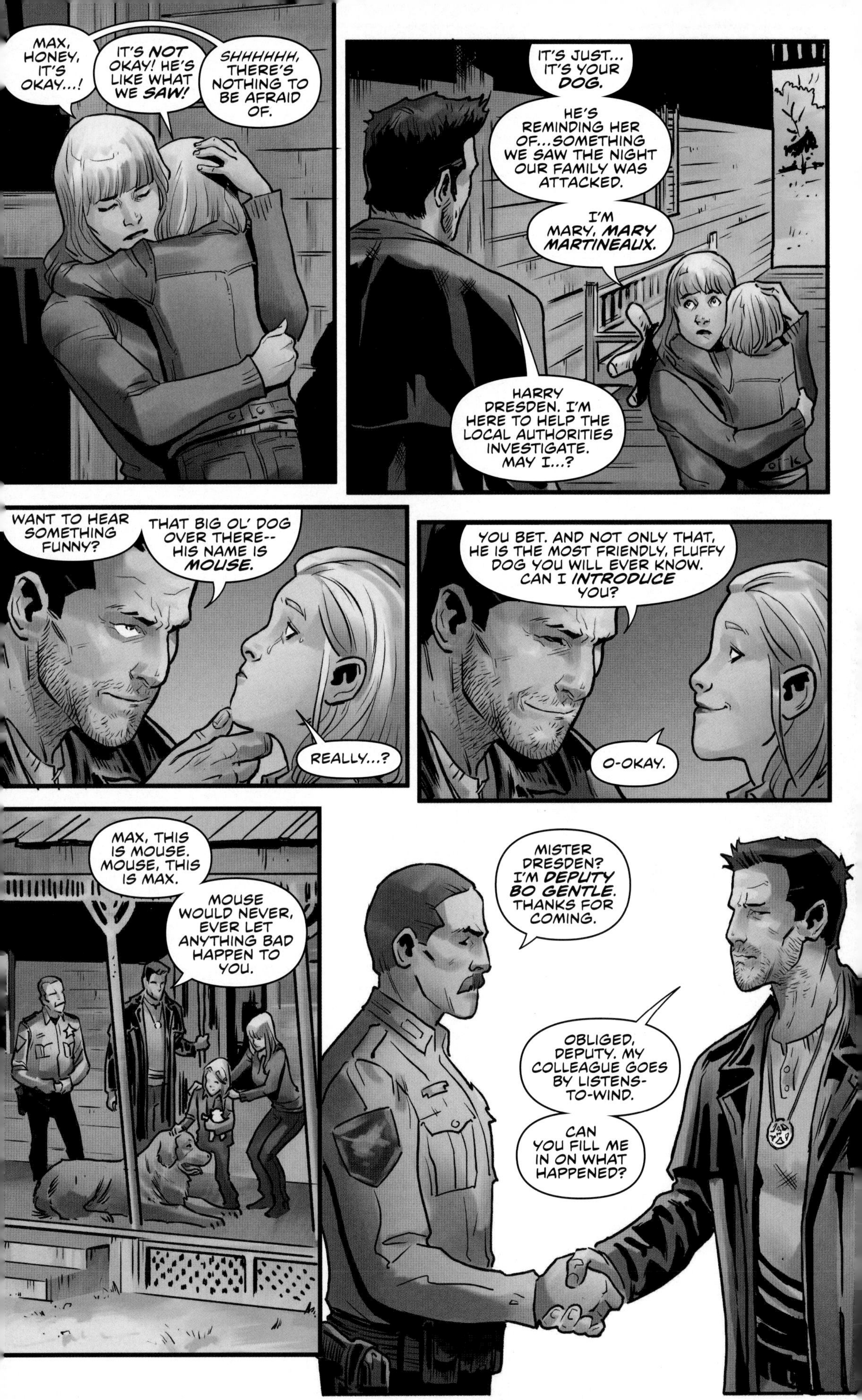
MAX, HONEY, IT'S OKAY...!
IT'S NOT OKAY! HE'S LIKE WHAT WE SAW!
SHHHHHH, THERE'S NOTHING TO BE AFRAID OF.
IT'S JUST... IT'S YOUR DOG.
HE'S REMINDING HER OF...SOMETHING WE SAW THE NIGHT OUR FAMILY WAS ATTACKED.
I'M MARY, MARY MARTINEAUX.
HARRY DRESDEN. I'M HERE TO HELP THE LOCAL AUTHORITIES INVESTIGATE. MAY I...?
WANT TO HEAR SOMETHING FUNNY?
THAT BIG OL' DOG OVER THERE-- HIS NAME IS MOUSE.
REALLY...?
YOU BET. AND NOT ONLY THAT, HE IS THE MOST FRIENDLY, FLUFFY DOG YOU WILL EVER KNOW. CAN I INTRODUCE YOU?
O-OKAY.
MAX, THIS IS MOUSE. MOUSE, THIS IS MAX.
MOUSE WOULD NEVER, EVER LET ANYTHING BAD HAPPEN TO YOU.
MISTER DRESDEN? I'M DEPUTY BO GENTLE. THANKS FOR COMING.
OBLIGED, DEPUTY. MY COLLEAGUE GOES BY LISTENS-TO-WIND.
CAN YOU FILL ME IN ON WHAT HAPPENED?

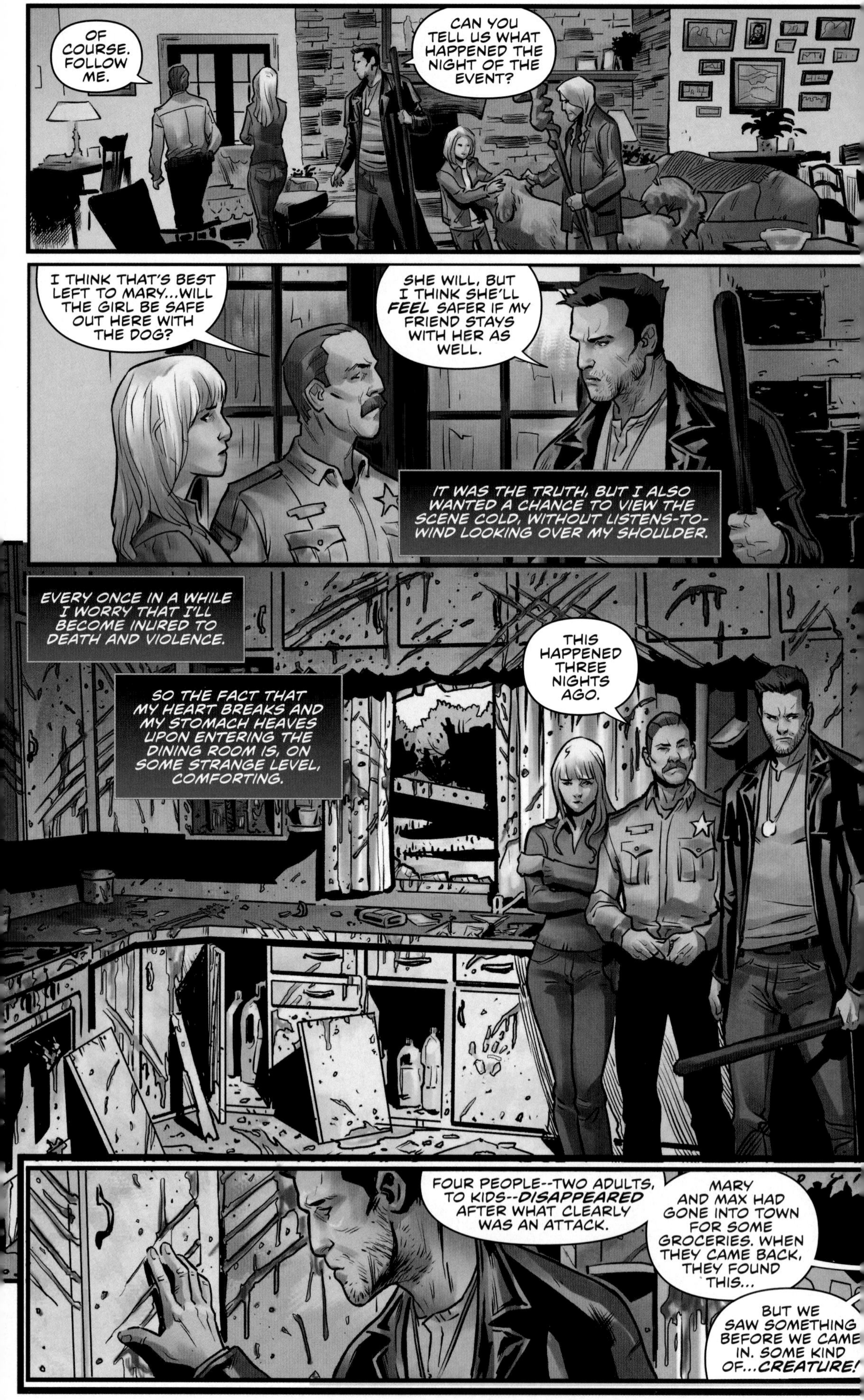
OF COURSE. FOLLOW ME.
CAN YOU TELL US WHAT HAPPENED THE NIGHT OF THE EVENT?
I THINK THAT'S BEST LEFT TO MARY...WILL THE GIRL BE SAFE OUT HERE WITH THE DOG?
SHE WILL, BUT I THINK SHE'LL FEEL SAFER IF MY FRIEND STAYS WITH HER AS WELL.
IT WAS THE TRUTH, BUT I ALSO WANTED A CHANCE TO VIEW THE SCENE COLD, WITHOUT LISTENS-TO-WIND LOOKING OVER MY SHOULDER.
EVERY ONCE IN A WHILE I WORRY THAT I'LL BECOME INURED TO DEATH AND VIOLENCE.
SO THE FACT THAT MY HEART BREAKS AND MY STOMACH HEAVES UPON ENTERING THE DINING ROOM IS, ON SOME STRANGE LEVEL, COMFORTING.
THIS HAPPENED THREE NIGHTS AGO.
FOUR PEOPLE--TWO ADULTS, TO KIDS--DISAPPEARED AFTER WHAT CLEARLY WAS AN ATTACK.
MARY AND MAX HAD GONE INTO TOWN FOR SOME GROCERIES. WHEN THEY CAME BACK, THEY FOUND THIS...
BUT WE SAW SOMETHING BEFORE WE CAME IN. SOME KIND OF...CREATURE!

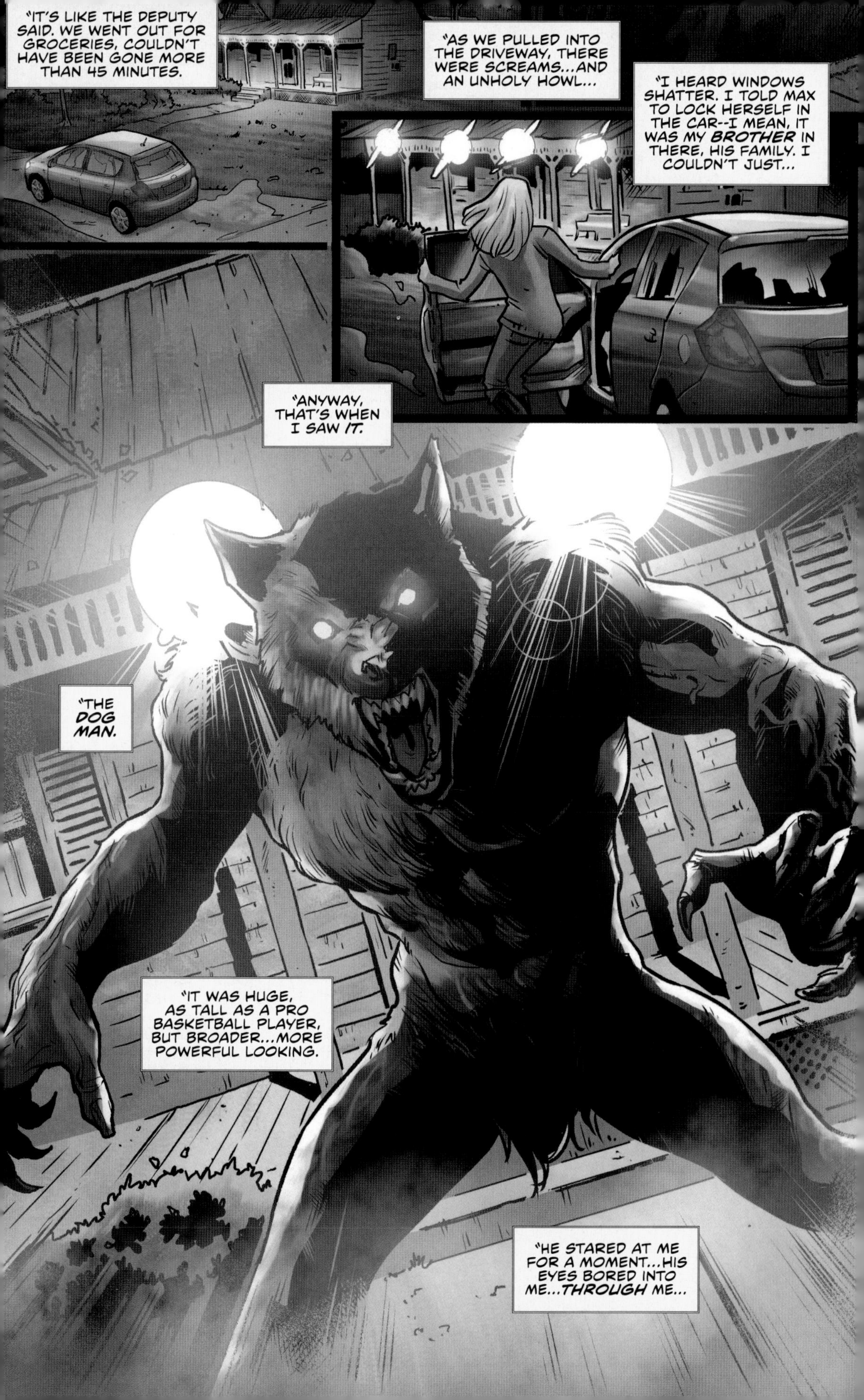
"IT'S LIKE THE DEPUTY SAID. WE WENT OUT FOR GROCERIES, COULDN'T HAVE BEEN GONE MORE THAN 45 MINUTES.
"AS WE PULLED INTO THE DRIVEWAY, THERE WERE SCREAMS...AND AN UNHOLY HOWL...
"I HEARD WINDOWS SHATTER. I TOLD MAX TO LOCK HERSELF IN THE CAR--I MEAN, IT WAS MY *BROTHER* IN THERE, HIS FAMILY. I COULDN'T JUST...
"ANYWAY, THAT'S WHEN I SAW *IT*.
"THE *DOG MAN*.
"IT WAS HUGE, AS TALL AS A PRO BASKETBALL PLAYER, BUT BROADER...MORE POWERFUL LOOKING.
"HE STARED AT ME FOR A MOMENT...HIS EYES BORED INTO ME...*THROUGH* ME...

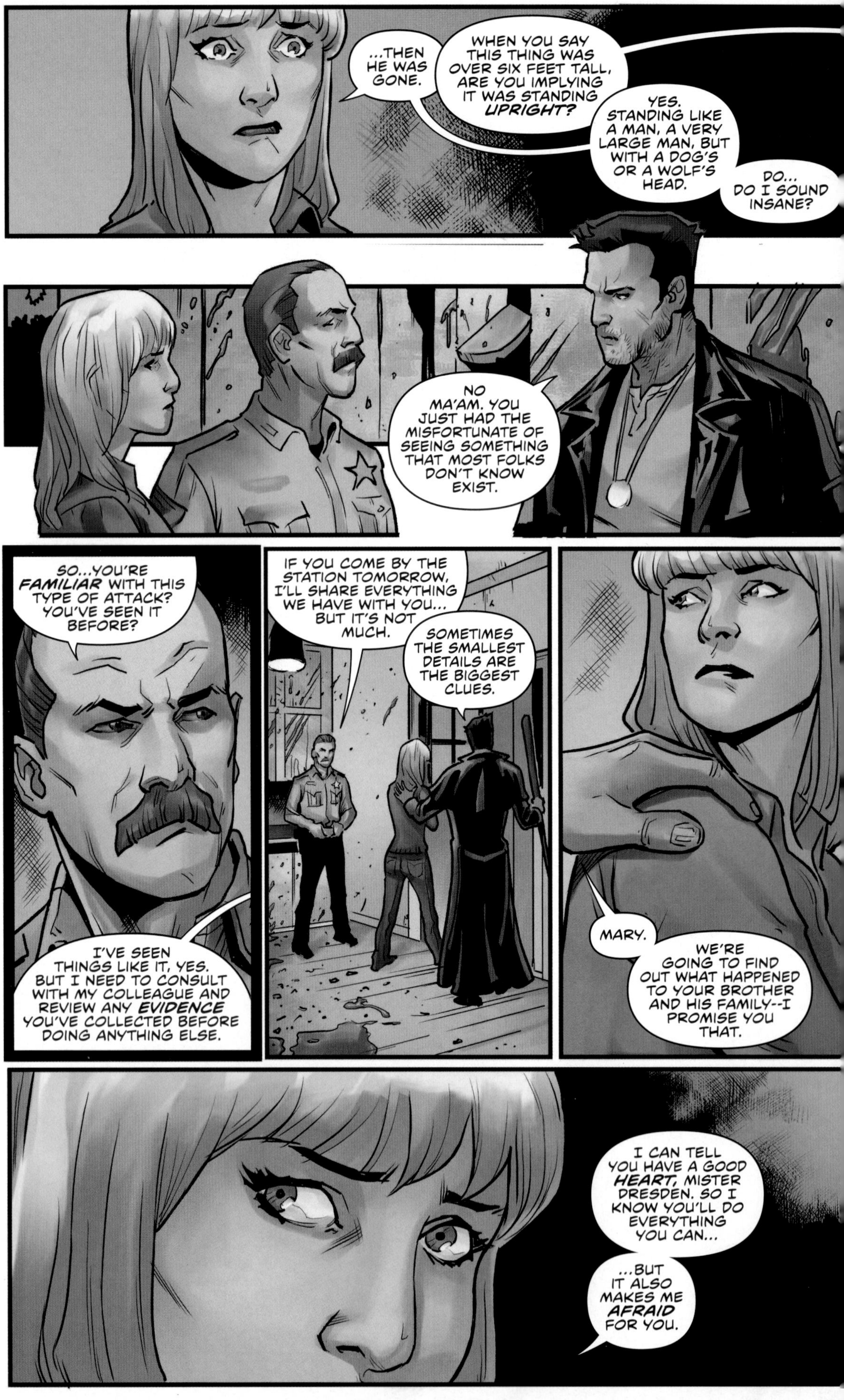
...THEN HE WAS GONE.
WHEN YOU SAY THIS THING WAS OVER SIX FEET TALL, ARE YOU IMPLYING IT WAS STANDING UPRIGHT?
YES. STANDING LIKE A MAN, A VERY LARGE MAN, BUT WITH A DOG'S OR A WOLF'S HEAD.
DO... DO I SOUND INSANE?
NO MA'AM. YOU JUST HAD THE MISFORTUNATE OF SEEING SOMETHING THAT MOST FOLKS DON'T KNOW EXIST.
SO...YOU'RE FAMILIAR WITH THIS TYPE OF ATTACK? YOU'VE SEEN IT BEFORE?
I'VE SEEN THINGS LIKE IT, YES. BUT I NEED TO CONSULT WITH MY COLLEAGUE AND REVIEW ANY EVIDENCE YOU'VE COLLECTED BEFORE DOING ANYTHING ELSE.
IF YOU COME BY THE STATION TOMORROW, I'LL SHARE EVERYTHING WE HAVE WITH YOU... BUT IT'S NOT MUCH.
SOMETIMES THE SMALLEST DETAILS ARE THE BIGGEST CLUES.
MARY.
WE'RE GOING TO FIND OUT WHAT HAPPENED TO YOUR BROTHER AND HIS FAMILY--I PROMISE YOU THAT.
I CAN TELL YOU HAVE A GOOD HEART, MISTER DRESDEN. SO I KNOW YOU'LL DO EVERYTHING YOU CAN...
...BUT IT ALSO MAKES ME AFRAID FOR YOU.

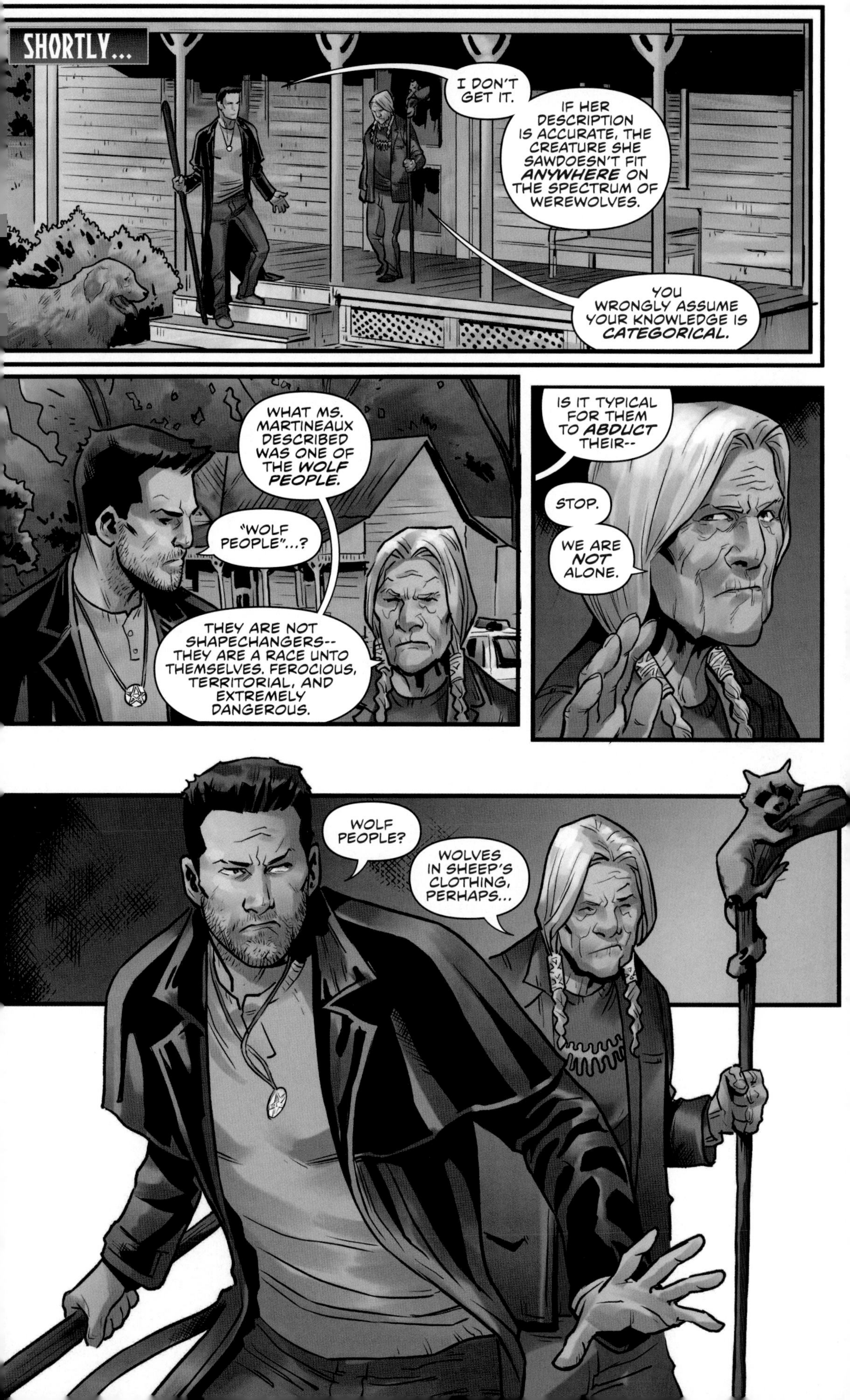
SHORTLY...
I DON'T GET IT.
IF HER DESCRIPTION IS ACCURATE, THE CREATURE SHE SAWDOESN'T FIT ANYWHERE ON THE SPECTRUM OF WEREWOLVES.
YOU WRONGLY ASSUME YOUR KNOWLEDGE IS CATEGORICAL.
WHAT MS. MARTINEAUX DESCRIBED WAS ONE OF THE WOLF PEOPLE.
"WOLF PEOPLE"...?
THEY ARE NOT SHAPECHANGERS-- THEY ARE A RACE UNTO THEMSELVES. FEROCIOUS, TERRITORIAL, AND EXTREMELY DANGEROUS.
IS IT TYPICAL FOR THEM TO ABDUCT THEIR--
STOP.
WE ARE NOT ALONE.
WOLF PEOPLE?
WOLVES IN SHEEP'S CLOTHING, PERHAPS...

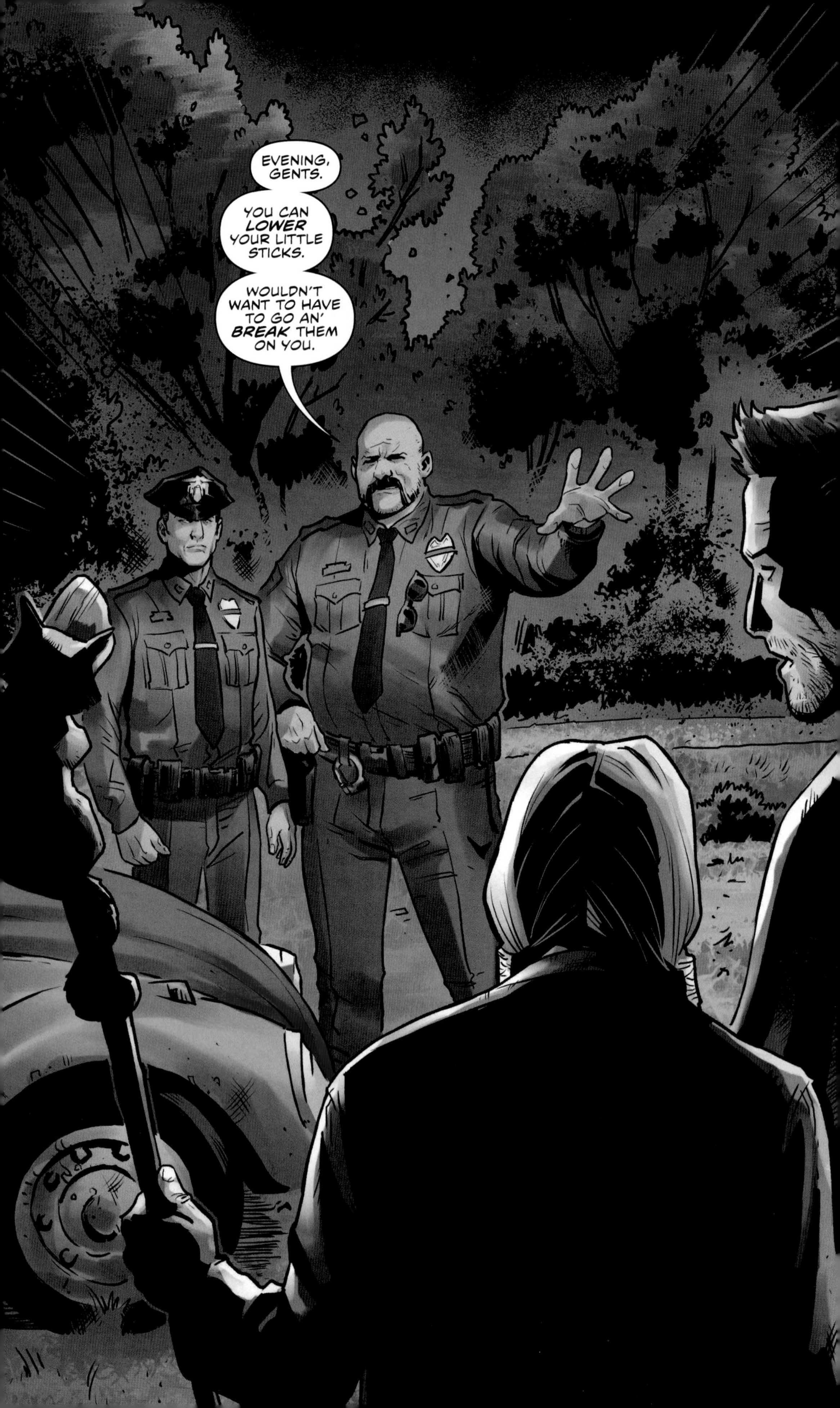
EVENING, GENTS.
YOU CAN *LOWER* YOUR LITTLE STICKS.
WOULDN'T WANT TO HAVE TO GO AN' *BREAK* THEM ON YOU.

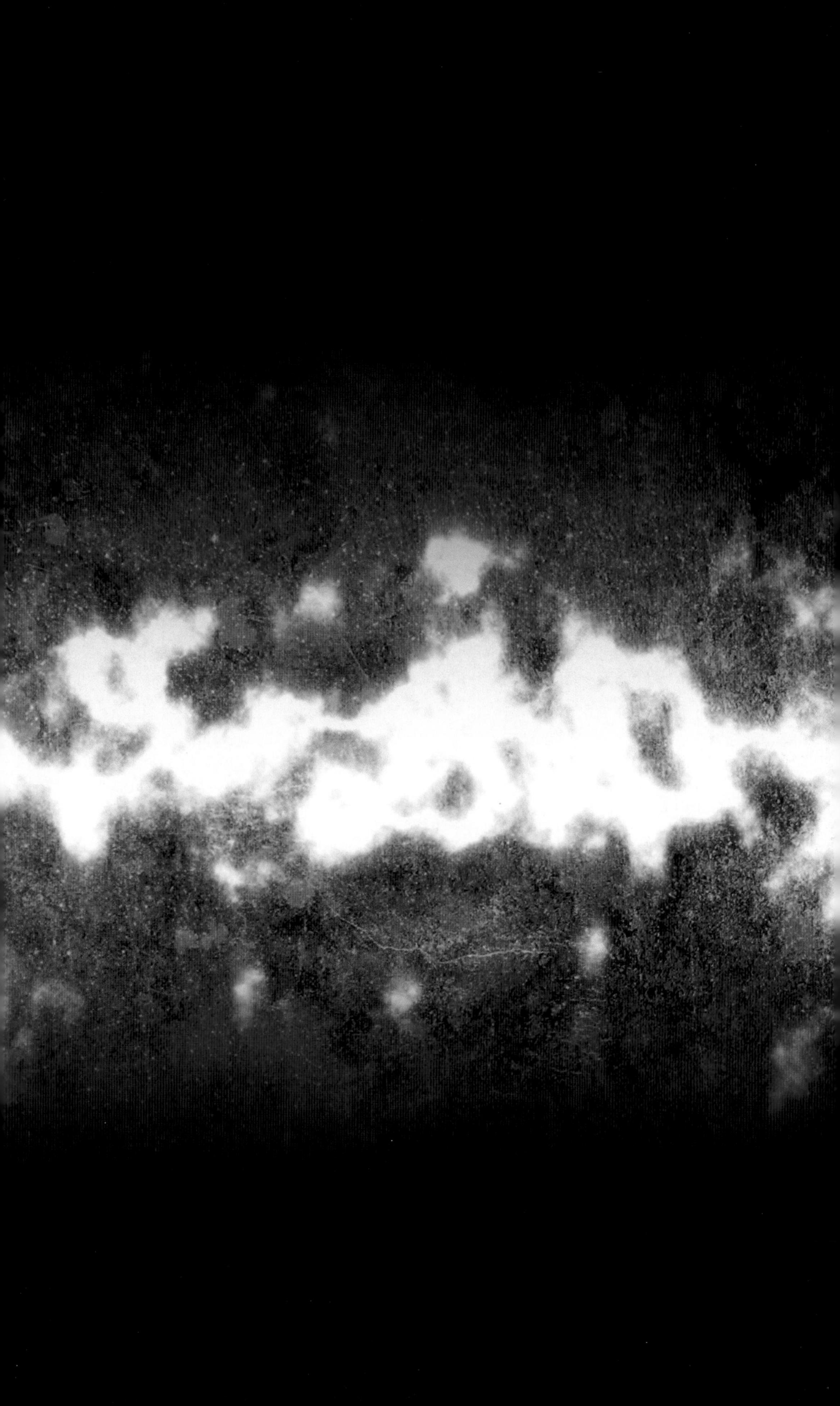

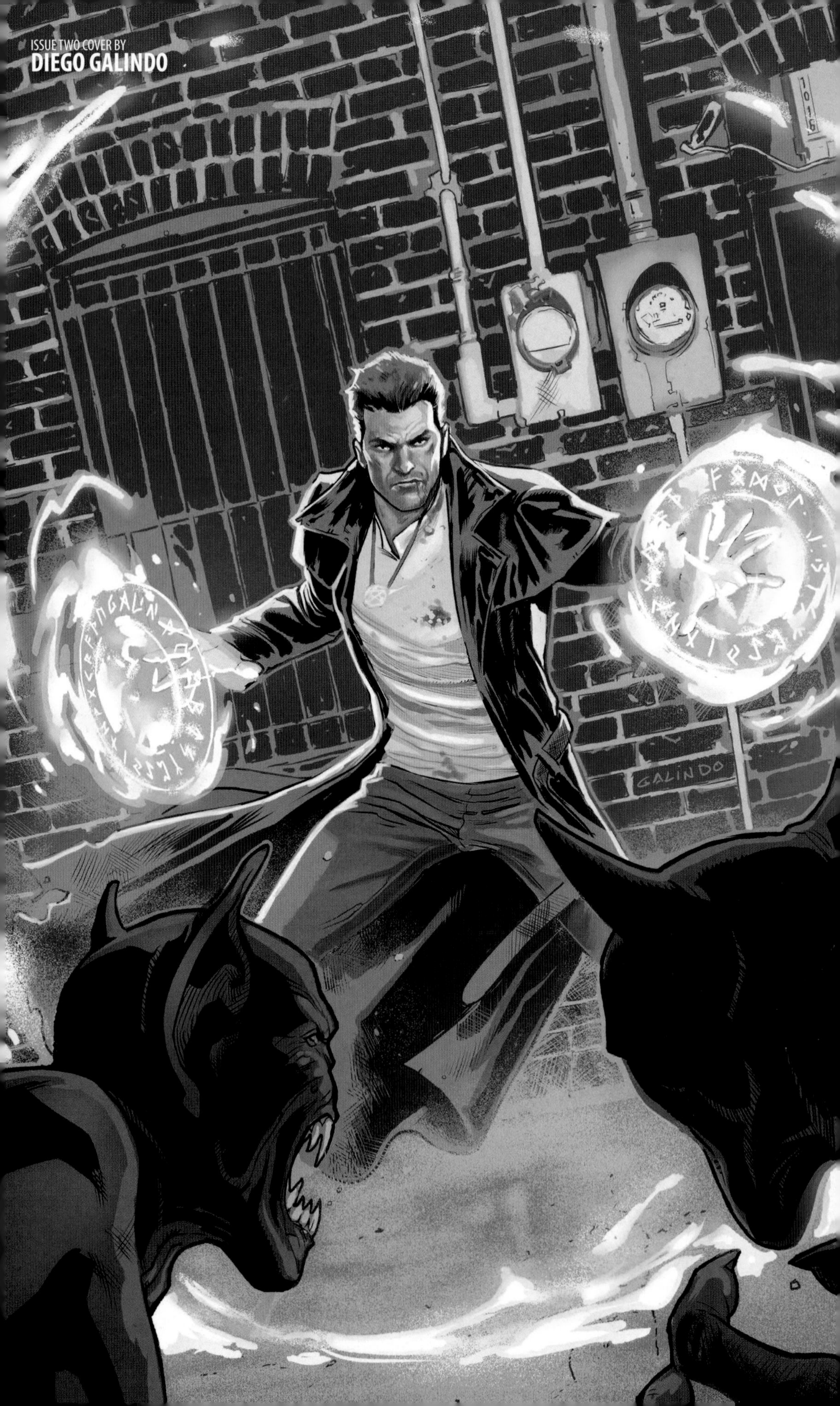
1016
GALINDO

ISSUE TWO COVER BY
DIEGO GALINDO

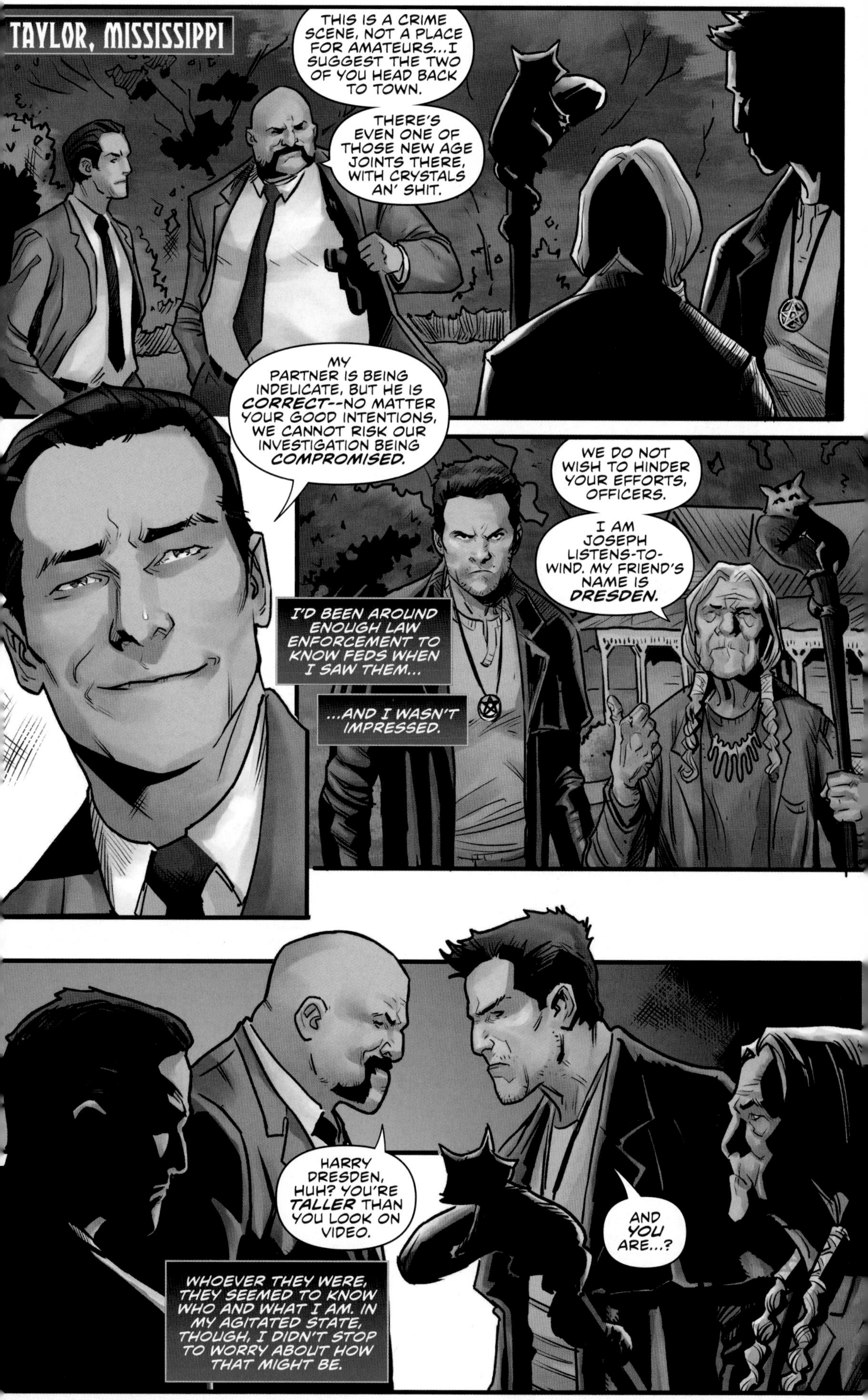

TAYLOR, MISSISSIPPI
THIS IS A CRIME SCENE, NOT A PLACE FOR AMATEURS...I SUGGEST THE TWO OF YOU HEAD BACK TO TOWN.
THERE'S EVEN ONE OF THOSE NEW AGE JOINTS THERE, WITH CRYSTALS AN' SHIT.
MY PARTNER IS BEING INDELICATE, BUT HE IS CORRECT--NO MATTER YOUR GOOD INTENTIONS, WE CANNOT RISK OUR INVESTIGATION BEING COMPROMISED.
WE DO NOT WISH TO HINDER YOUR EFFORTS, OFFICERS.
I AM JOSEPH LISTENS-TO-WIND. MY FRIEND'S NAME IS DRESDEN.
I'D BEEN AROUND ENOUGH LAW ENFORCEMENT TO KNOW FEDS WHEN I SAW THEM...
...AND I WASN'T IMPRESSED.
HARRY DRESDEN, HUH? YOU'RE TALLER THAN YOU LOOK ON VIDEO.
AND YOU ARE...?
WHOEVER THEY WERE, THEY SEEMED TO KNOW WHO AND WHAT I AM. IN MY AGITATED STATE, THOUGH, I DIDN'T STOP TO WORRY ABOUT HOW THAT MIGHT BE.

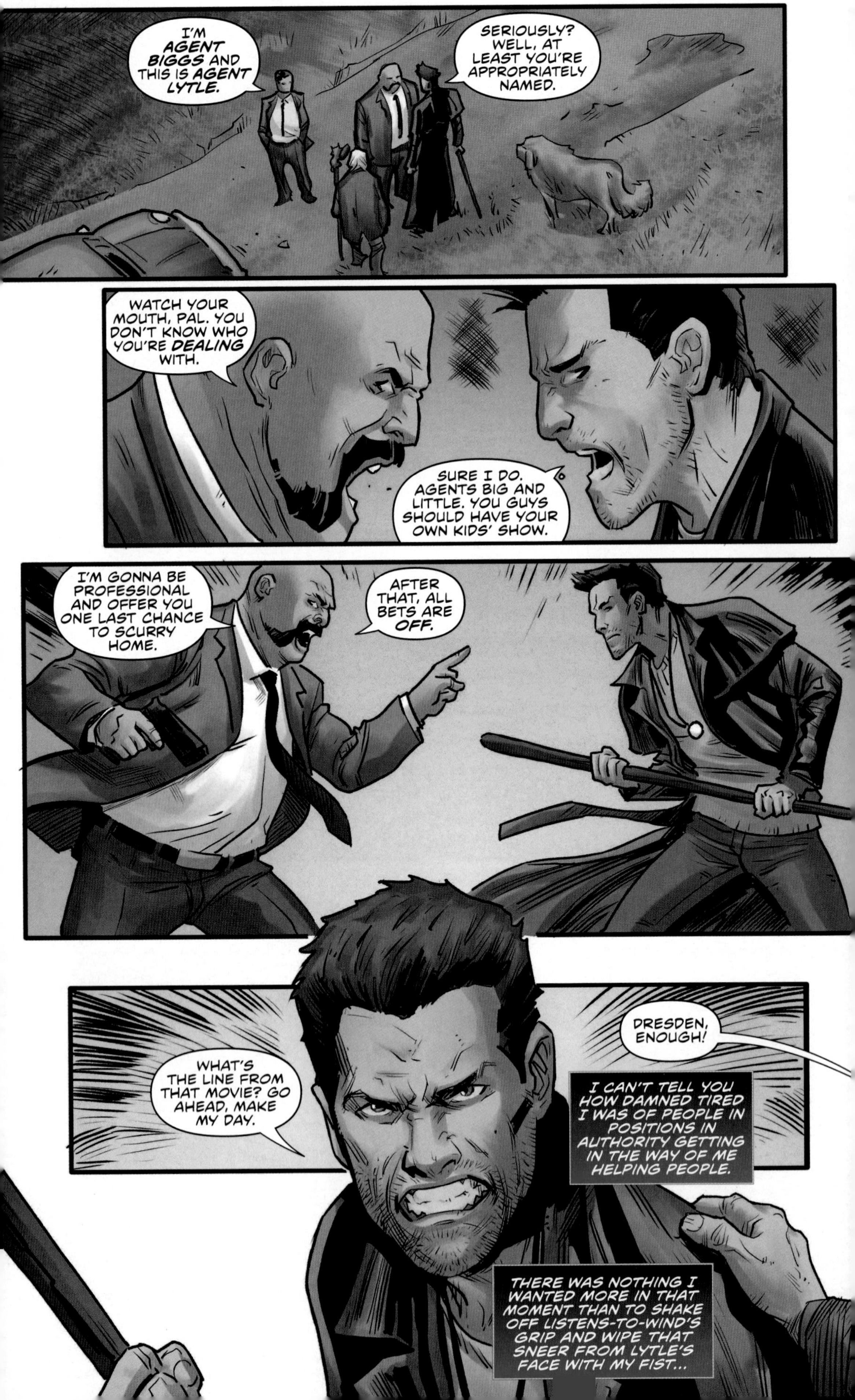
I'M AGENT BIGGS AND THIS IS AGENT LYTLE.
SERIOUSLY? WELL, AT LEAST YOU'RE APPROPRIATELY NAMED.
WATCH YOUR MOUTH, PAL. YOU DON'T KNOW WHO YOU'RE DEALING WITH.
SURE I DO. AGENTS BIG AND LITTLE. YOU GUYS SHOULD HAVE YOUR OWN KIDS' SHOW.
I'M GONNA BE PROFESSIONAL AND OFFER YOU ONE LAST CHANCE TO SCURRY HOME.
AFTER THAT, ALL BETS ARE OFF.
WHAT'S THE LINE FROM THAT MOVIE? GO AHEAD, MAKE MY DAY.
DRESDEN, ENOUGH!
I CAN'T TELL YOU HOW DAMNED TIRED I WAS OF PEOPLE IN POSITIONS IN AUTHORITY GETTING IN THE WAY OF ME HELPING PEOPLE.
THERE WAS NOTHING I WANTED MORE IN THAT MOMENT THAN TO SHAKE OFF LISTENS-TO-WIND'S GRIP AND WIPE THAT SNEER FROM LYTLE'S FACE WITH MY FIST...

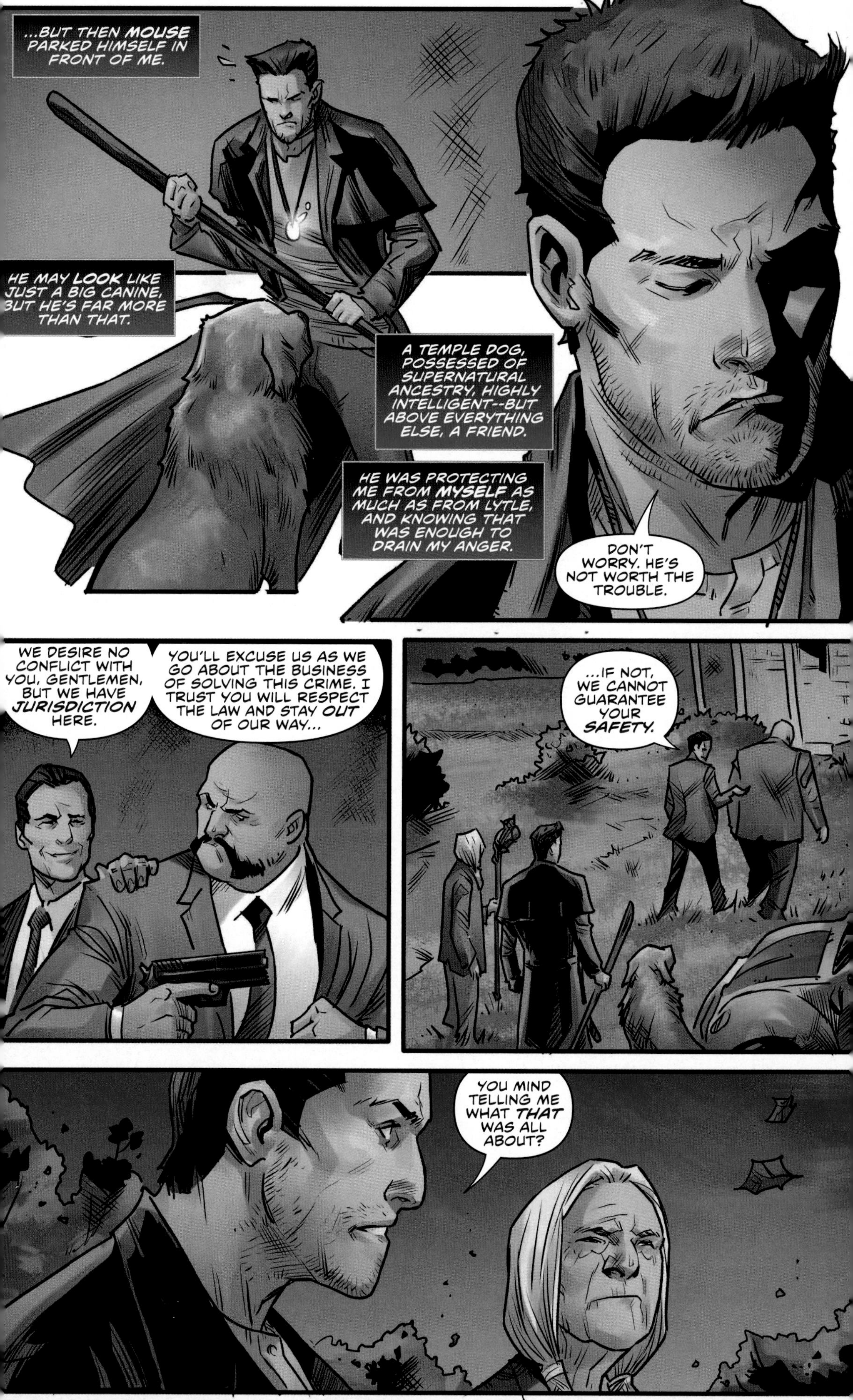
...BUT THEN MOUSE PARKED HIMSELF IN FRONT OF ME.
HE MAY LOOK LIKE JUST A BIG CANINE, BUT HE'S FAR MORE THAN THAT.
A TEMPLE DOG, POSSESSED OF SUPERNATURAL ANCESTRY, HIGHLY INTELLIGENT--BUT ABOVE EVERYTHING ELSE, A FRIEND.
HE WAS PROTECTING ME FROM MYSELF AS MUCH AS FROM LYTLE, AND KNOWING THAT WAS ENOUGH TO DRAIN MY ANGER.
DON'T WORRY. HE'S NOT WORTH THE TROUBLE.
WE DESIRE NO CONFLICT WITH YOU, GENTLEMEN, BUT WE HAVE JURISDICTION HERE.
YOU'LL EXCUSE US AS WE GO ABOUT THE BUSINESS OF SOLVING THIS CRIME. I TRUST YOU WILL RESPECT THE LAW AND STAY OUT OF OUR WAY...
...IF NOT, WE CANNOT GUARANTEE YOUR SAFETY.
YOU MIND TELLING ME WHAT THAT WAS ALL ABOUT?

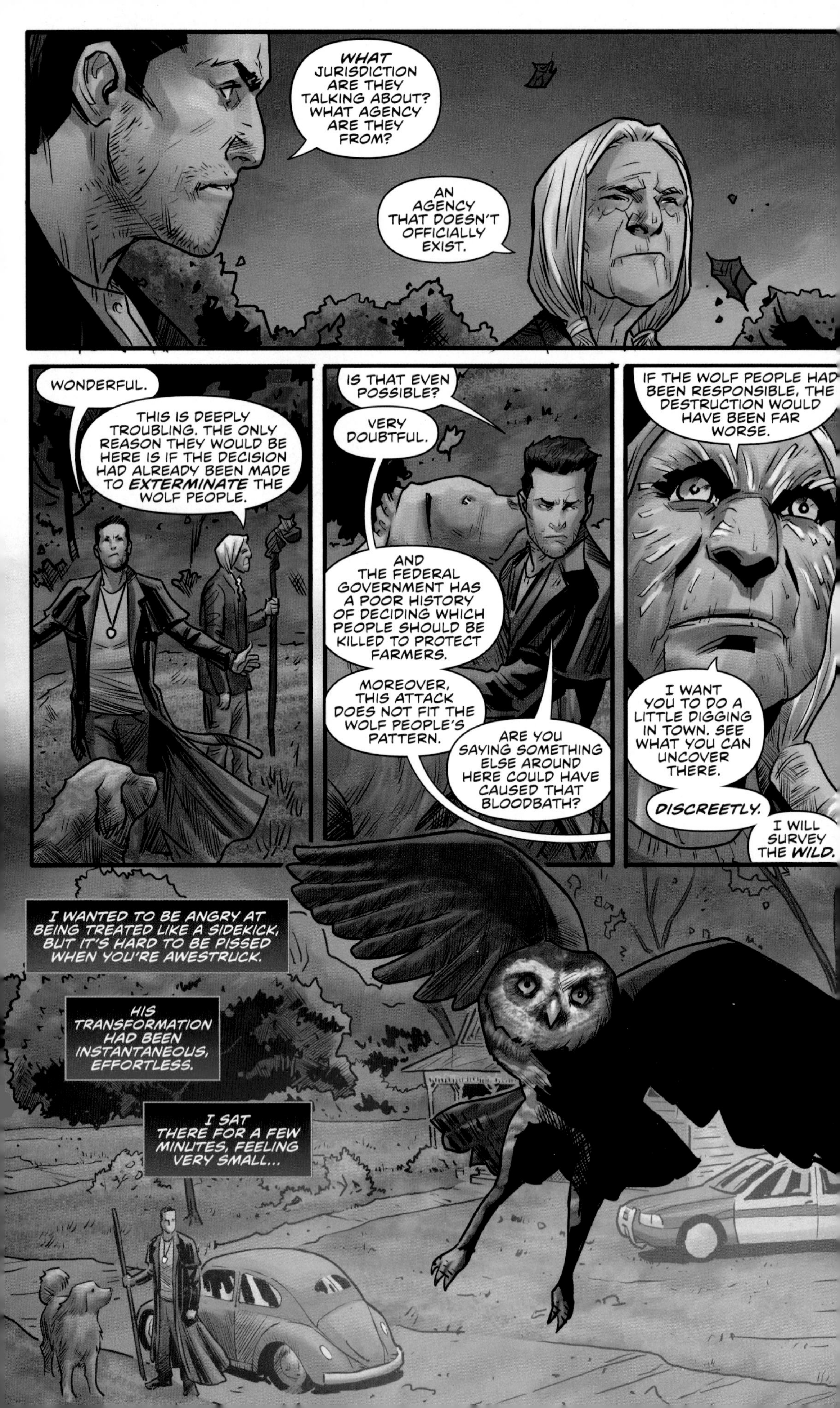
WHAT JURISDICTION ARE THEY TALKING ABOUT? WHAT AGENCY ARE THEY FROM?
AN AGENCY THAT DOESN'T OFFICIALLY EXIST.
WONDERFUL.
THIS IS DEEPLY TROUBLING. THE ONLY REASON THEY WOULD BE HERE IS IF THE DECISION HAD ALREADY BEEN MADE TO EXTERMINATE THE WOLF PEOPLE.
IS THAT EVEN POSSIBLE?
VERY DOUBTFUL.
AND THE FEDERAL GOVERNMENT HAS A POOR HISTORY OF DECIDING WHICH PEOPLE SHOULD BE KILLED TO PROTECT FARMERS.
MOREOVER, THIS ATTACK DOES NOT FIT THE WOLF PEOPLE'S PATTERN.
ARE YOU SAYING SOMETHING ELSE AROUND HERE COULD HAVE CAUSED THAT BLOODBATH?
IF THE WOLF PEOPLE HAD BEEN RESPONSIBLE, THE DESTRUCTION WOULD HAVE BEEN FAR WORSE.
I WANT YOU TO DO A LITTLE DIGGING IN TOWN. SEE WHAT YOU CAN UNCOVER THERE.
DISCREETLY.
I WILL SURVEY THE WILD.
I WANTED TO BE ANGRY AT BEING TREATED LIKE A SIDEKICK, BUT IT'S HARD TO BE PISSED WHEN YOU'RE AWESTRUCK.
HIS TRANSFORMATION HAD BEEN INSTANTANEOUS, EFFORTLESS.
I SAT THERE FOR A FEW MINUTES, FEELING VERY SMALL...

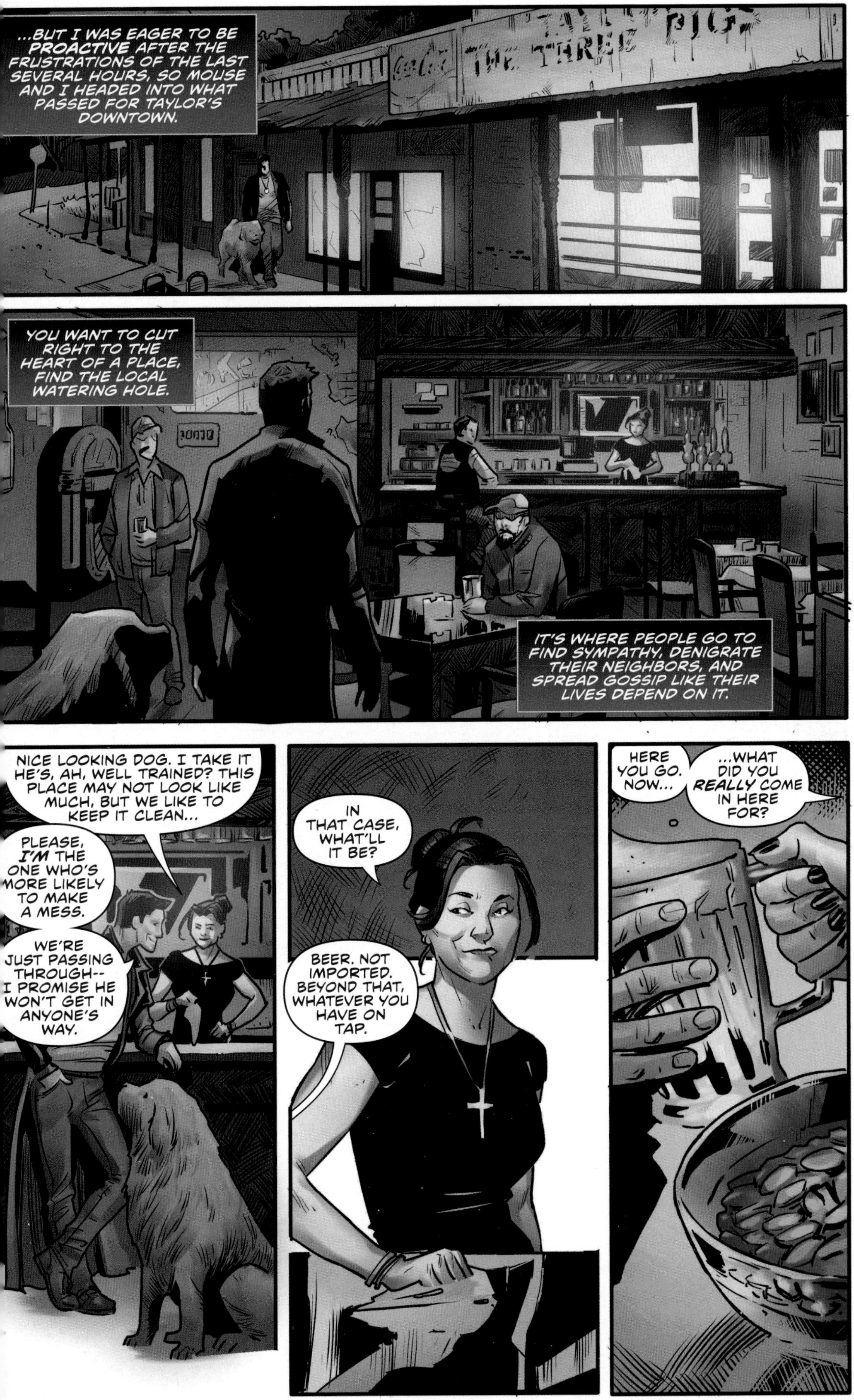
...BUT I WAS EAGER TO BE PROACTIVE AFTER THE FRUSTRATIONS OF THE LAST SEVERAL HOURS, SO MOUSE AND I HEADED INTO WHAT PASSED FOR TAYLOR'S DOWNTOWN.
THE THREE PIGS
YOU WANT TO CUT RIGHT TO THE HEART OF A PLACE, FIND THE LOCAL WATERING HOLE.
IT'S WHERE PEOPLE GO TO FIND SYMPATHY, DENIGRATE THEIR NEIGHBORS, AND SPREAD GOSSIP LIKE THEIR LIVES DEPEND ON IT.
NICE LOOKING DOG. I TAKE IT HE'S, AH, WELL TRAINED? THIS PLACE MAY NOT LOOK LIKE MUCH, BUT WE LIKE TO KEEP IT CLEAN...
PLEASE, I'M THE ONE WHO'S MORE LIKELY TO MAKE A MESS.
WE'RE JUST PASSING THROUGH-- I PROMISE HE WON'T GET IN ANYONE'S WAY.
IN THAT CASE, WHAT'LL IT BE?
BEER. NOT IMPORTED. BEYOND THAT, WHATEVER YOU HAVE ON TAP.
HERE YOU GO. NOW...
...WHAT DID YOU REALLY COME IN HERE FOR?

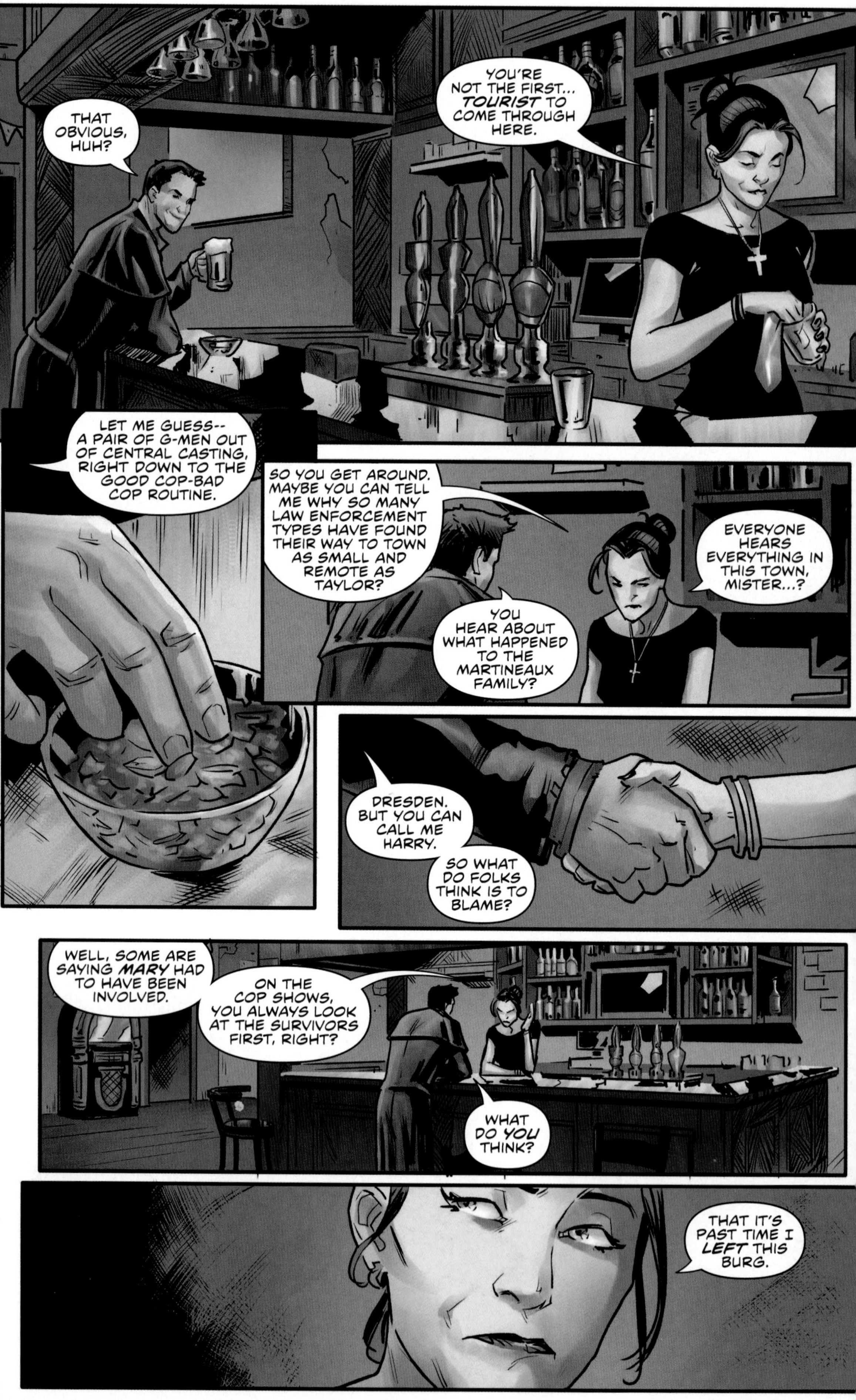

THAT OBVIOUS, HUH?
YOU'RE NOT THE FIRST... *TOURIST* TO COME THROUGH HERE.
LET ME GUESS-- A PAIR OF G-MEN OUT OF CENTRAL CASTING, RIGHT DOWN TO THE GOOD COP-BAD COP ROUTINE.
SO YOU GET AROUND. MAYBE YOU CAN TELL ME WHY SO MANY LAW ENFORCEMENT TYPES HAVE FOUND THEIR WAY TO TOWN AS SMALL AND REMOTE AS TAYLOR?
EVERYONE HEARS EVERYTHING IN THIS TOWN, MISTER...?
YOU HEAR ABOUT WHAT HAPPENED TO THE MARTINEAUX FAMILY?
DRESDEN. BUT YOU CAN CALL ME HARRY.
SO WHAT DO FOLKS THINK IS TO BLAME?
WELL, SOME ARE SAYING *MARY* HAD TO HAVE BEEN INVOLVED.
ON THE COP SHOWS, YOU ALWAYS LOOK AT THE SURVIVORS FIRST, RIGHT?
WHAT DO *YOU* THINK?
THAT IT'S PAST TIME I *LEFT* THIS BURG.

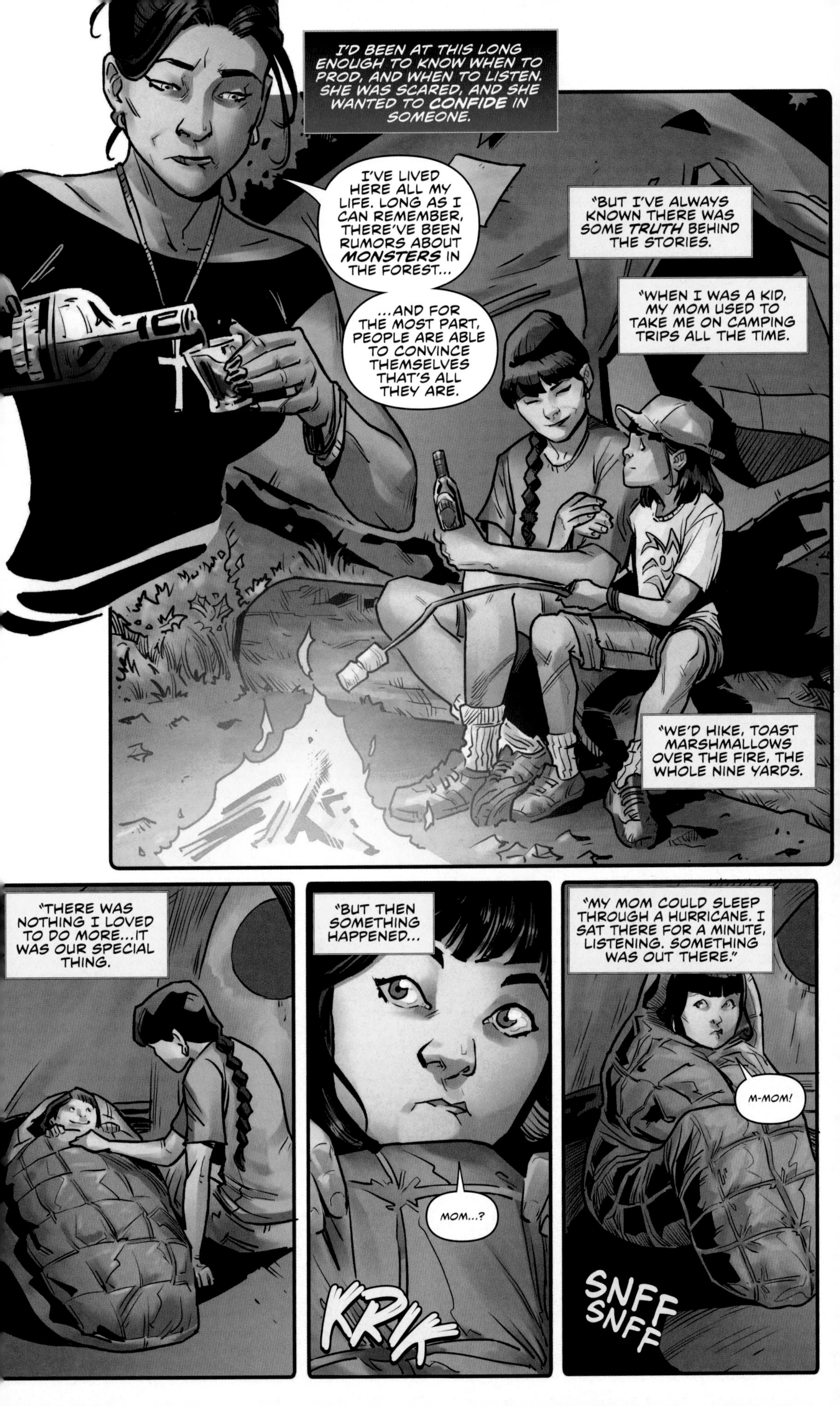
I'D BEEN AT THIS LONG ENOUGH TO KNOW WHEN TO PROD, AND WHEN TO LISTEN. SHE WAS SCARED, AND SHE WANTED TO CONFIDE IN SOMEONE.
I'VE LIVED HERE ALL MY LIFE. LONG AS I CAN REMEMBER, THERE'VE BEEN RUMORS ABOUT MONSTERS IN THE FOREST...
...AND FOR THE MOST PART, PEOPLE ARE ABLE TO CONVINCE THEMSELVES THAT'S ALL THEY ARE.
"BUT I'VE ALWAYS KNOWN THERE WAS SOME TRUTH BEHIND THE STORIES.
"WHEN I WAS A KID, MY MOM USED TO TAKE ME ON CAMPING TRIPS ALL THE TIME.
"WE'D HIKE, TOAST MARSHMALLOWS OVER THE FIRE, THE WHOLE NINE YARDS.
"THERE WAS NOTHING I LOVED TO DO MORE...IT WAS OUR SPECIAL THING.
"BUT THEN SOMETHING HAPPENED...
MOM...?
KRIK
"MY MOM COULD SLEEP THROUGH A HURRICANE. I SAT THERE FOR A MINUTE, LISTENING. SOMETHING WAS OUT THERE."
M-MOM!
SNFF SNFF

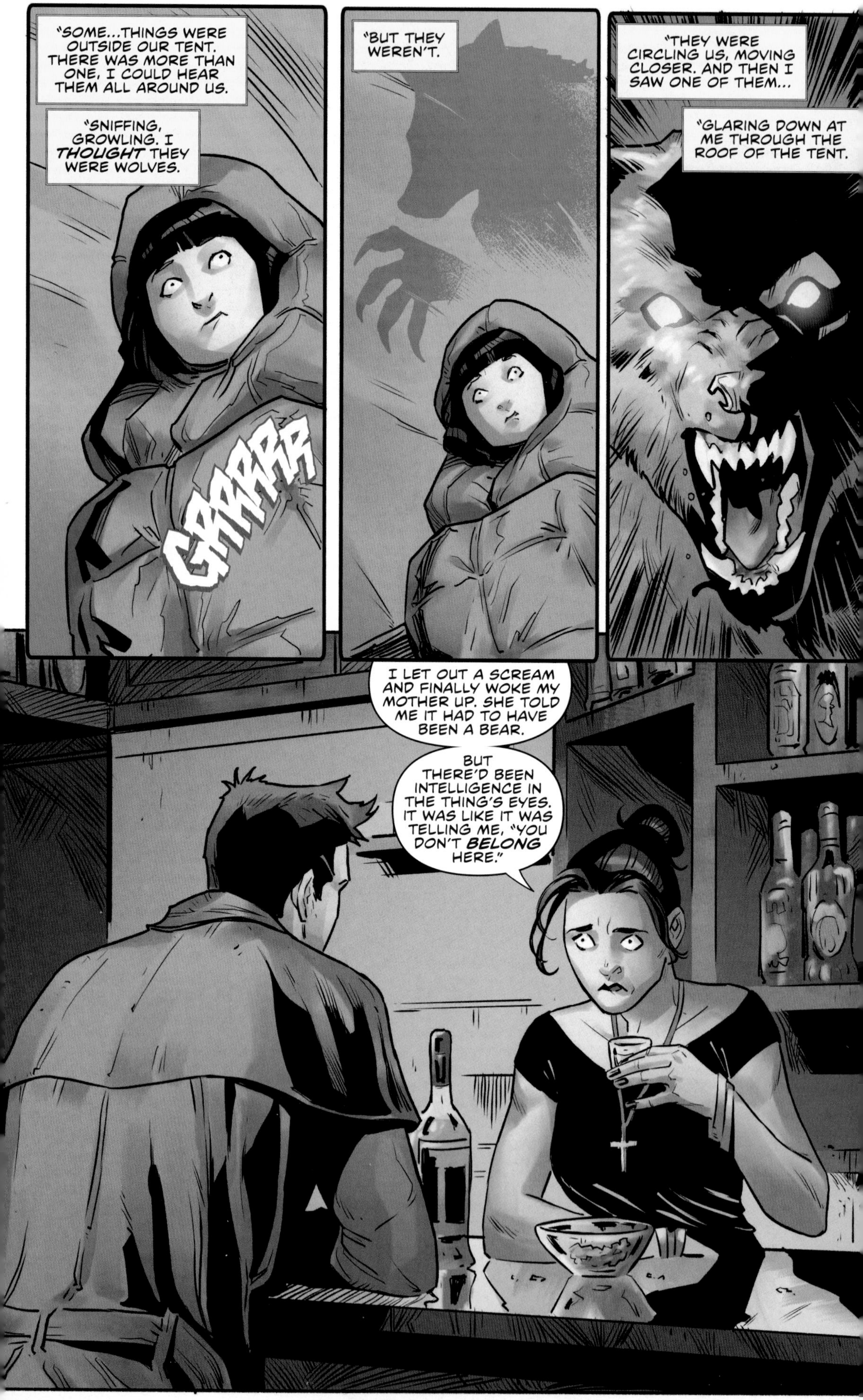
"SOME...THINGS WERE OUTSIDE OUR TENT. THERE WAS MORE THAN ONE, I COULD HEAR THEM ALL AROUND US.
"SNIFFING, GROWLING. I *THOUGHT* THEY WERE WOLVES.
GRRRR
"BUT THEY WEREN'T.
"THEY WERE CIRCLING US, MOVING CLOSER. AND THEN I SAW ONE OF THEM...
"GLARING DOWN AT ME THROUGH THE ROOF OF THE TENT.
I LET OUT A SCREAM AND FINALLY WOKE MY MOTHER UP. SHE TOLD ME IT HAD TO HAVE BEEN A BEAR.
BUT THERE'D BEEN INTELLIGENCE IN THE THING'S EYES. IT WAS LIKE IT WAS TELLING ME, "YOU DON'T *BELONG* HERE."

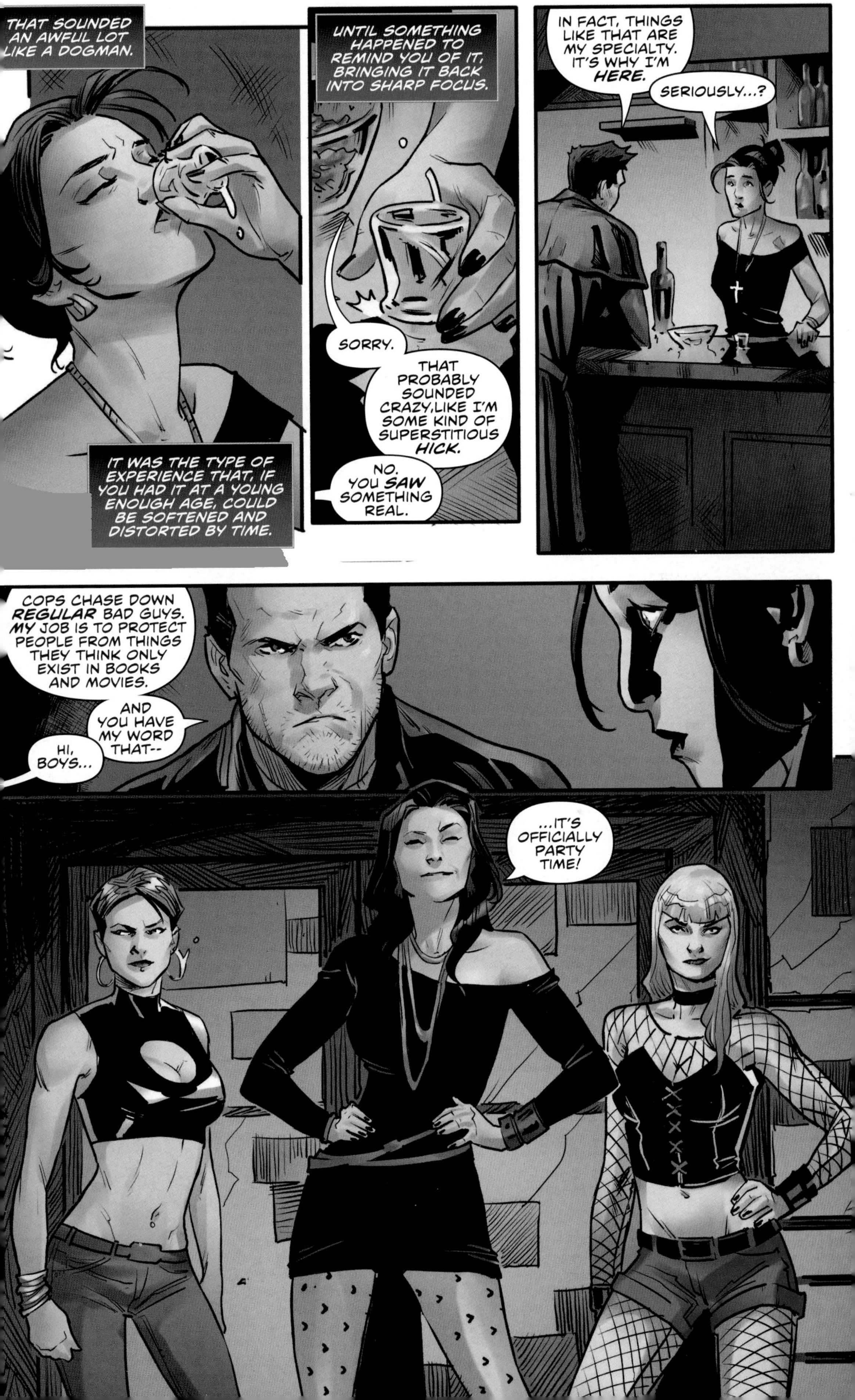
THAT SOUNDED AN AWFUL LOT LIKE A DOGMAN.
IT WAS THE TYPE OF EXPERIENCE THAT, IF YOU HAD IT AT A YOUNG ENOUGH AGE, COULD BE SOFTENED AND DISTORTED BY TIME.
UNTIL SOMETHING HAPPENED TO REMIND YOU OF IT, BRINGING IT BACK INTO SHARP FOCUS.
SORRY.
THAT PROBABLY SOUNDED CRAZY,LIKE I'M SOME KIND OF SUPERSTITIOUS HICK.
NO. YOU SAW SOMETHING REAL.
IN FACT, THINGS LIKE THAT ARE MY SPECIALTY. IT'S WHY I'M HERE.
SERIOUSLY...?
COPS CHASE DOWN REGULAR BAD GUYS. MY JOB IS TO PROTECT PEOPLE FROM THINGS THEY THINK ONLY EXIST IN BOOKS AND MOVIES.
AND YOU HAVE MY WORD THAT--
HI, BOYS...
...IT'S OFFICIALLY PARTY TIME!

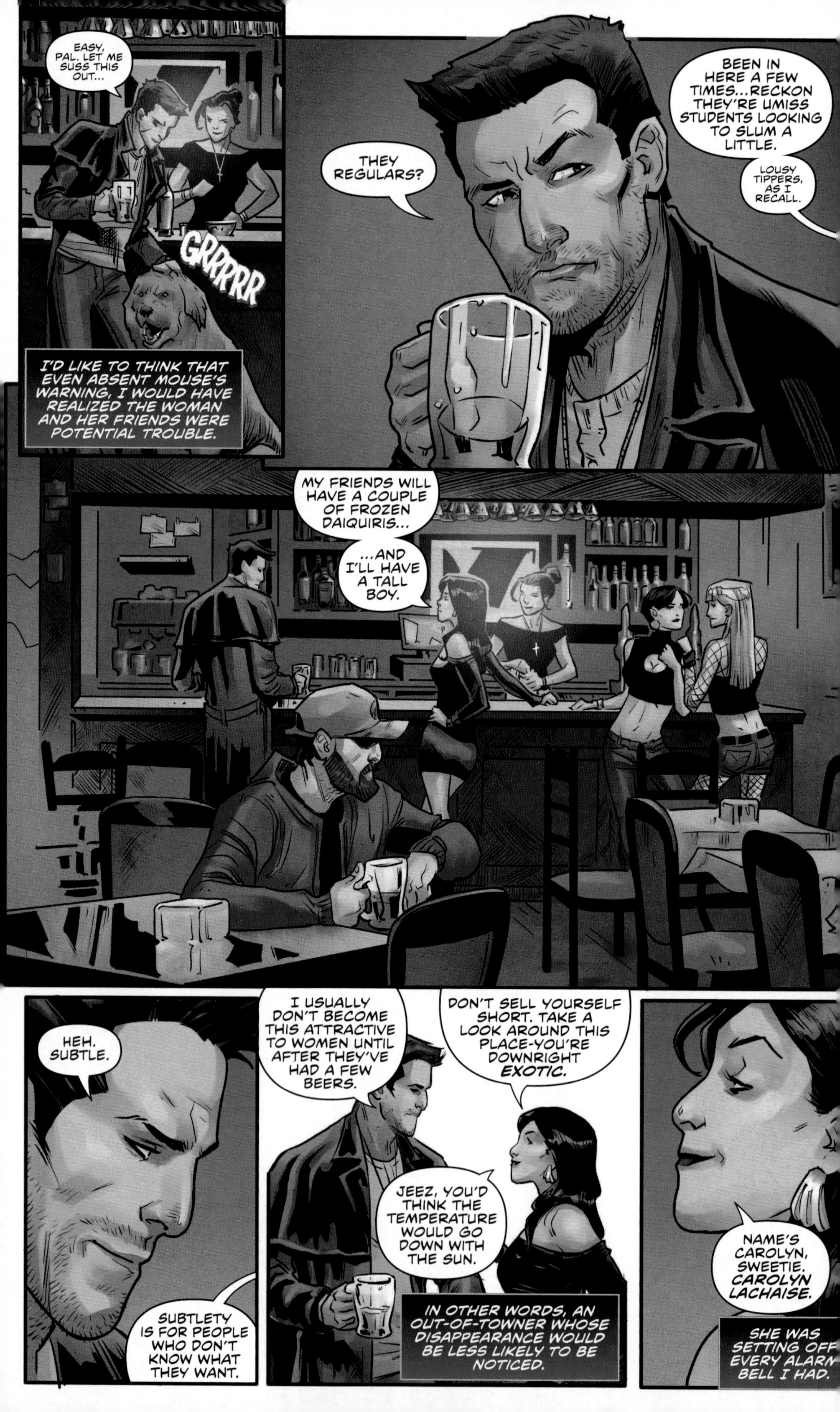
EASY, PAL. LET ME SUSS THIS OUT...
GRRRRR
I'D LIKE TO THINK THAT EVEN ABSENT MOUSE'S WARNING, I WOULD HAVE REALIZED THE WOMAN AND HER FRIENDS WERE POTENTIAL TROUBLE.
THEY REGULARS?
BEEN IN HERE A FEW TIMES...RECKON THEY'RE UMISS STUDENTS LOOKING TO SLUM A LITTLE.
LOUSY TIPPERS, AS I RECALL.
MY FRIENDS WILL HAVE A COUPLE OF FROZEN DAIQUIRIS...
...AND I'LL HAVE A TALL BOY.
HEH. SUBTLE.
SUBTLETY IS FOR PEOPLE WHO DON'T KNOW WHAT THEY WANT.
I USUALLY DON'T BECOME THIS ATTRACTIVE TO WOMEN UNTIL AFTER THEY'VE HAD A FEW BEERS.
DON'T SELL YOURSELF SHORT. TAKE A LOOK AROUND THIS PLACE-YOU'RE DOWNRIGHT EXOTIC.
JEEZ, YOU'D THINK THE TEMPERATURE WOULD GO DOWN WITH THE SUN.
IN OTHER WORDS, AN OUT-OF-TOWNER WHOSE DISAPPEARANCE WOULD BE LESS LIKELY TO BE NOTICED.
NAME'S CAROLYN, SWEETIE. CAROLYN LACHAISE.
SHE WAS SETTING OFF EVERY ALARM BELL I HAD.

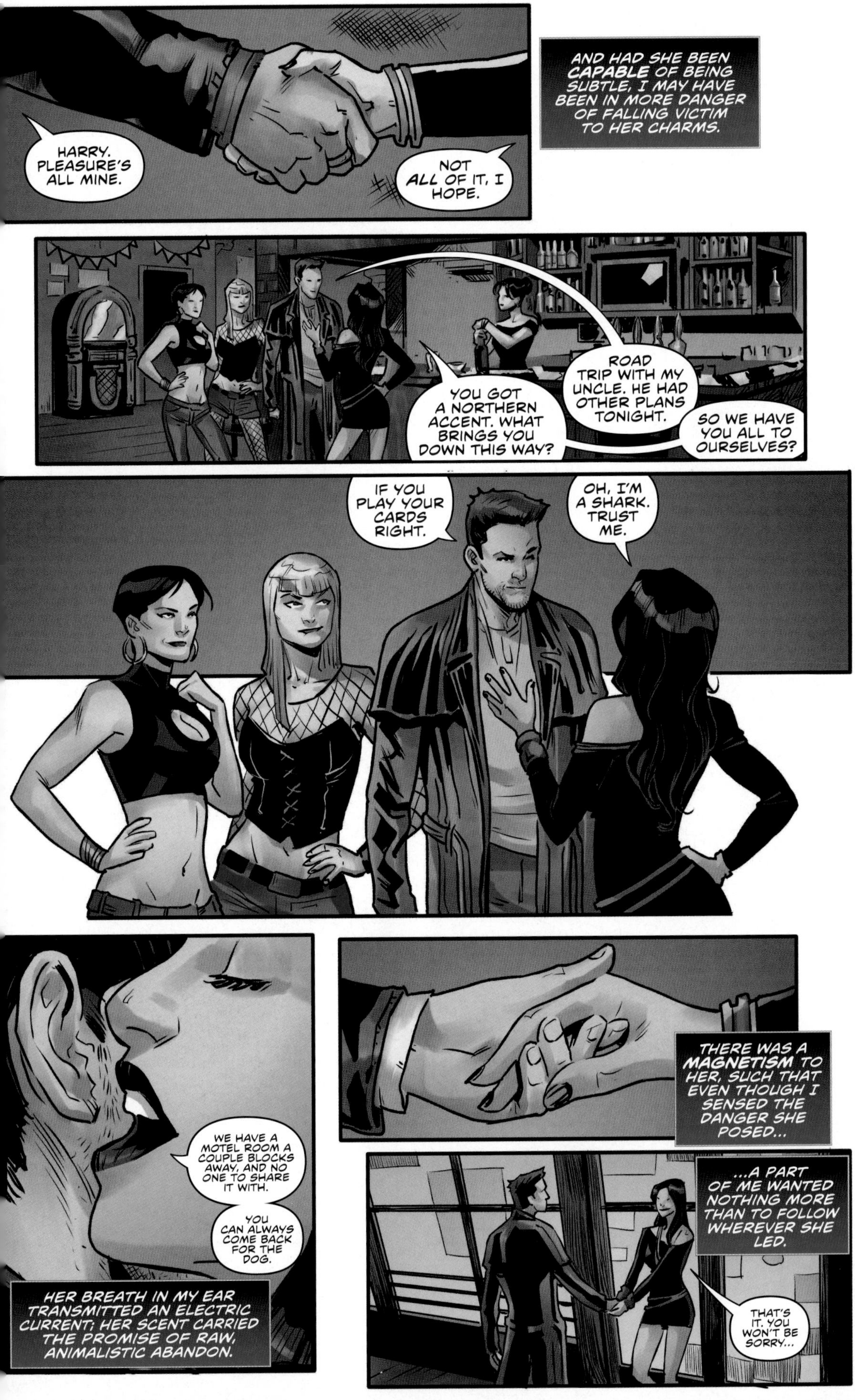

AND HAD SHE BEEN CAPABLE OF BEING SUBTLE, I MAY HAVE BEEN IN MORE DANGER OF FALLING VICTIM TO HER CHARMS.
HARRY. PLEASURE'S ALL MINE.
NOT ALL OF IT, I HOPE.
YOU GOT A NORTHERN ACCENT. WHAT BRINGS YOU DOWN THIS WAY?
ROAD TRIP WITH MY UNCLE. HE HAD OTHER PLANS TONIGHT.
SO WE HAVE YOU ALL TO OURSELVES?
IF YOU PLAY YOUR CARDS RIGHT.
OH, I'M A SHARK. TRUST ME.
WE HAVE A MOTEL ROOM A COUPLE BLOCKS AWAY, AND NO ONE TO SHARE IT WITH.
YOU CAN ALWAYS COME BACK FOR THE DOG.
HER BREATH IN MY EAR TRANSMITTED AN ELECTRIC CURRENT; HER SCENT CARRIED THE PROMISE OF RAW, ANIMALISTIC ABANDON.
THERE WAS A MAGNETISM TO HER, SUCH THAT EVEN THOUGH I SENSED THE DANGER SHE POSED...
...A PART OF ME WANTED NOTHING MORE THAN TO FOLLOW WHEREVER SHE LED.
THAT'S IT. YOU WON'T BE SORRY...

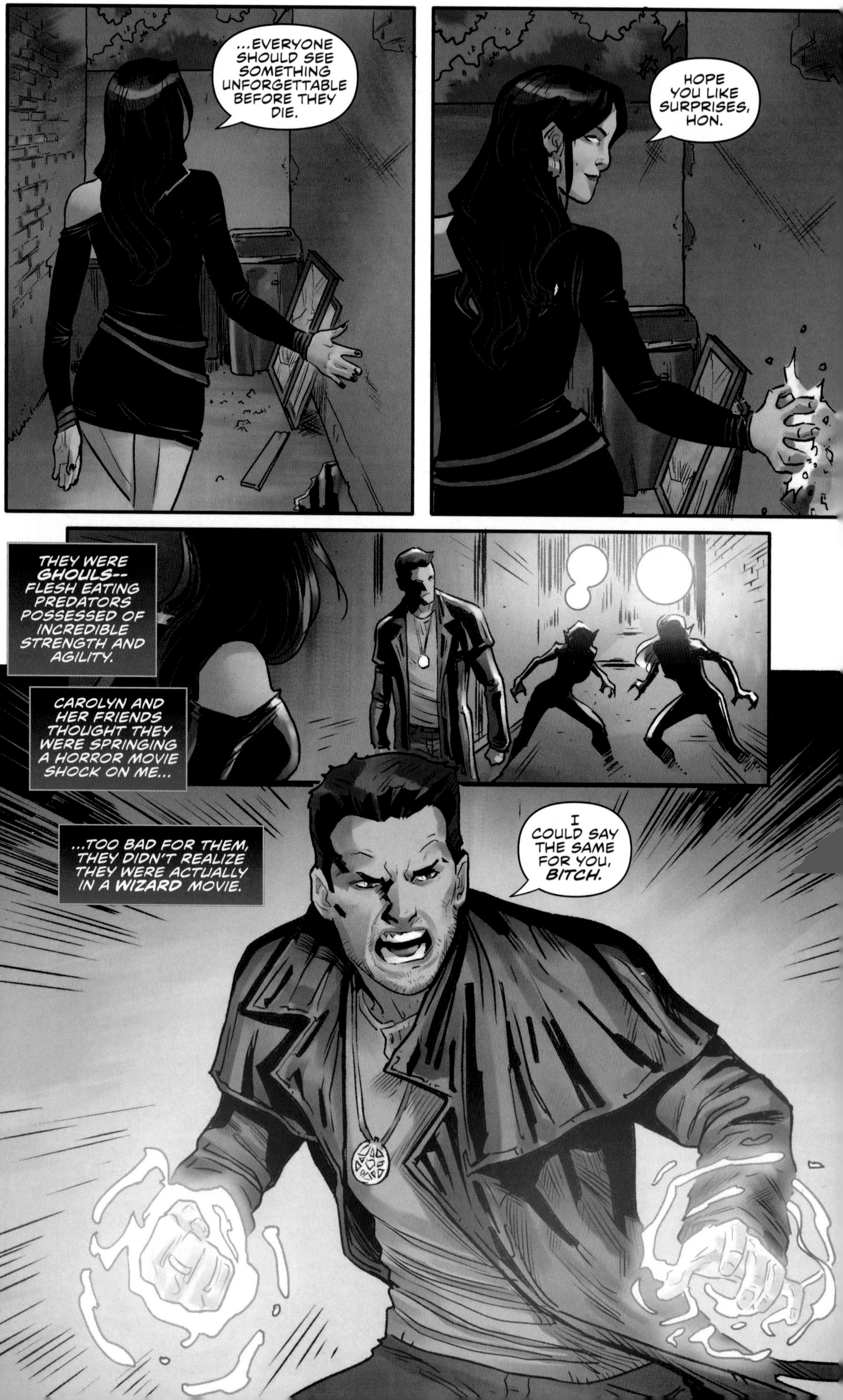
...EVERYONE SHOULD SEE SOMETHING UNFORGETTABLE BEFORE THEY DIE.
HOPE YOU LIKE SURPRISES, HON.
THEY WERE GHOULS--FLESH EATING PREDATORS POSSESSED OF INCREDIBLE STRENGTH AND AGILITY.
CAROLYN AND HER FRIENDS THOUGHT THEY WERE SPRINGING A HORROR MOVIE SHOCK ON ME...
...TOO BAD FOR THEM, THEY DIDN'T REALIZE THEY WERE ACTUALLY IN A WIZARD MOVIE.
I COULD SAY THE SAME FOR YOU, BITCH.

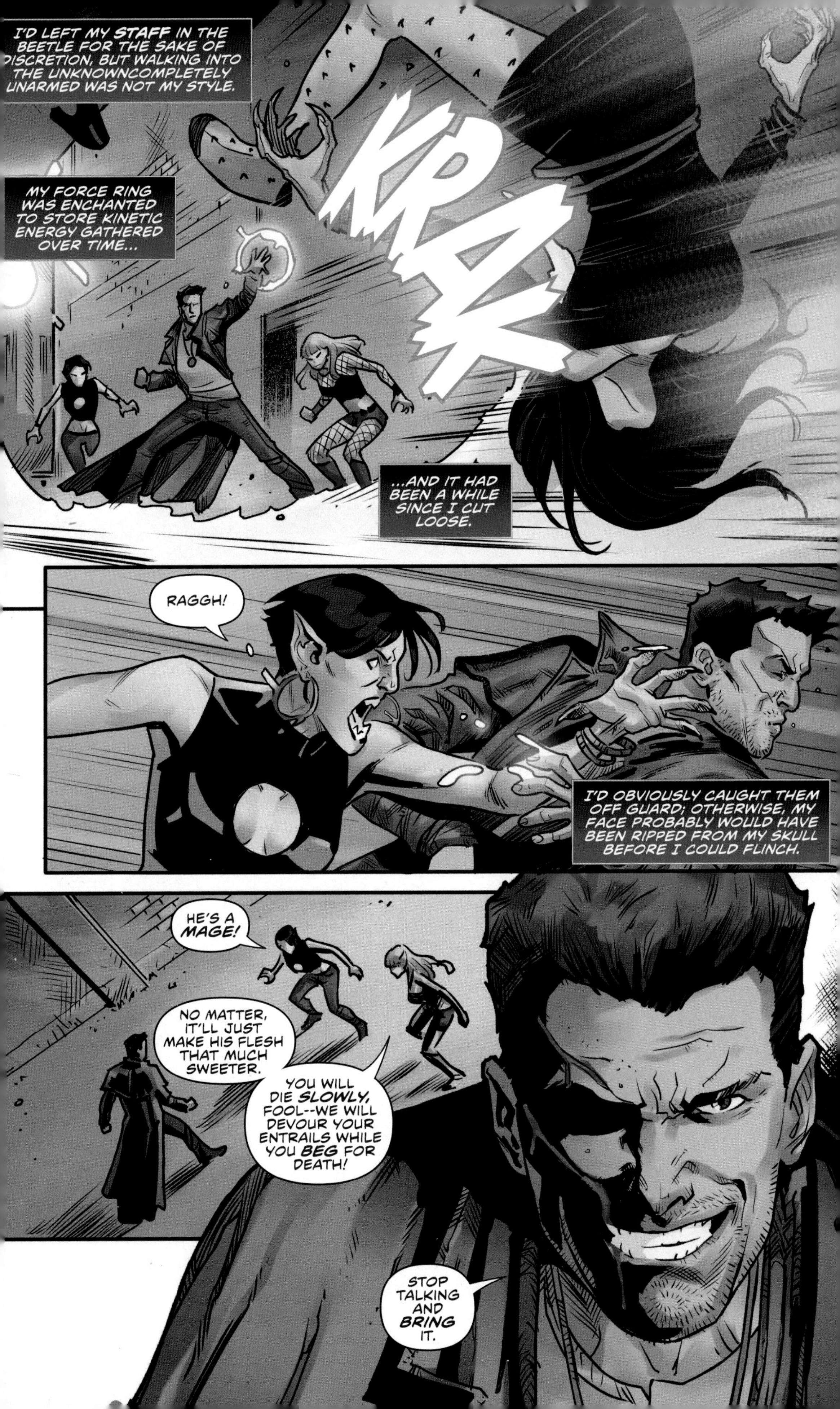
I'D LEFT MY STAFF IN THE BEETLE FOR THE SAKE OF DISCRETION, BUT WALKING INTO THE UNKNOWNCOMPLETELY UNARMED WAS NOT MY STYLE.
MY FORCE RING WAS ENCHANTED TO STORE KINETIC ENERGY GATHERED OVER TIME...
KRAK
...AND IT HAD BEEN A WHILE SINCE I CUT LOOSE.
RAGGH!
I'D OBVIOUSLY CAUGHT THEM OFF GUARD; OTHERWISE, MY FACE PROBABLY WOULD HAVE BEEN RIPPED FROM MY SKULL BEFORE I COULD FLINCH.
HE'S A MAGE!
NO MATTER, IT'LL JUST MAKE HIS FLESH THAT MUCH SWEETER.
YOU WILL DIE SLOWLY, FOOL--WE WILL DEVOUR YOUR ENTRAILS WHILE YOU BEG FOR DEATH!
STOP TALKING AND BRING IT.

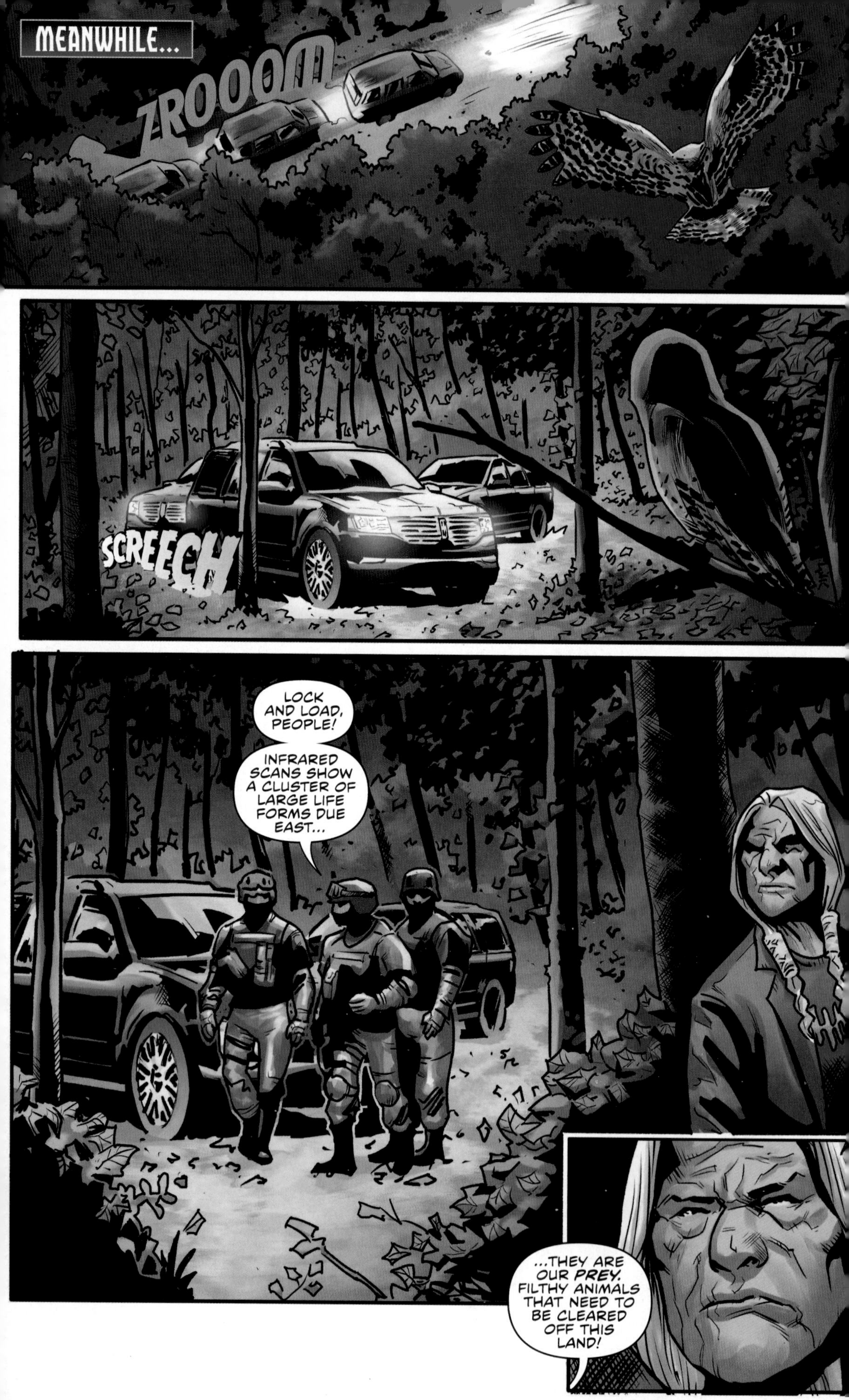
MEANWHILE...
ZROOOM
SCREECH
LOCK AND LOAD, PEOPLE!
INFRARED SCANS SHOW A CLUSTER OF LARGE LIFE FORMS DUE EAST...
...THEY ARE OUR PREY. FILTHY ANIMALS THAT NEED TO BE CLEARED OFF THIS LAND!

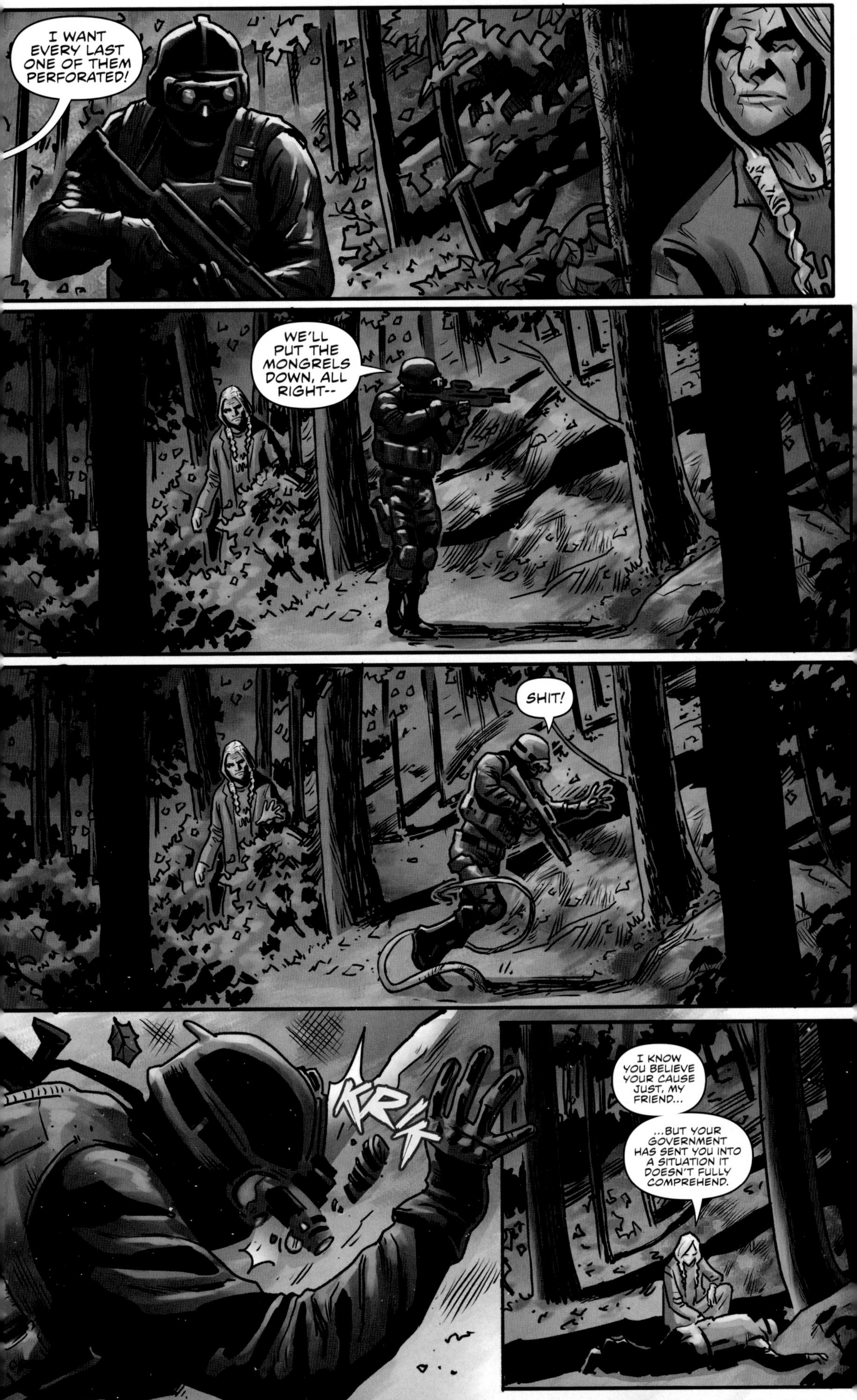
I WANT EVERY LAST ONE OF THEM PERFORATED!
WE'LL PUT THE MONGRELS DOWN, ALL RIGHT--
SHIT!
KRIK
I KNOW YOU BELIEVE YOUR CAUSE JUST, MY FRIEND...
...BUT YOUR GOVERNMENT HAS SENT YOU INTO A SITUATION IT DOESN'T FULLY COMPREHEND.

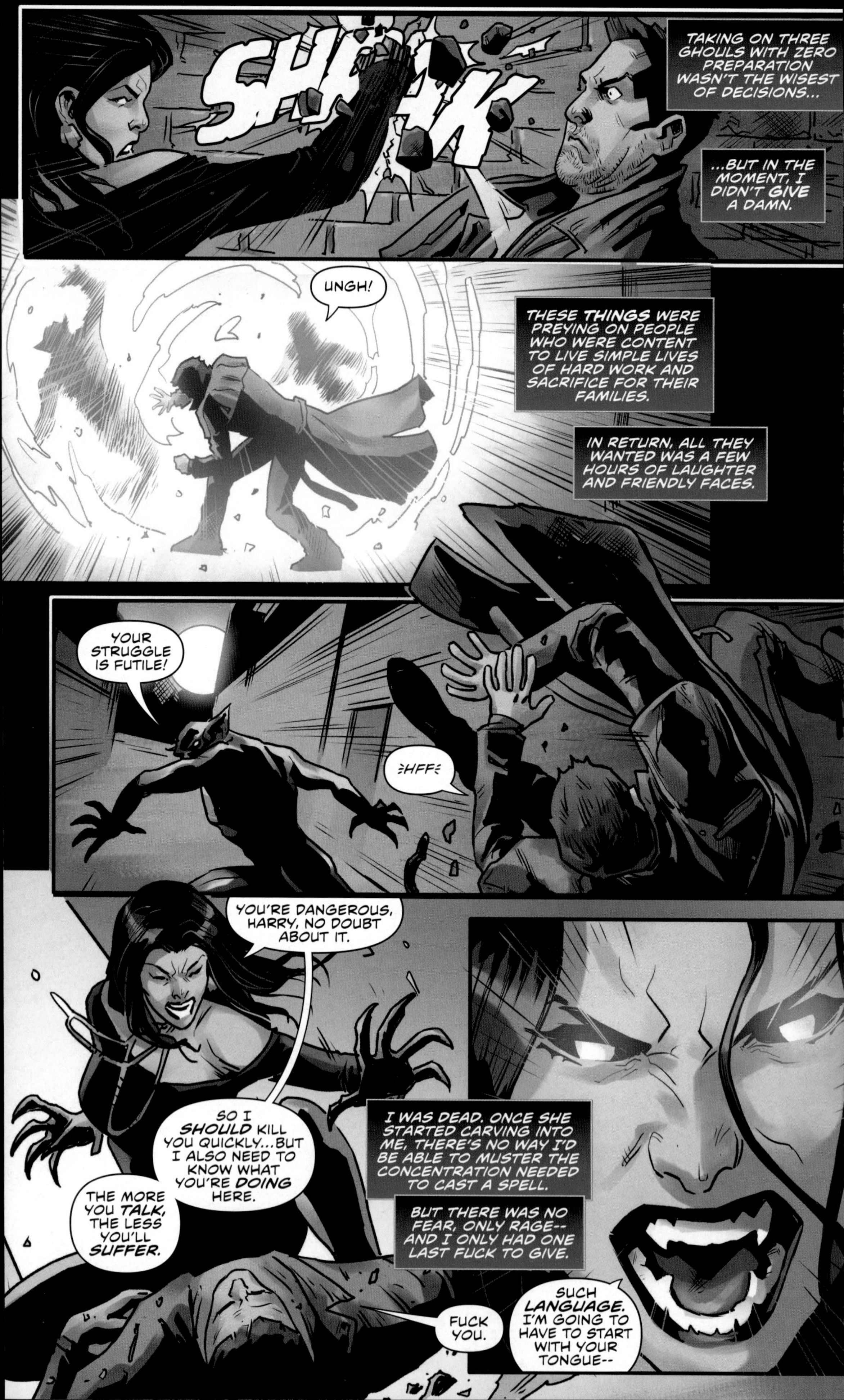

SHRAKK
TAKING ON THREE GHOULS WITH ZERO PREPARATION WASN'T THE WISEST OF DECISIONS...
...BUT IN THE MOMENT, I DIDN'T GIVE A DAMN.
UNGH!
THESE THINGS WERE PREYING ON PEOPLE WHO WERE CONTENT TO LIVE SIMPLE LIVES OF HARD WORK AND SACRIFICE FOR THEIR FAMILIES.
IN RETURN, ALL THEY WANTED WAS A FEW HOURS OF LAUGHTER AND FRIENDLY FACES.
YOUR STRUGGLE IS FUTILE!
HFF
YOU'RE DANGEROUS, HARRY, NO DOUBT ABOUT IT.
SO I SHOULD KILL YOU QUICKLY...BUT I ALSO NEED TO KNOW WHAT YOU'RE DOING HERE.
THE MORE YOU TALK, THE LESS YOU'LL SUFFER.
I WAS DEAD. ONCE SHE STARTED CARVING INTO ME, THERE'S NO WAY I'D BE ABLE TO MUSTER THE CONCENTRATION NEEDED TO CAST A SPELL.
BUT THERE WAS NO FEAR, ONLY RAGE--AND I ONLY HAD ONE LAST FUCK TO GIVE.
FUCK YOU.
SUCH LANGUAGE. I'M GOING TO HAVE TO START WITH YOUR TONGUE--

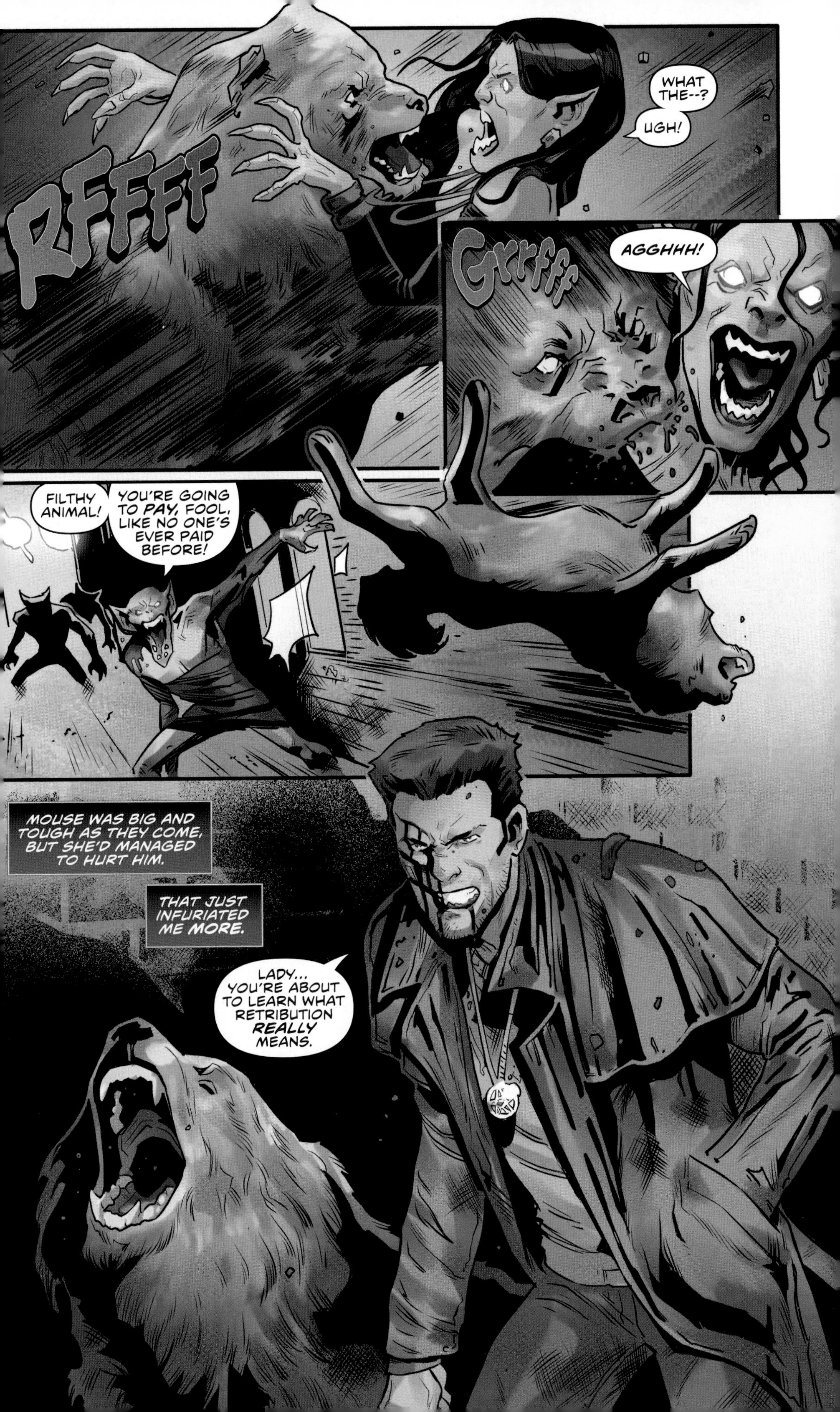
WHAT THE--?
UGH!
RFFFFF
GRRFFF
AGGHHH!
FILTHY ANIMAL!
YOU'RE GOING TO PAY, FOOL, LIKE NO ONE'S EVER PAID BEFORE!
MOUSE WAS BIG AND TOUGH AS THEY COME, BUT SHE'D MANAGED TO HURT HIM.
THAT JUST INFURIATED ME MORE.
LADY... YOU'RE ABOUT TO LEARN WHAT RETRIBUTION REALLY MEANS.

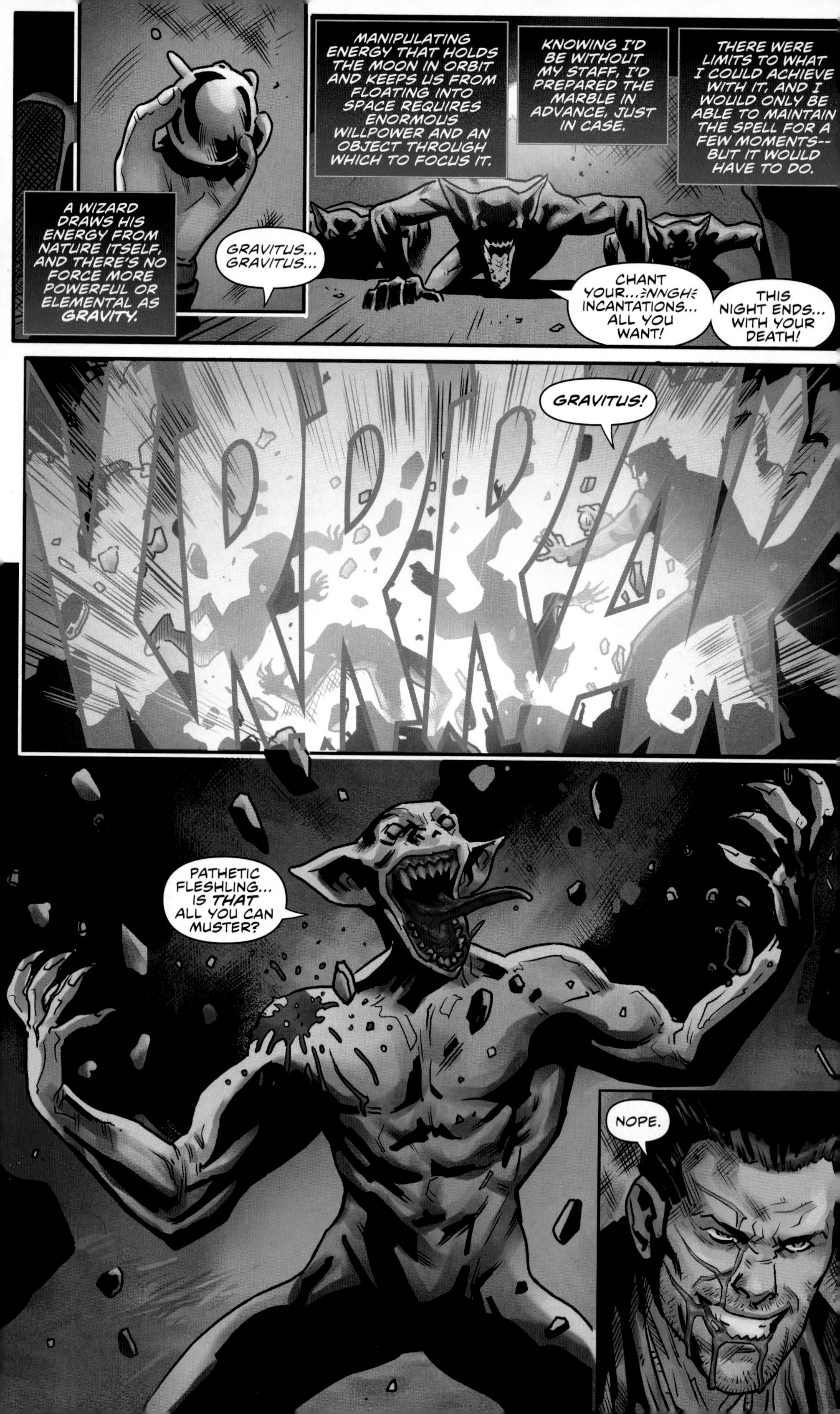

A WIZARD DRAWS HIS ENERGY FROM NATURE ITSELF, AND THERE'S NO FORCE MORE POWERFUL OR ELEMENTAL AS GRAVITY.
GRAVITUS... GRAVITUS...
MANIPULATING ENERGY THAT HOLDS THE MOON IN ORBIT AND KEEPS US FROM FLOATING INTO SPACE REQUIRES ENORMOUS WILLPOWER AND AN OBJECT THROUGH WHICH TO FOCUS IT.
KNOWING I'D BE WITHOUT MY STAFF, I'D PREPARED THE MARBLE IN ADVANCE, JUST IN CASE.
THERE WERE LIMITS TO WHAT I COULD ACHIEVE WITH IT, AND I WOULD ONLY BE ABLE TO MAINTAIN THE SPELL FOR A FEW MOMENTS--BUT IT WOULD HAVE TO DO.
CHANT YOUR... NNGH INCANTATIONS... ALL YOU WANT!
THIS NIGHT ENDS... WITH YOUR DEATH!
GRAVITUS!
PATHETIC FLESHLING... IS THAT ALL YOU CAN MUSTER?
NOPE.

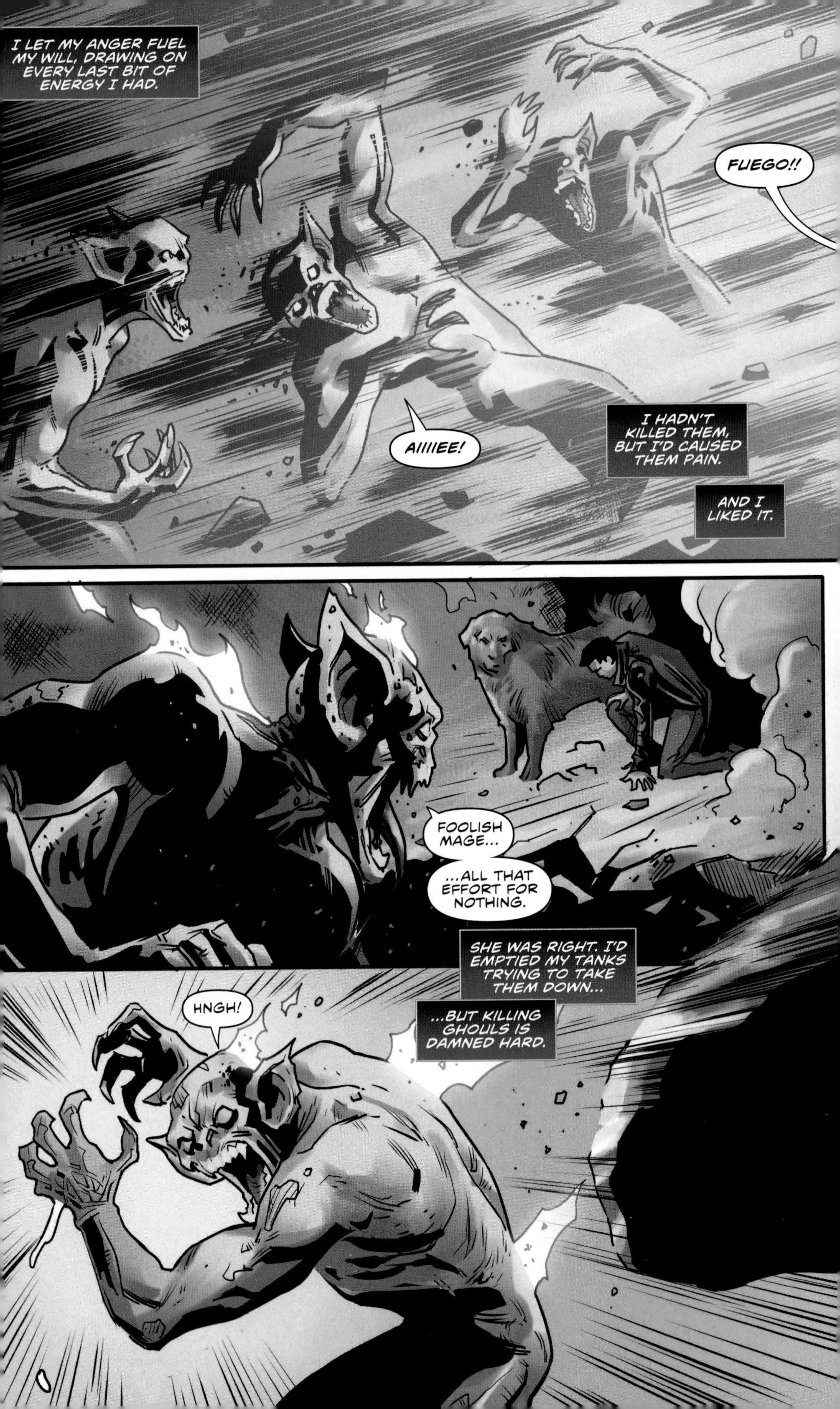
I LET MY ANGER FUEL MY WILL, DRAWING ON EVERY LAST BIT OF ENERGY I HAD.
FUEGO!!
AIIIIEE!
I HADN'T KILLED THEM, BUT I'D CAUSED THEM PAIN.
AND I LIKED IT.
FOOLISH MAGE...
...ALL THAT EFFORT FOR NOTHING.
SHE WAS RIGHT. I'D EMPTIED MY TANKS TRYING TO TAKE THEM DOWN...
...BUT KILLING GHOULS IS DAMNED HARD.
HNGH!

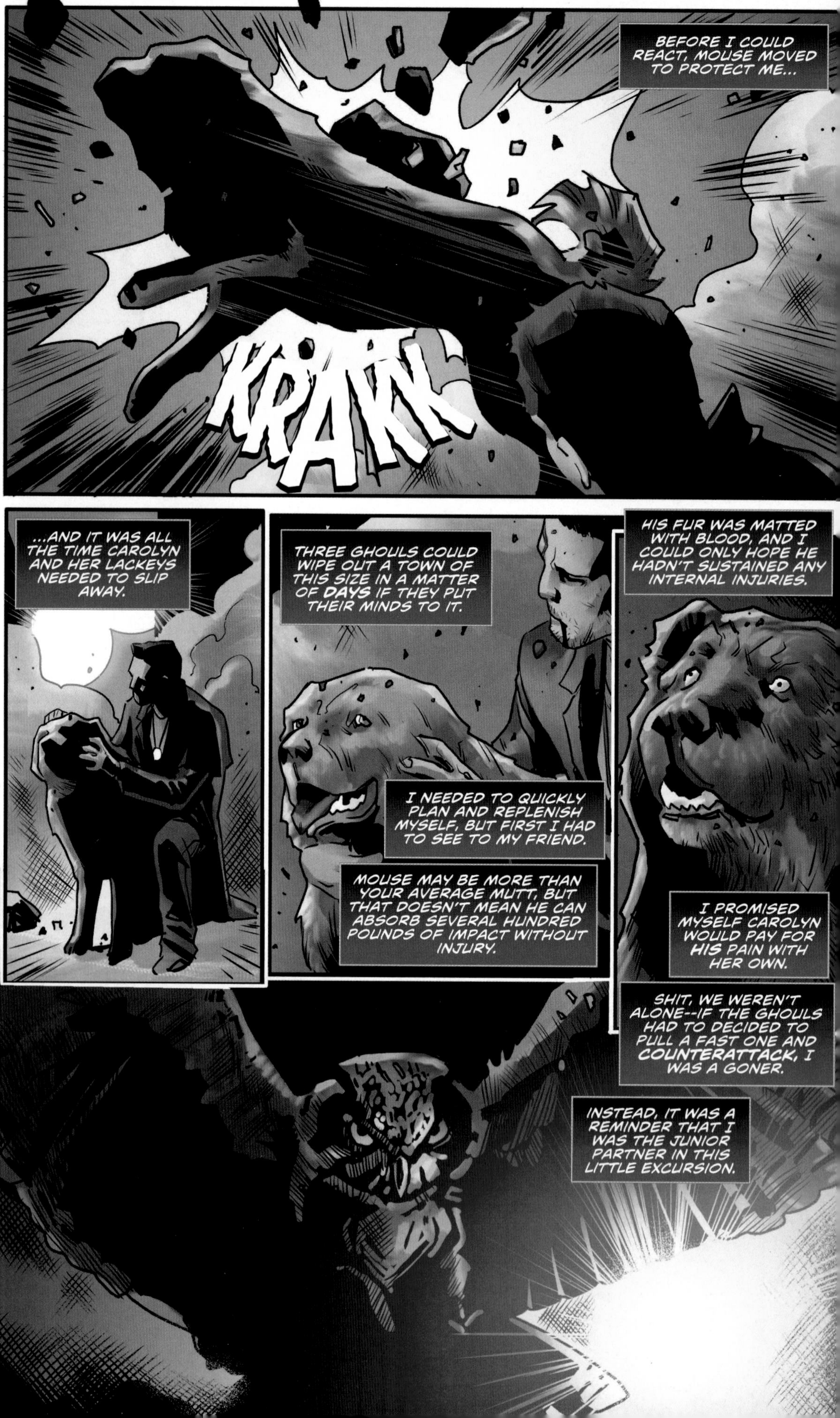
BEFORE I COULD REACT, MOUSE MOVED TO PROTECT ME...
KRAKK
...AND IT WAS ALL THE TIME CAROLYN AND HER LACKEYS NEEDED TO SLIP AWAY.
THREE GHOULS COULD WIPE OUT A TOWN OF THIS SIZE IN A MATTER OF DAYS IF THEY PUT THEIR MINDS TO IT.
I NEEDED TO QUICKLY PLAN AND REPLENISH MYSELF, BUT FIRST I HAD TO SEE TO MY FRIEND.
MOUSE MAY BE MORE THAN YOUR AVERAGE MUTT, BUT THAT DOESN'T MEAN HE CAN ABSORB SEVERAL HUNDRED POUNDS OF IMPACT WITHOUT INJURY.
HIS FUR WAS MATTED WITH BLOOD, AND I COULD ONLY HOPE HE HADN'T SUSTAINED ANY INTERNAL INJURIES.
I PROMISED MYSELF CAROLYN WOULD PAY FOR HIS PAIN WITH HER OWN.
SHIT, WE WEREN'T ALONE--IF THE GHOULS HAD TO DECIDED TO PULL A FAST ONE AND COUNTERATTACK, I WAS A GONER.
INSTEAD, IT WAS A REMINDER THAT I WAS THE JUNIOR PARTNER IN THIS LITTLE EXCURSION.

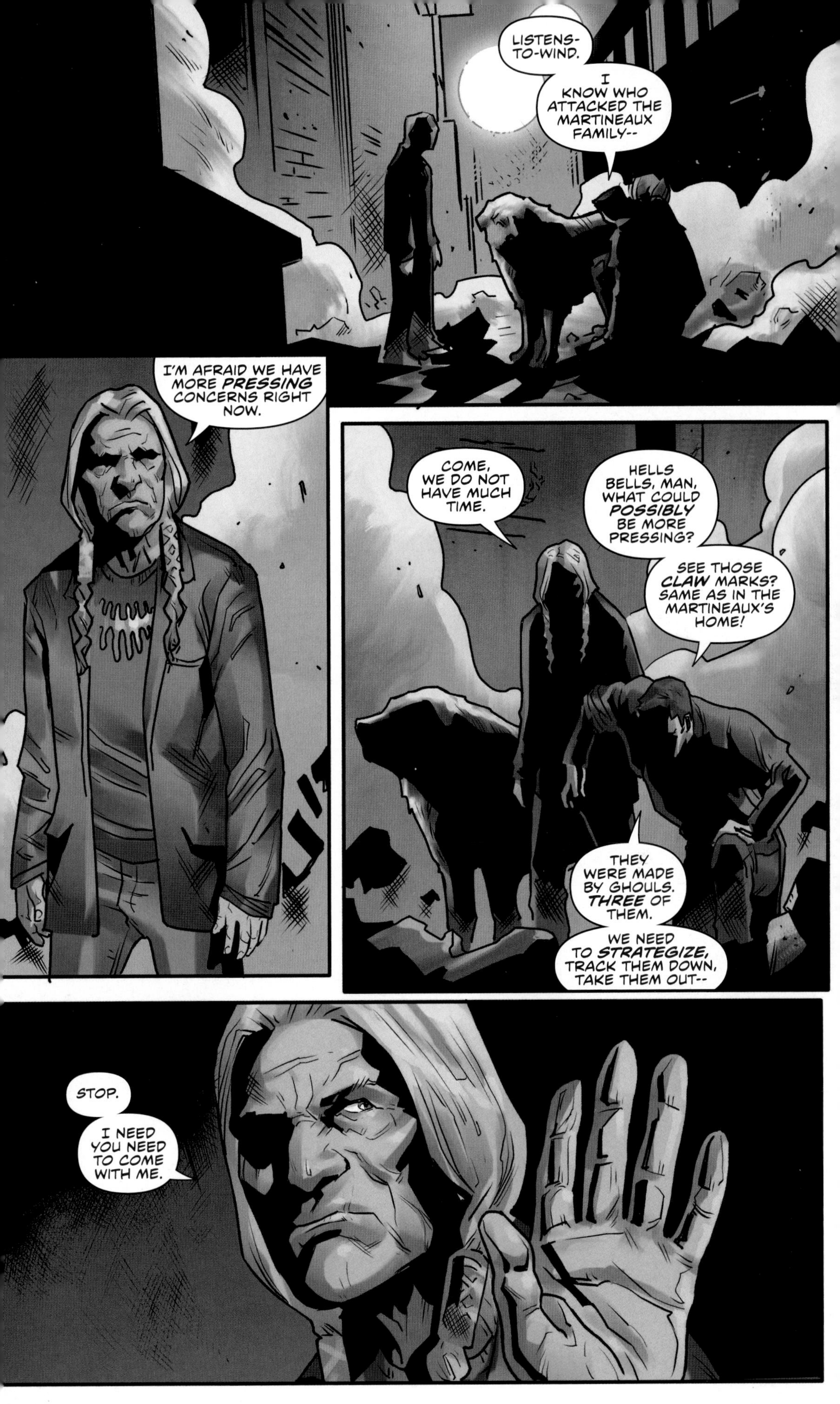
LISTENS-TO-WIND.
I KNOW WHO ATTACKED THE MARTINEAUX FAMILY--
I'M AFRAID WE HAVE MORE PRESSING CONCERNS RIGHT NOW.
COME, WE DO NOT HAVE MUCH TIME.
HELLS BELLS, MAN, WHAT COULD POSSIBLY BE MORE PRESSING?
SEE THOSE CLAW MARKS? SAME AS IN THE MARTINEAUX'S HOME!
THEY WERE MADE BY GHOULS. THREE OF THEM.
WE NEED TO STRATEGIZE, TRACK THEM DOWN, TAKE THEM OUT--
STOP.
I NEED YOU NEED TO COME WITH ME.

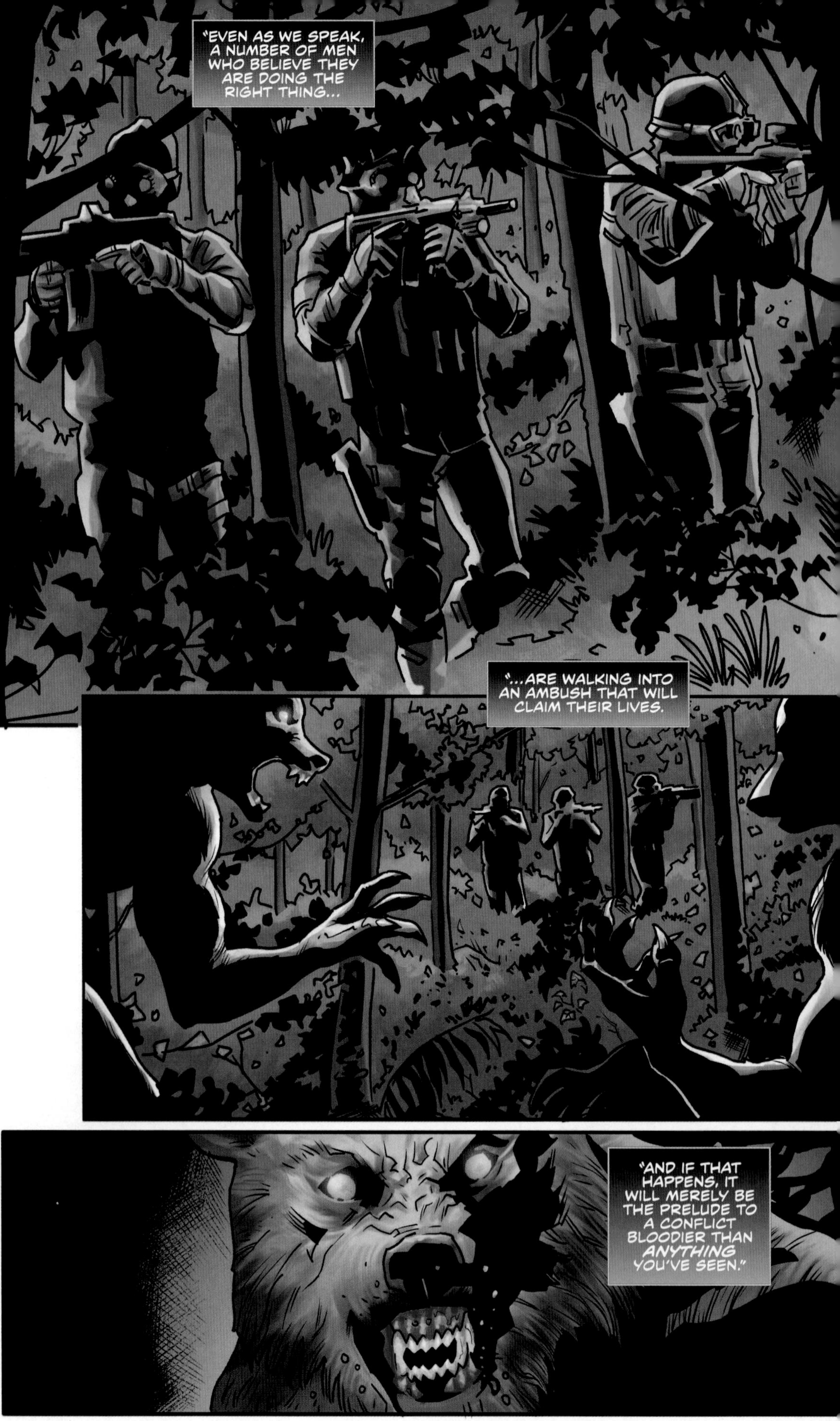
"EVEN AS WE SPEAK, A NUMBER OF MEN WHO BELIEVE THEY ARE DOING THE RIGHT THING...
"...ARE WALKING INTO AN AMBUSH THAT WILL CLAIM THEIR LIVES.
"AND IF THAT HAPPENS, IT WILL MERELY BE THE PRELUDE TO A CONFLICT BLOODIER THAN *ANYTHING* YOU'VE SEEN."

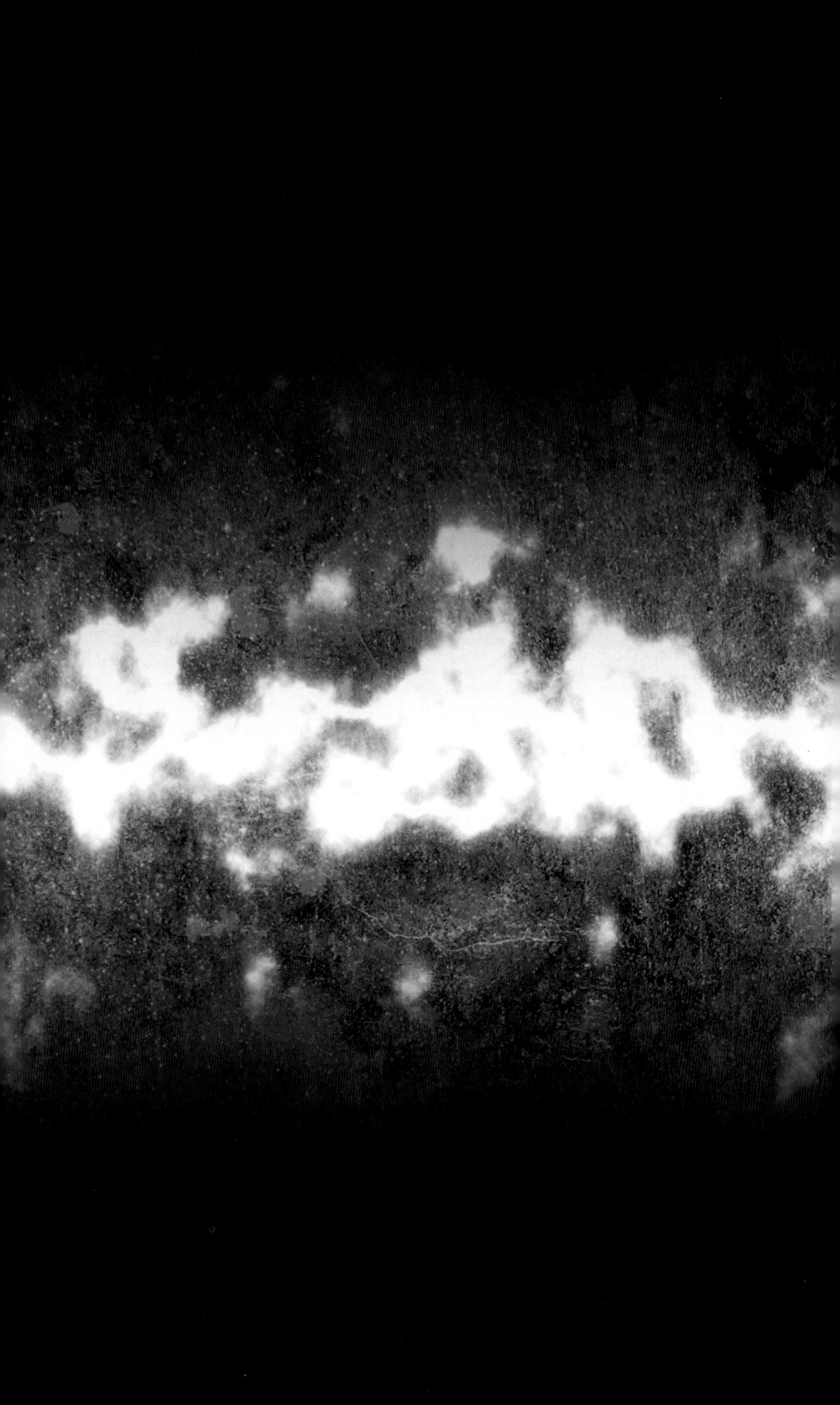

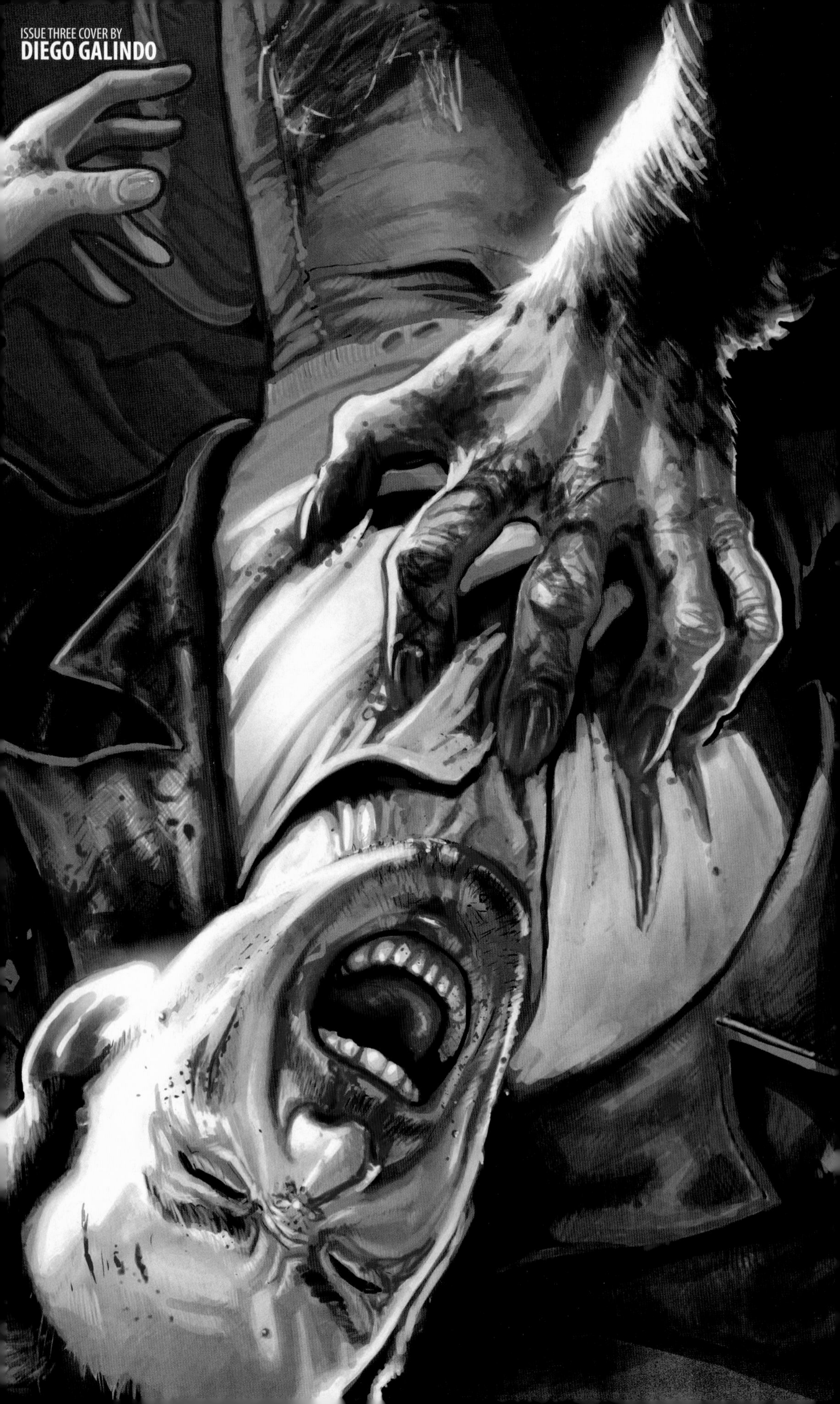
ISSUE THREE COVER BY
DIEGO GALINDO

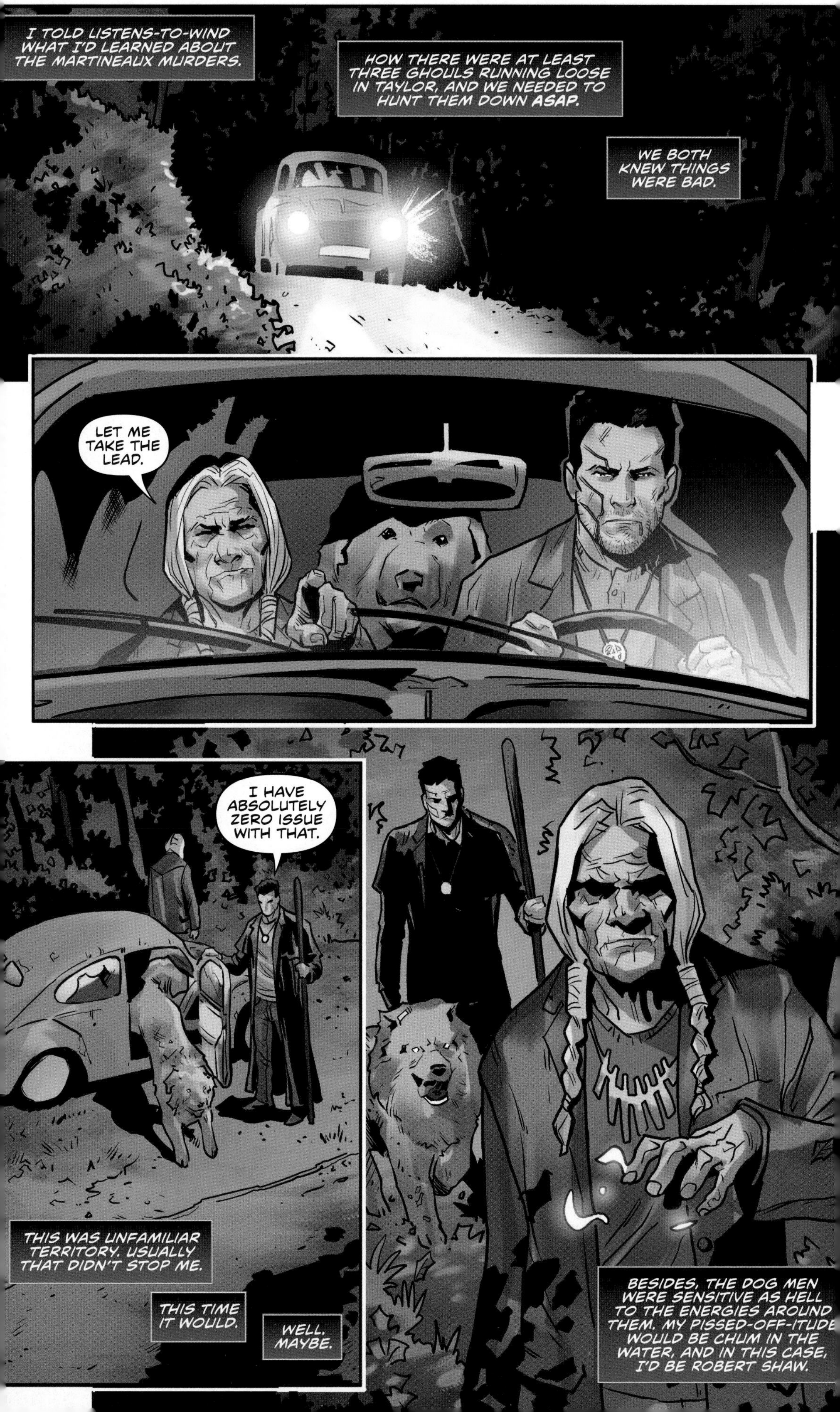
I TOLD LISTENS-TO-WIND WHAT I'D LEARNED ABOUT THE MARTINEAUX MURDERS.
HOW THERE WERE AT LEAST THREE GHOULS RUNNING LOOSE IN TAYLOR, AND WE NEEDED TO HUNT THEM DOWN ASAP.
WE BOTH KNEW THINGS WERE BAD.
LET ME TAKE THE LEAD.
I HAVE ABSOLUTELY ZERO ISSUE WITH THAT.
THIS WAS UNFAMILIAR TERRITORY. USUALLY THAT DIDN'T STOP ME.
THIS TIME IT WOULD.
WELL. MAYBE.
BESIDES, THE DOG MEN WERE SENSITIVE AS HELL TO THE ENERGIES AROUND THEM. MY PISSED-OFF-ITUDE WOULD BE CHUM IN THE WATER, AND IN THIS CASE, I'D BE ROBERT SHAW.

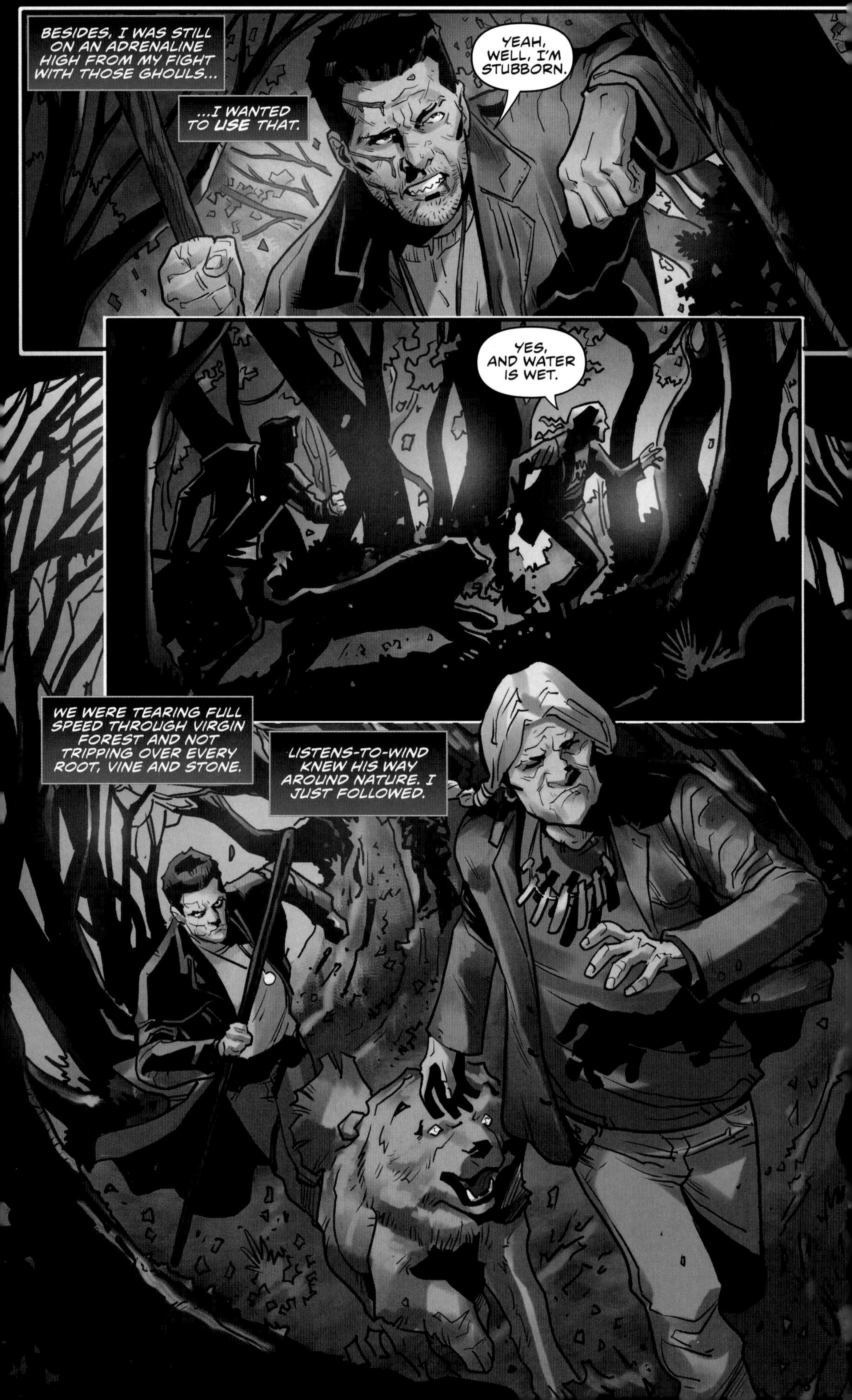
BESIDES, I WAS STILL ON AN ADRENALINE HIGH FROM MY FIGHT WITH THOSE GHOULS...
...I WANTED TO USE THAT.
YEAH, WELL, I'M STUBBORN.
YES, AND WATER IS WET.
WE WERE TEARING FULL SPEED THROUGH VIRGIN FOREST AND NOT TRIPPING OVER EVERY ROOT, VINE AND STONE.
LISTENS-TO-WIND KNEW HIS WAY AROUND NATURE. I JUST FOLLOWED.

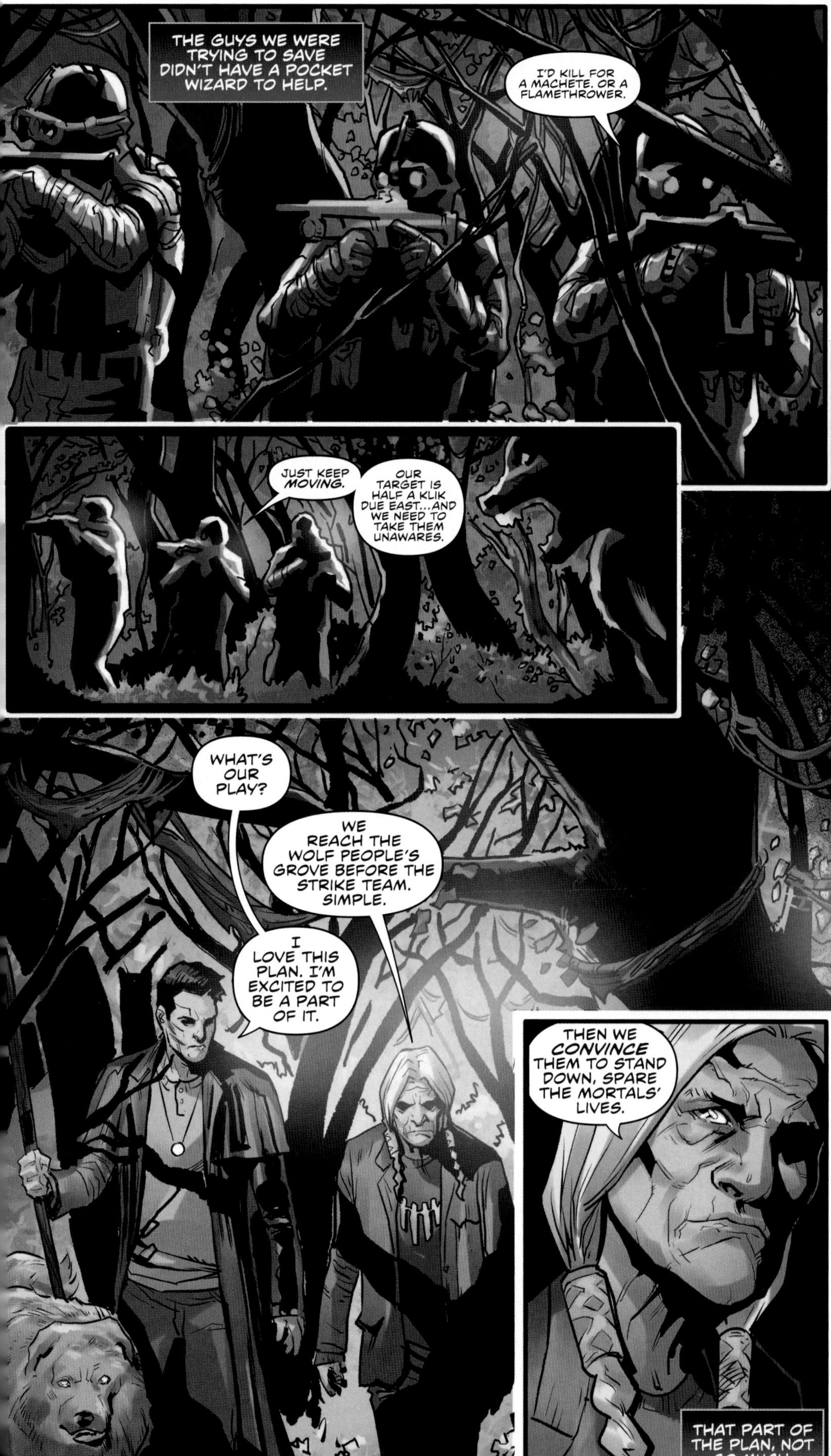
THE GUYS WE WERE TRYING TO SAVE DIDN'T HAVE A POCKET WIZARD TO HELP.
I'D KILL FOR A MACHETE. OR A FLAMETHROWER.
JUST KEEP MOVING.
OUR TARGET IS HALF A KLIK DUE EAST...AND WE NEED TO TAKE THEM UNAWARES.
WHAT'S OUR PLAY?
WE REACH THE WOLF PEOPLE'S GROVE BEFORE THE STRIKE TEAM. SIMPLE.
I LOVE THIS PLAN. I'M EXCITED TO BE A PART OF IT.
THEN WE CONVINCE THEM TO STAND DOWN, SPARE THE MORTALS' LIVES.
THAT PART OF THE PLAN, NOT SO MUCH.

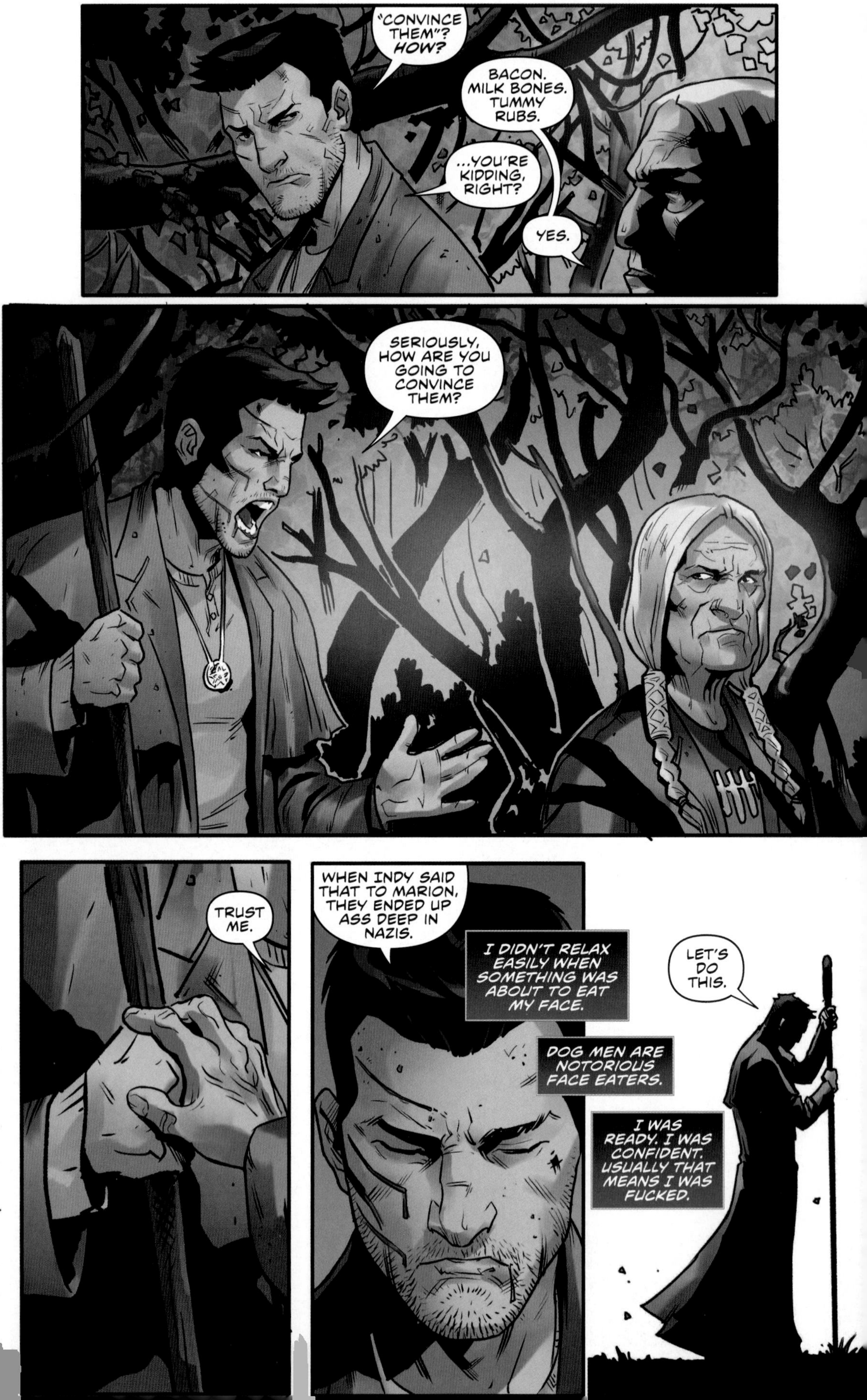
"CONVINCE THEM"? HOW?
BACON. MILK BONES. TUMMY RUBS.
...YOU'RE KIDDING, RIGHT?
YES.
SERIOUSLY, HOW ARE YOU GOING TO CONVINCE THEM?
TRUST ME.
WHEN INDY SAID THAT TO MARION, THEY ENDED UP ASS DEEP IN NAZIS.
I DIDN'T RELAX EASILY WHEN SOMETHING WAS ABOUT TO EAT MY FACE.
DOG MEN ARE NOTORIOUS FACE EATERS.
LET'S DO THIS.
I WAS READY. I WAS CONFIDENT. USUALLY THAT MEANS I WAS FUCKED.

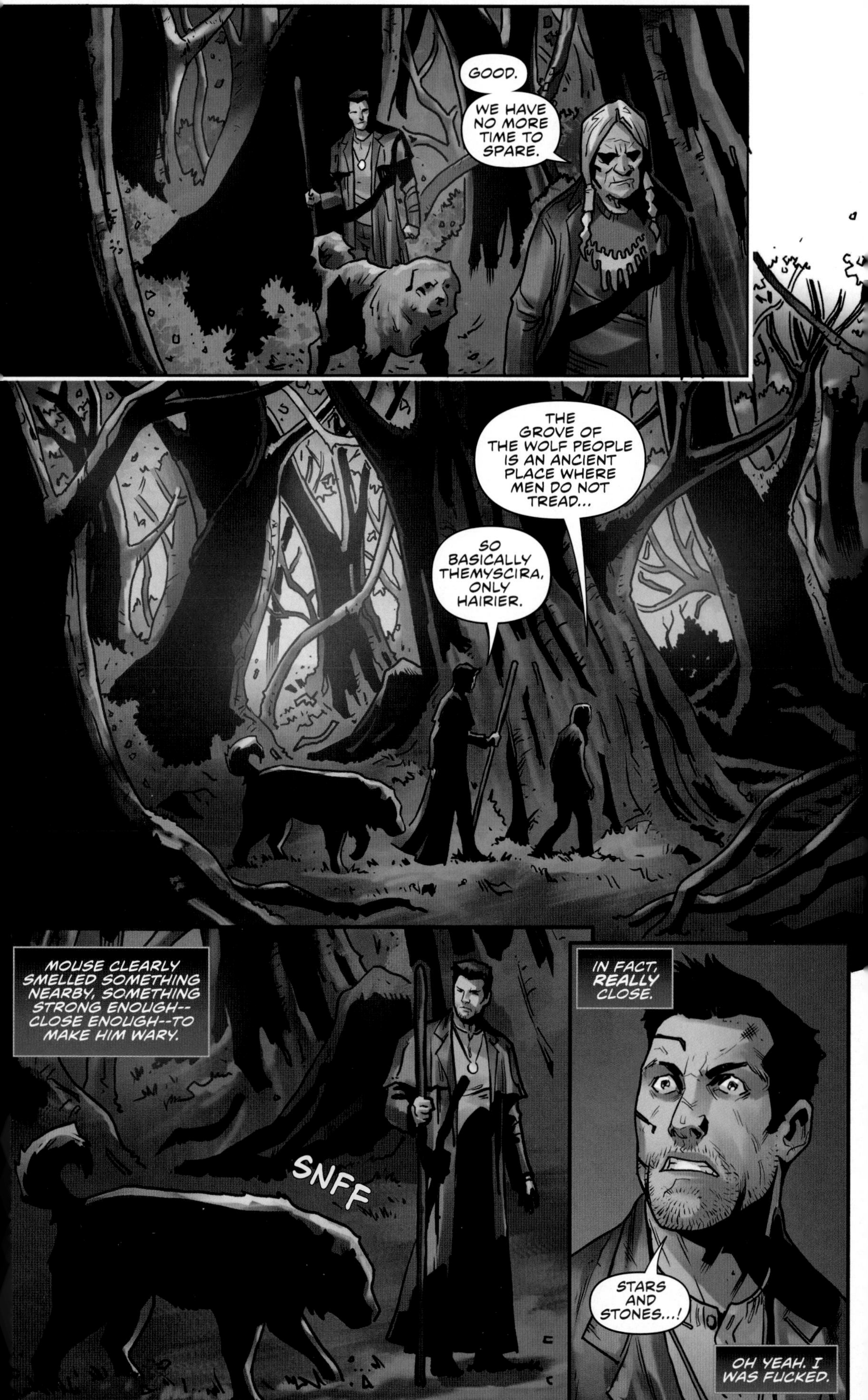
GOOD.
WE HAVE NO MORE TIME TO SPARE.
THE GROVE OF THE WOLF PEOPLE IS AN ANCIENT PLACE WHERE MEN DO NOT TREAD...
SO BASICALLY THEMYSCIRA, ONLY HAIRIER.
MOUSE CLEARLY SMELLED SOMETHING NEARBY, SOMETHING STRONG ENOUGH--CLOSE ENOUGH--TO MAKE HIM WARY.
SNFF
IN FACT, REALLY CLOSE.
STARS AND STONES...!
OH YEAH. I WAS FUCKED.

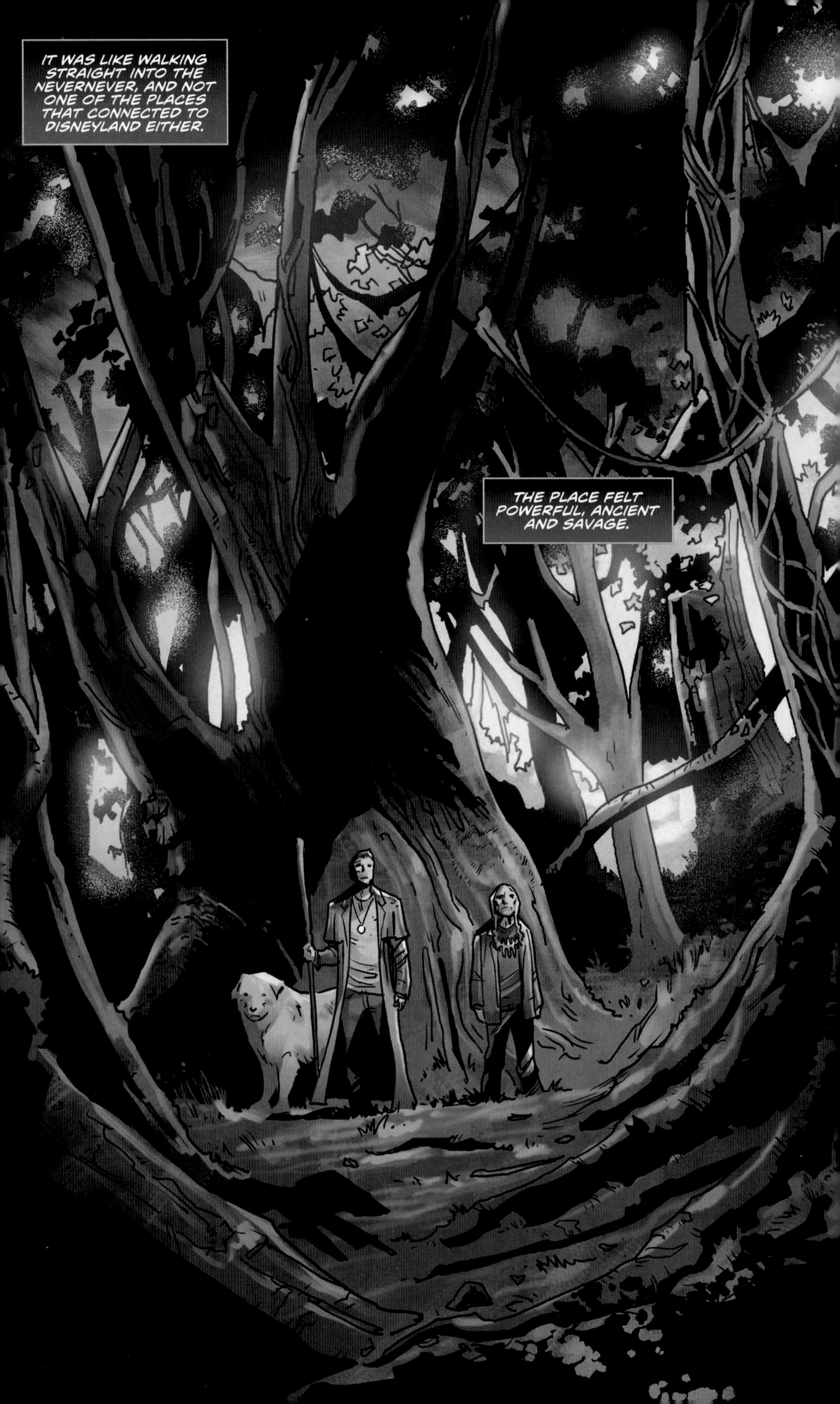
IT WAS LIKE WALKING STRAIGHT INTO THE NEVERNEVER, AND NOT ONE OF THE PLACES THAT CONNECTED TO DISNEYLAND EITHER.
THE PLACE FELT POWERFUL, ANCIENT AND SAVAGE.

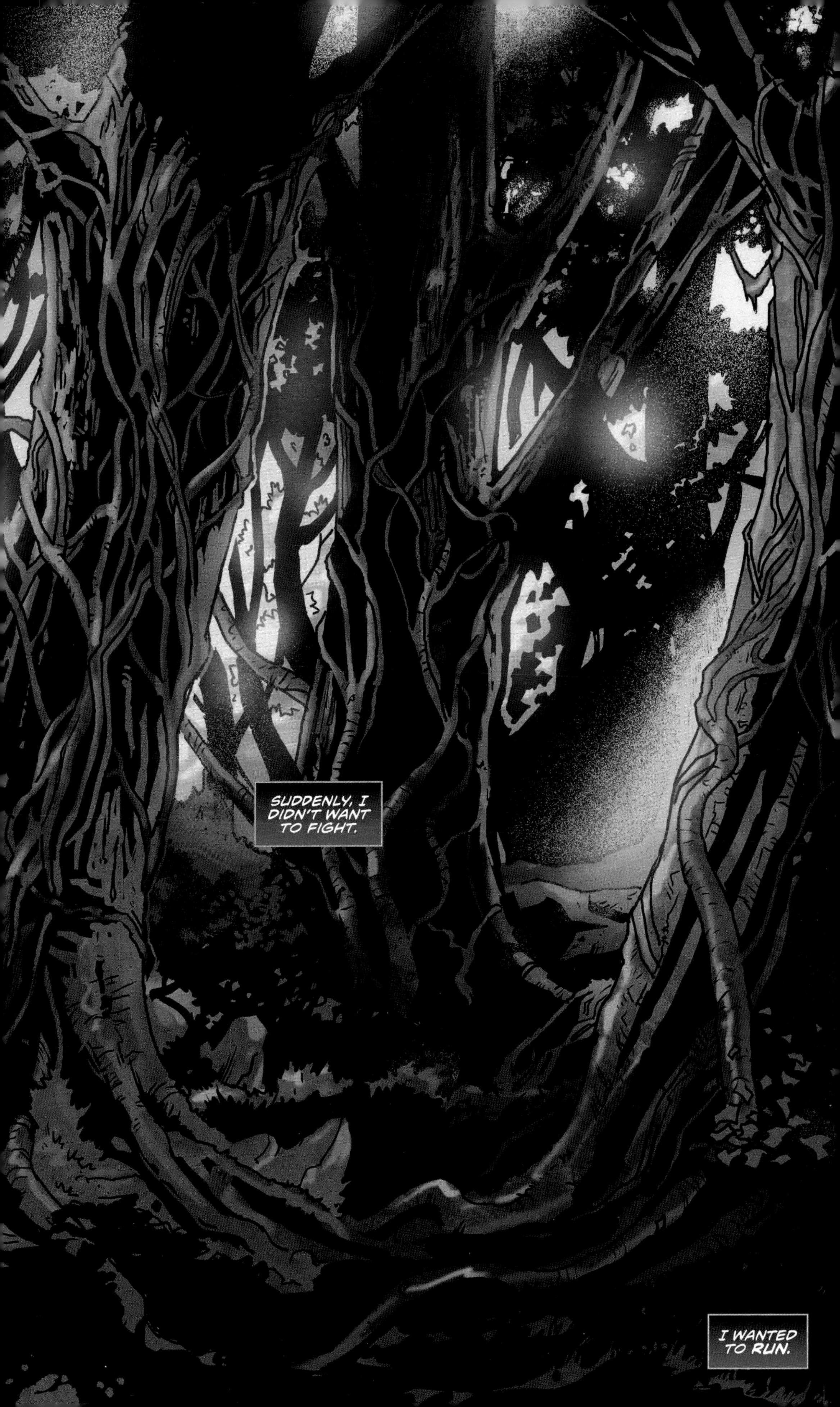
SUDDENLY, I DIDN'T WANT TO FIGHT.
I WANTED TO RUN.

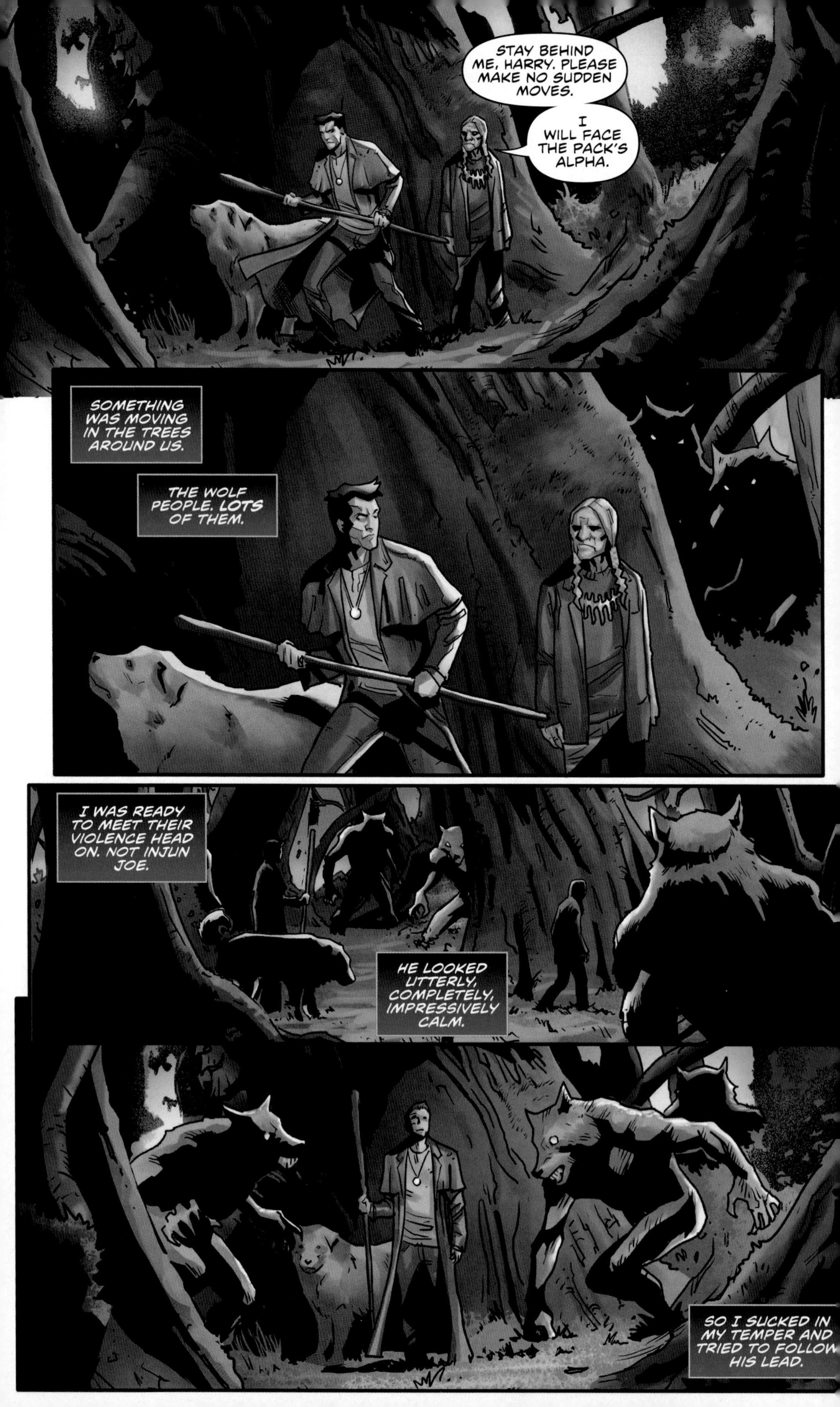
STAY BEHIND ME, HARRY. PLEASE MAKE NO SUDDEN MOVES.
I WILL FACE THE PACK'S ALPHA.
SOMETHING WAS MOVING IN THE TREES AROUND US.
THE WOLF PEOPLE. LOTS OF THEM.
I WAS READY TO MEET THEIR VIOLENCE HEAD ON. NOT INJUN JOE.
HE LOOKED UTTERLY, COMPLETELY, IMPRESSIVELY CALM.
SO I SUCKED IN MY TEMPER AND TRIED TO FOLLOW HIS LEAD.

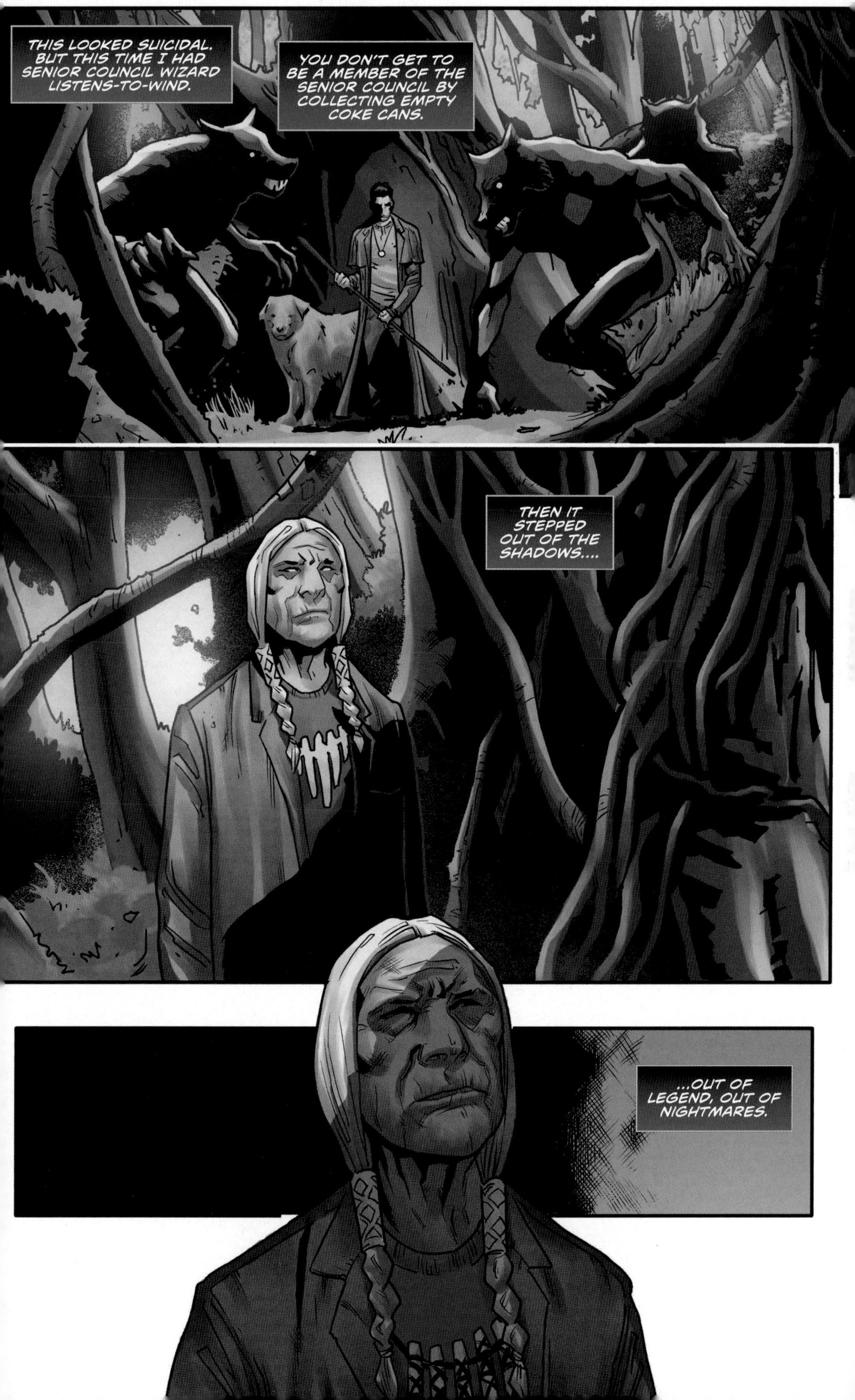

THIS LOOKED SUICIDAL. BUT THIS TIME I HAD SENIOR COUNCIL WIZARD LISTENS-TO-WIND.
YOU DON'T GET TO BE A MEMBER OF THE SENIOR COUNCIL BY COLLECTING EMPTY COKE CANS.
THEN IT STEPPED OUT OF THE SHADOWS....
...OUT OF LEGEND, OUT OF NIGHTMARES.

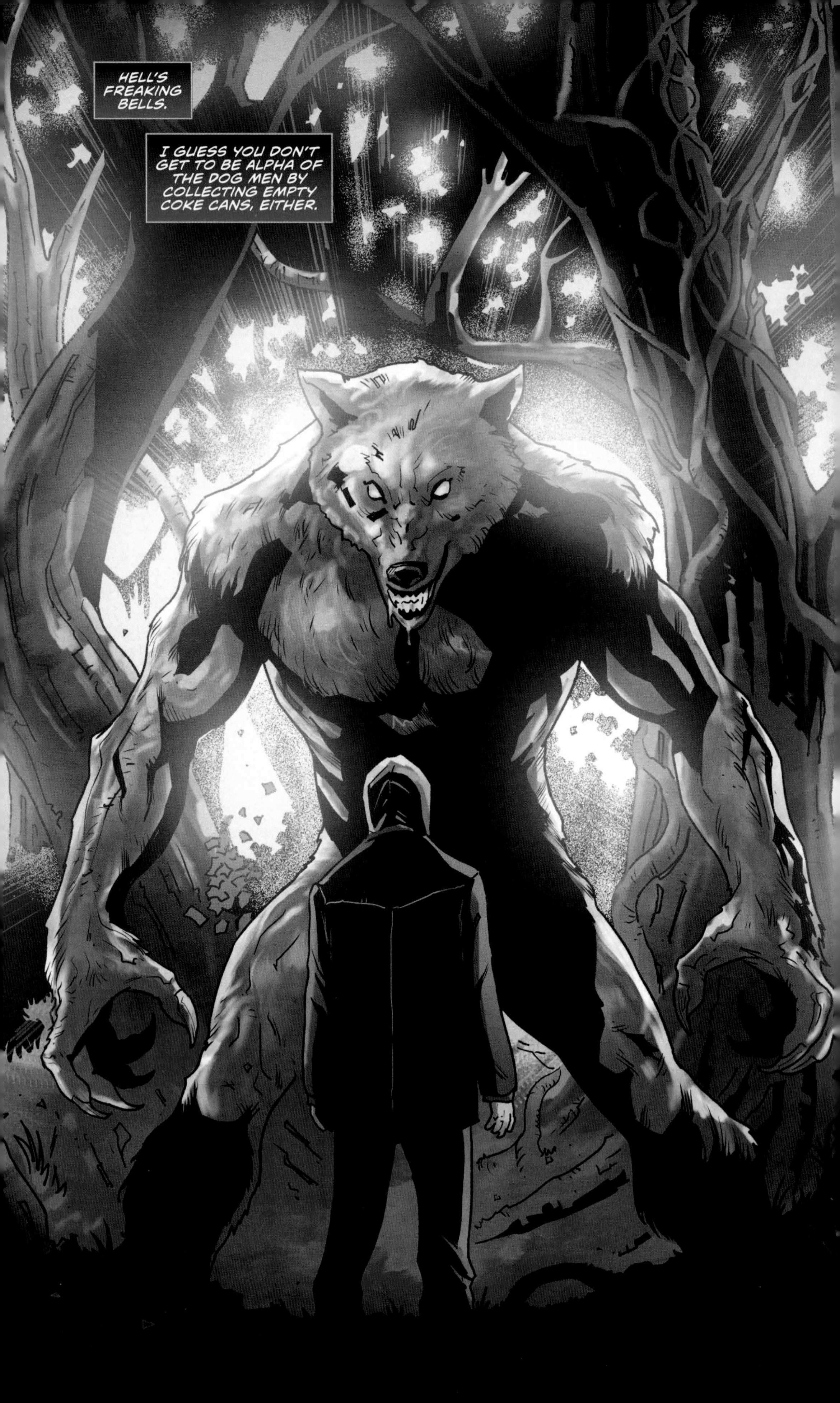
HELL'S FREAKING BELLS.
I GUESS YOU DON'T GET TO BE ALPHA OF THE DOG MEN BY COLLECTING EMPTY COKE CANS, EITHER.

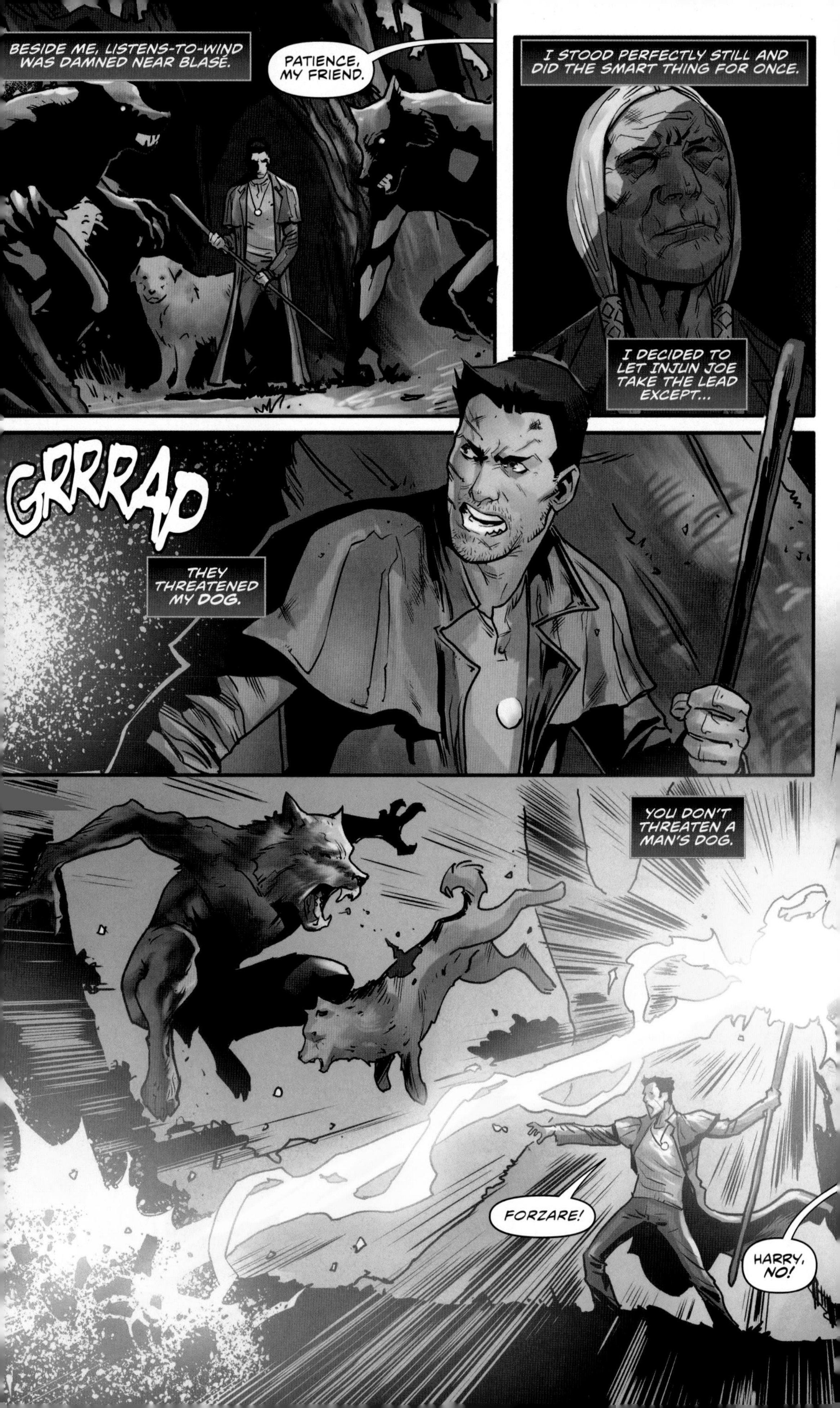
BESIDE ME, LISTENS-TO-WIND WAS DAMNED NEAR BLASÉ.
PATIENCE, MY FRIEND.
I STOOD PERFECTLY STILL AND DID THE SMART THING FOR ONCE.
I DECIDED TO LET INJUN JOE TAKE THE LEAD EXCEPT...
GRRRAD
THEY THREATENED MY DOG.
YOU DON'T THREATEN A MAN'S DOG.
FORZARE!
HARRY, NO!

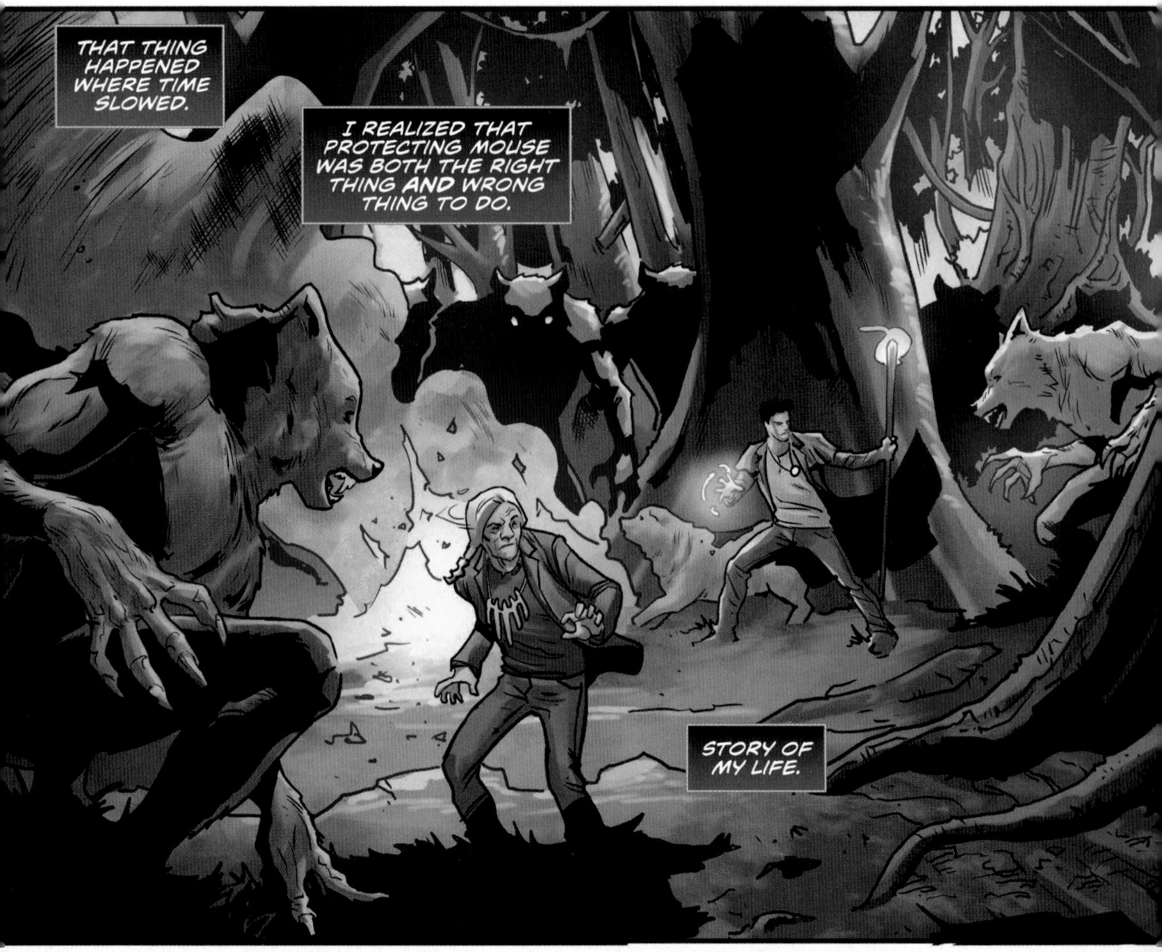
THAT THING HAPPENED WHERE TIME SLOWED.
I REALIZED THAT PROTECTING MOUSE WAS BOTH THE RIGHT THING AND WRONG THING TO DO.
STORY OF MY LIFE.

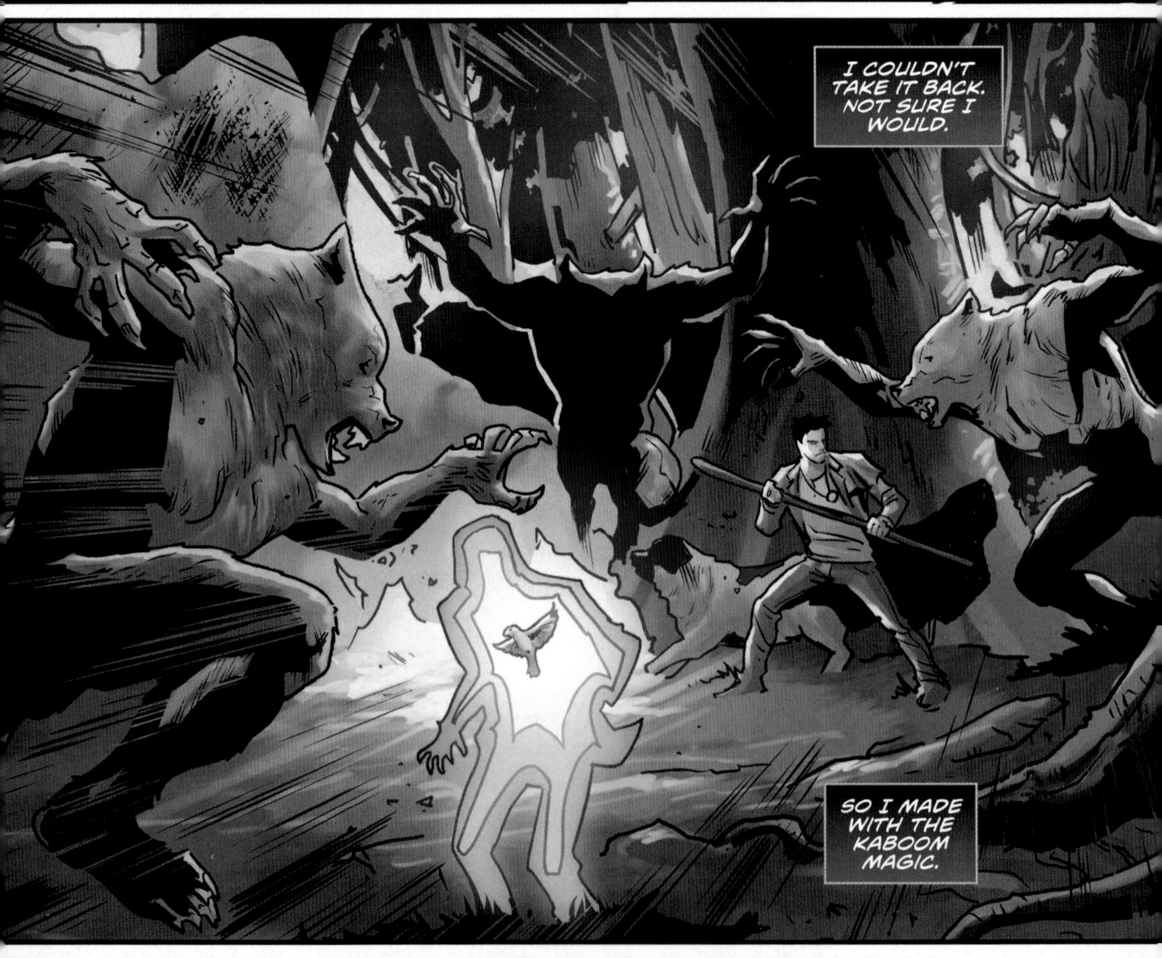
I COULDN'T TAKE IT BACK. NOT SURE I WOULD.
SO I MADE WITH THE KABOOM MAGIC.

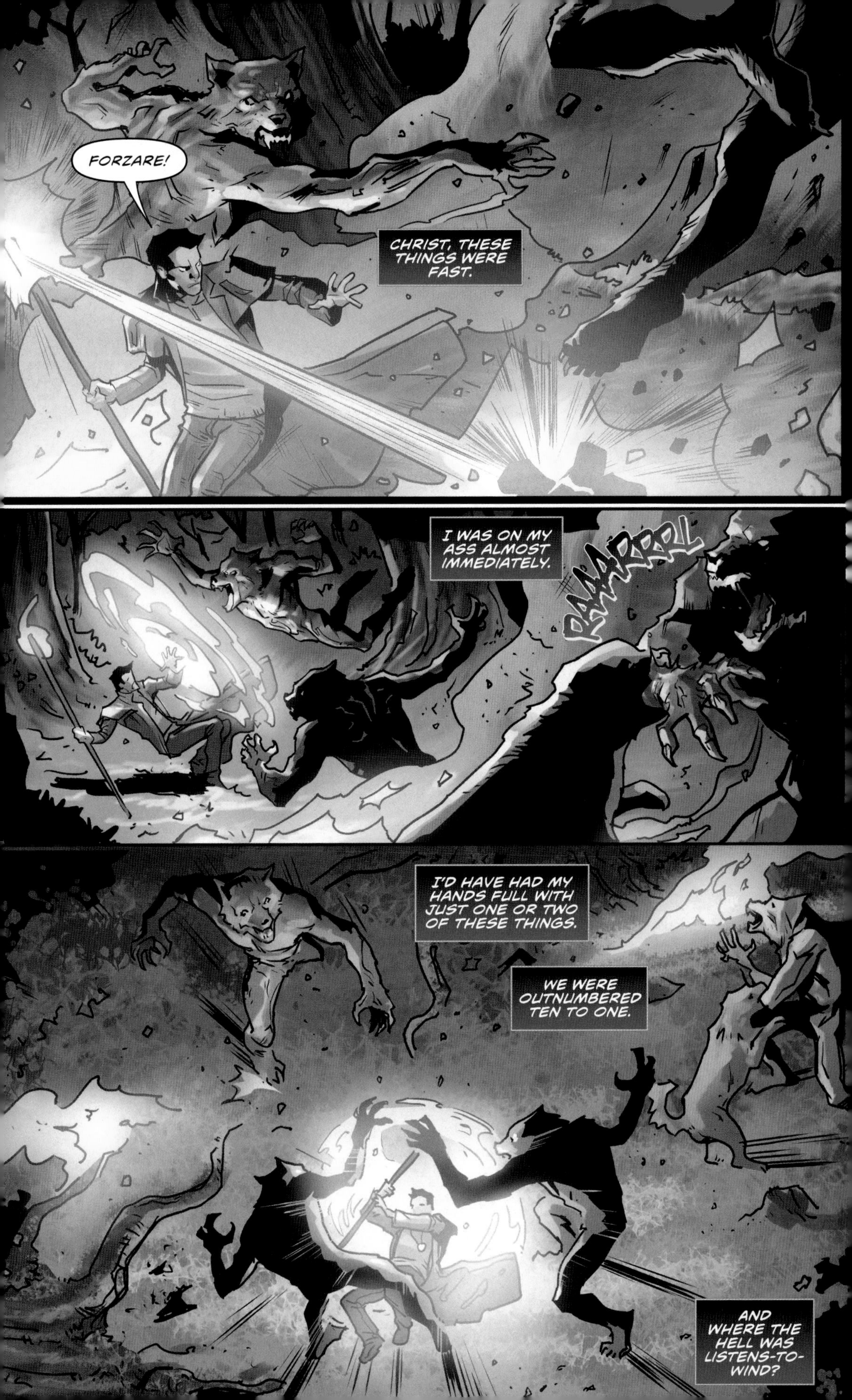
FORZARE!
CHRIST, THESE THINGS WERE FAST.
I WAS ON MY ASS ALMOST IMMEDIATELY.
RAAARRRL
I'D HAVE HAD MY HANDS FULL WITH JUST ONE OR TWO OF THESE THINGS.
WE WERE OUTNUMBERED TEN TO ONE.
AND WHERE THE HELL WAS LISTENS-TO-WIND?

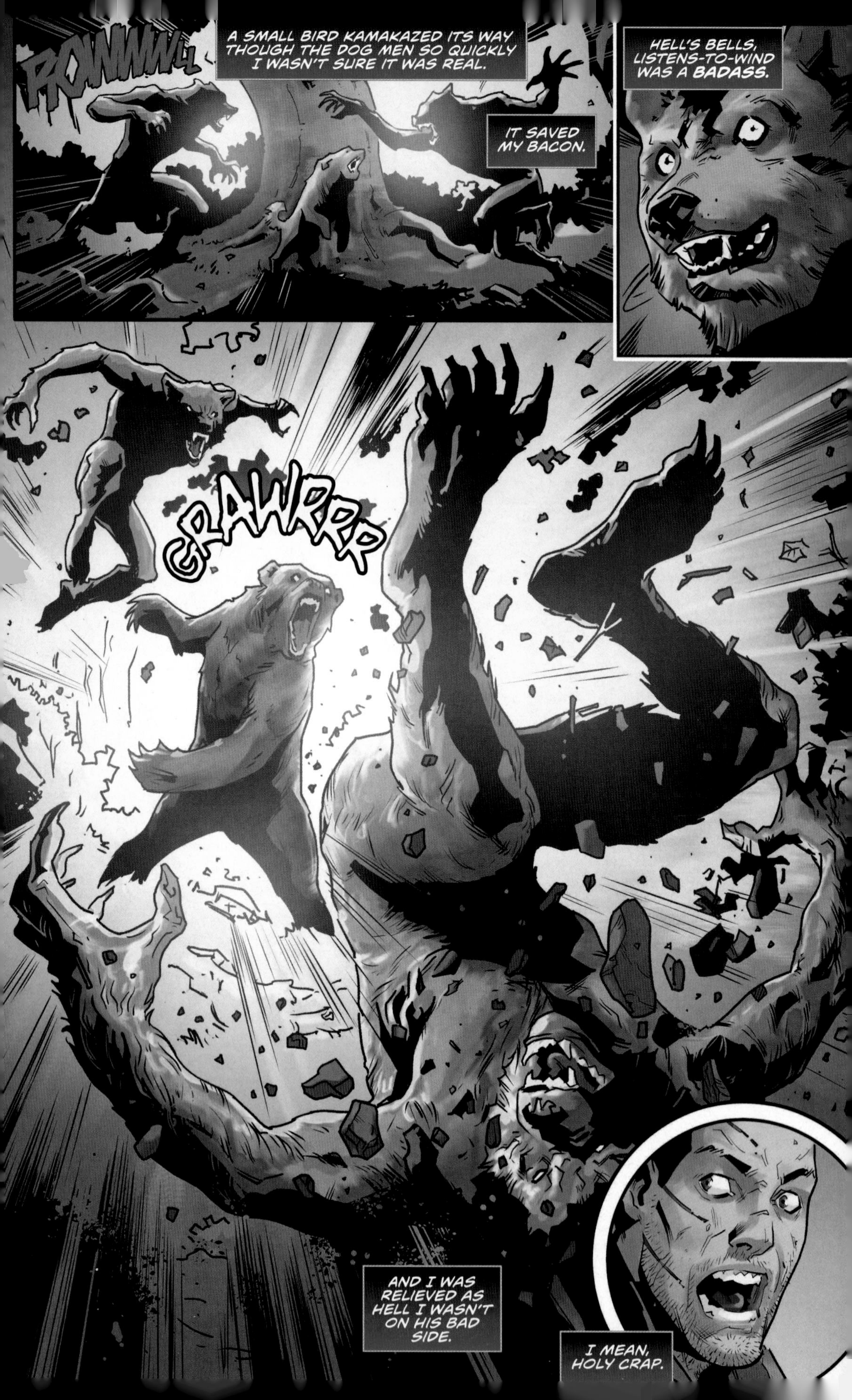

RONWWLL
A SMALL BIRD KAMAKAZED ITS WAY THOUGH THE DOG MEN SO QUICKLY I WASN'T SURE IT WAS REAL.
IT SAVED MY BACON.
HELL'S BELLS, LISTENS-TO-WIND WAS A BADASS.
GRAWRRR
AND I WAS RELIEVED AS HELL I WASN'T ON HIS BAD SIDE.
I MEAN, HOLY CRAP.

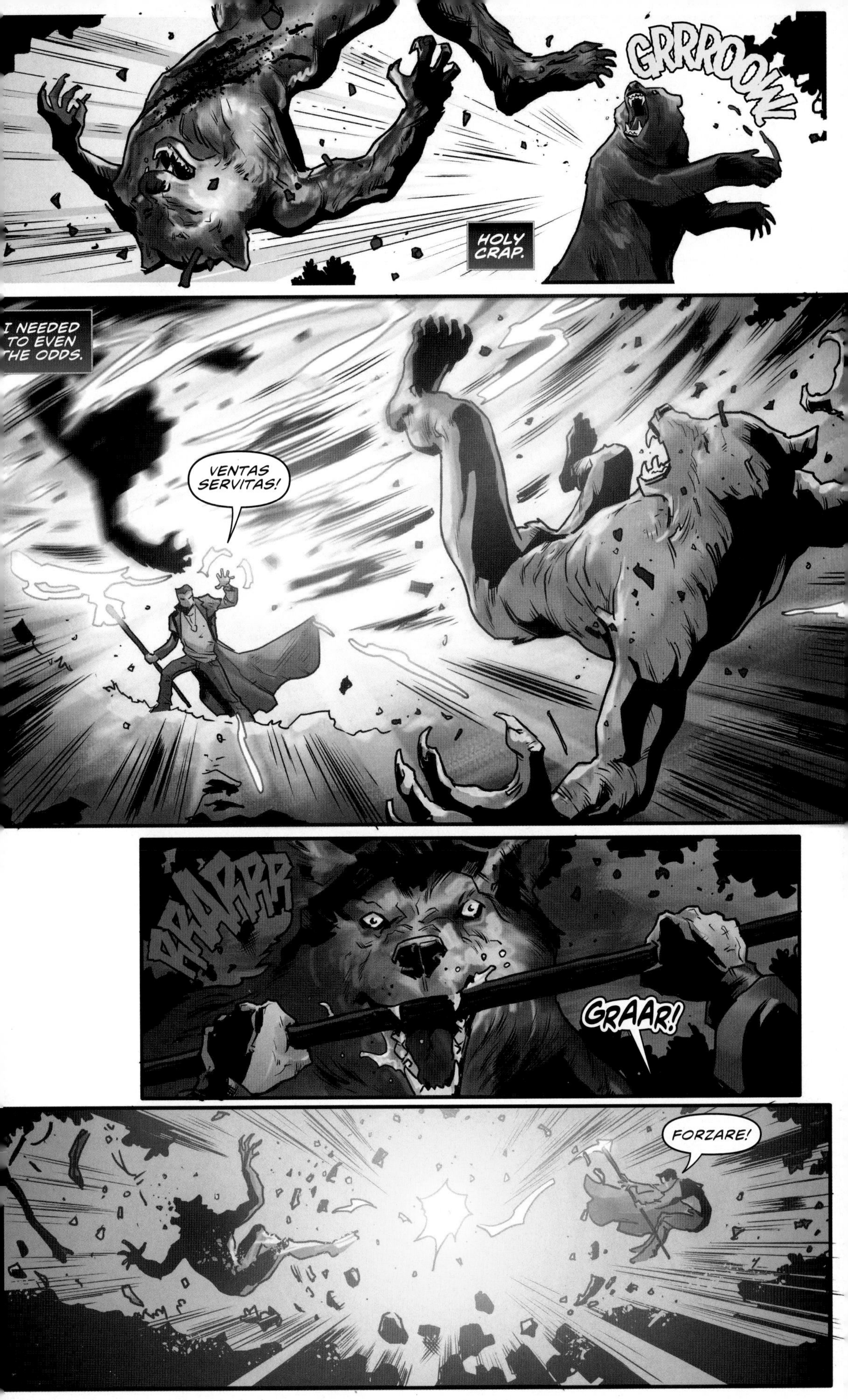
GRRROOW!
HOLY CRAP.
I NEEDED TO EVEN THE ODDS.
VENTAS SERVITAS!
GRAAR!
FORZARE!

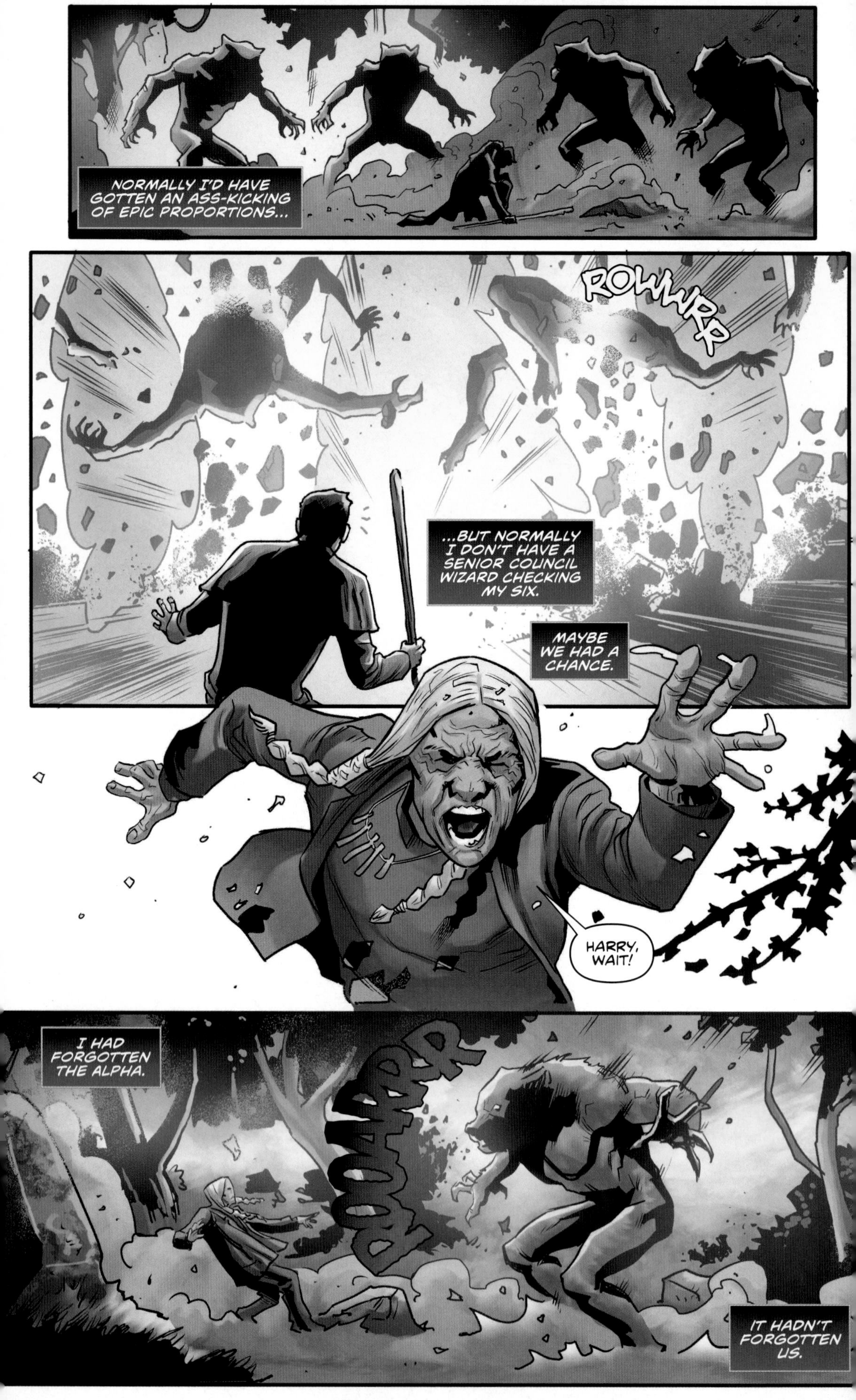
NORMALLY I'D HAVE GOTTEN AN ASS-KICKING OF EPIC PROPORTIONS...
ROWWRR
...BUT NORMALLY I DON'T HAVE A SENIOR COUNCIL WIZARD CHECKING MY SIX.
MAYBE WE HAD A CHANCE.
HARRY, WAIT!
I HAD FORGOTTEN THE ALPHA.
ROWWRR
IT HADN'T FORGOTTEN US.

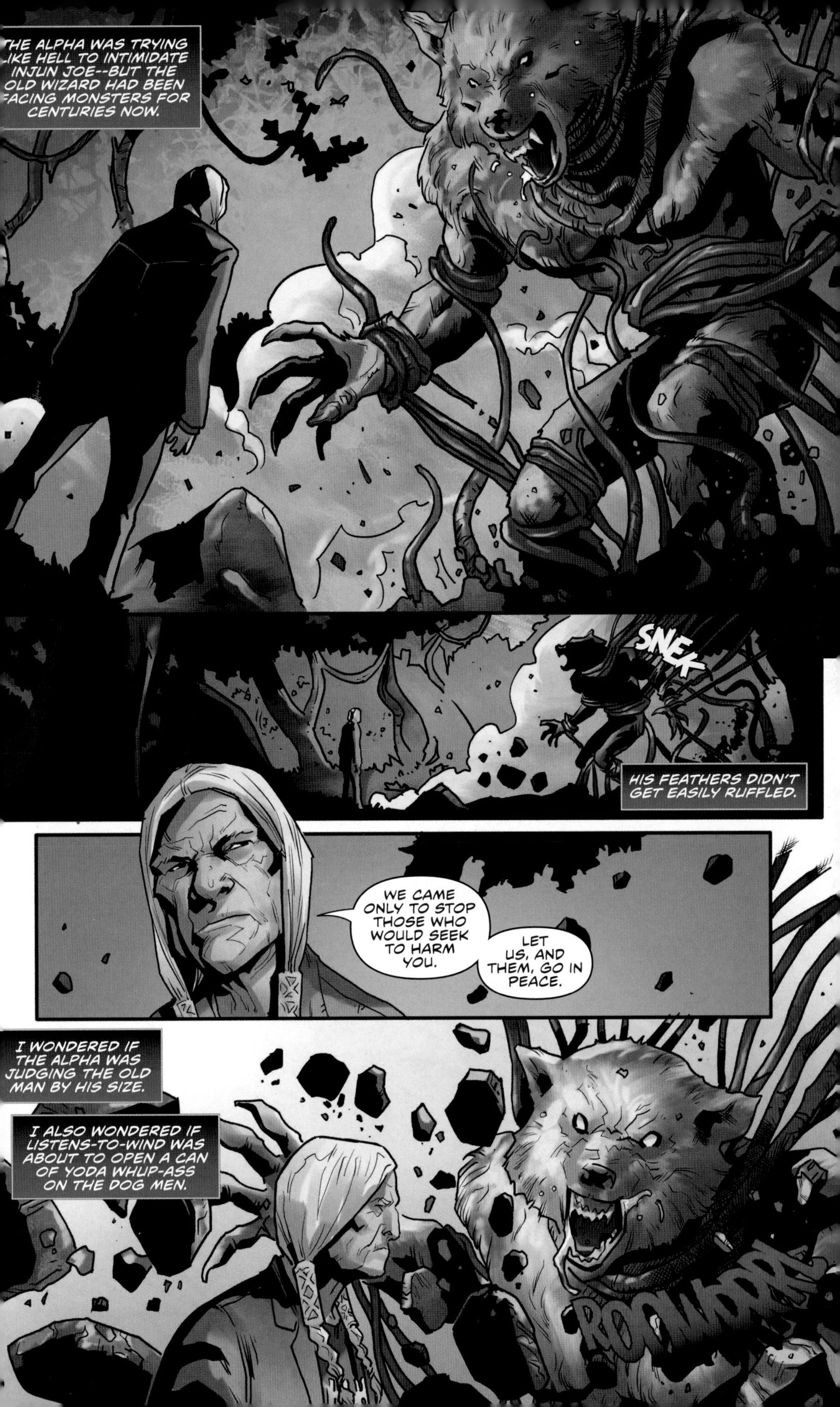
THE ALPHA WAS TRYING LIKE HELL TO INTIMIDATE INJUN JOE--BUT THE OLD WIZARD HAD BEEN FACING MONSTERS FOR CENTURIES NOW.
SNEK
HIS FEATHERS DIDN'T GET EASILY RUFFLED.
WE CAME ONLY TO STOP THOSE WHO WOULD SEEK TO HARM YOU.
LET US, AND THEM, GO IN PEACE.
I WONDERED IF THE ALPHA WAS JUDGING THE OLD MAN BY HIS SIZE.
I ALSO WONDERED IF LISTENS-TO-WIND WAS ABOUT TO OPEN A CAN OF YODA WHUP-ASS ON THE DOG MEN.

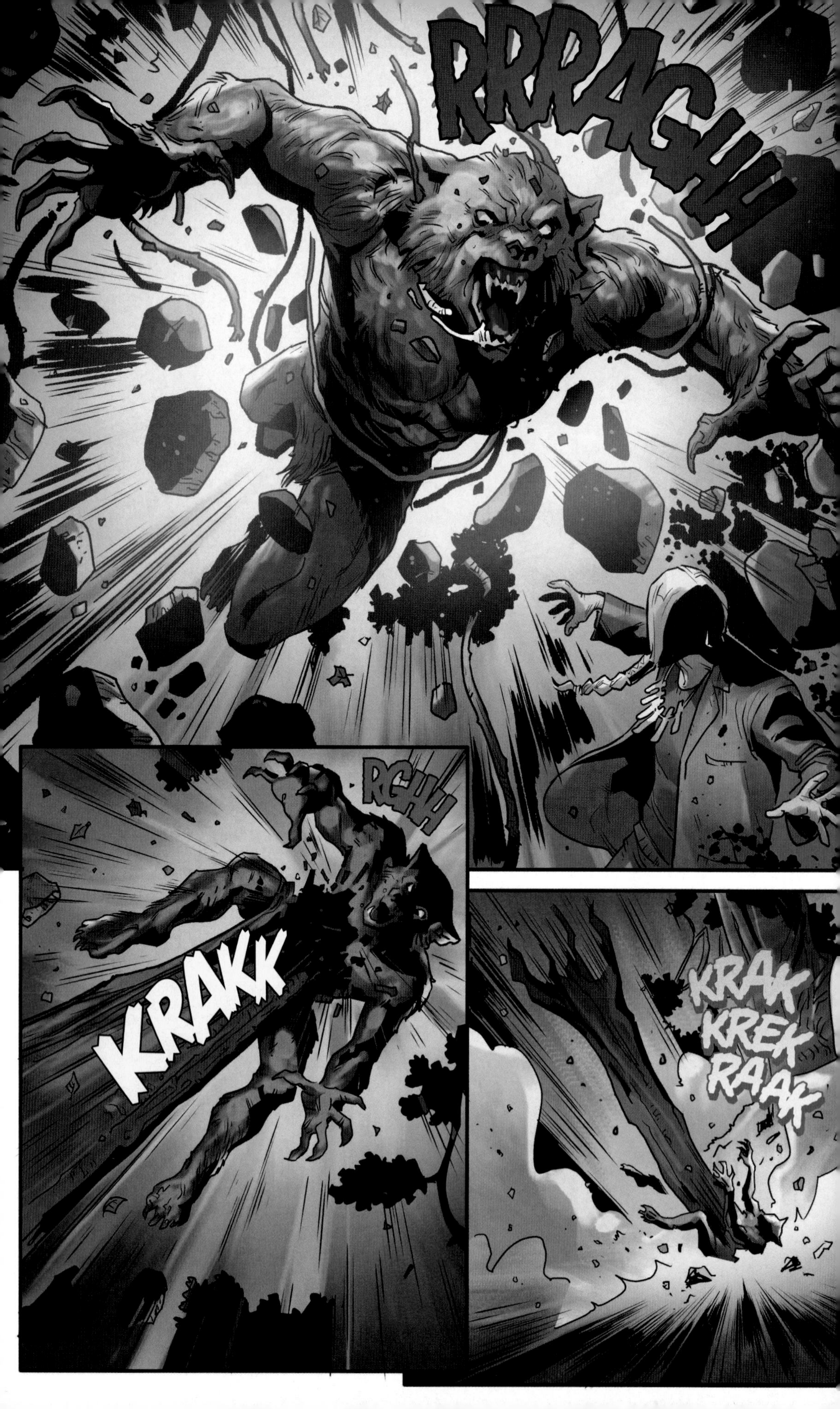
RRRAGHH
RGHH
KRAKK
KRAK
KREK
RAAK

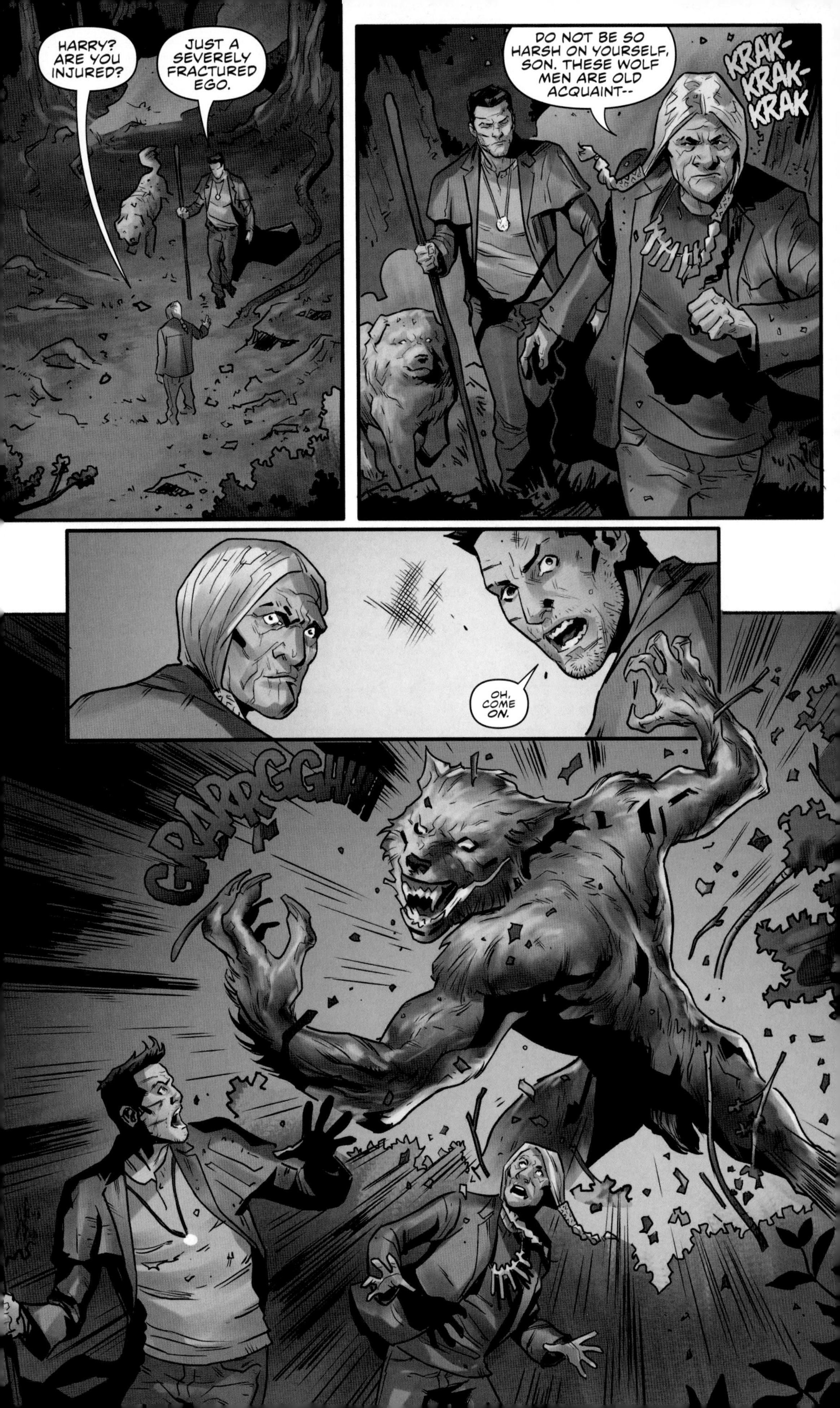

HARRY? ARE YOU INJURED?
JUST A SEVERELY FRACTURED EGO.
DO NOT BE SO HARSH ON YOURSELF, SON. THESE WOLF MEN ARE OLD ACQUAINT--
KRAK-KRAK-KRAK
OH, COME ON.
GRARRGGHH

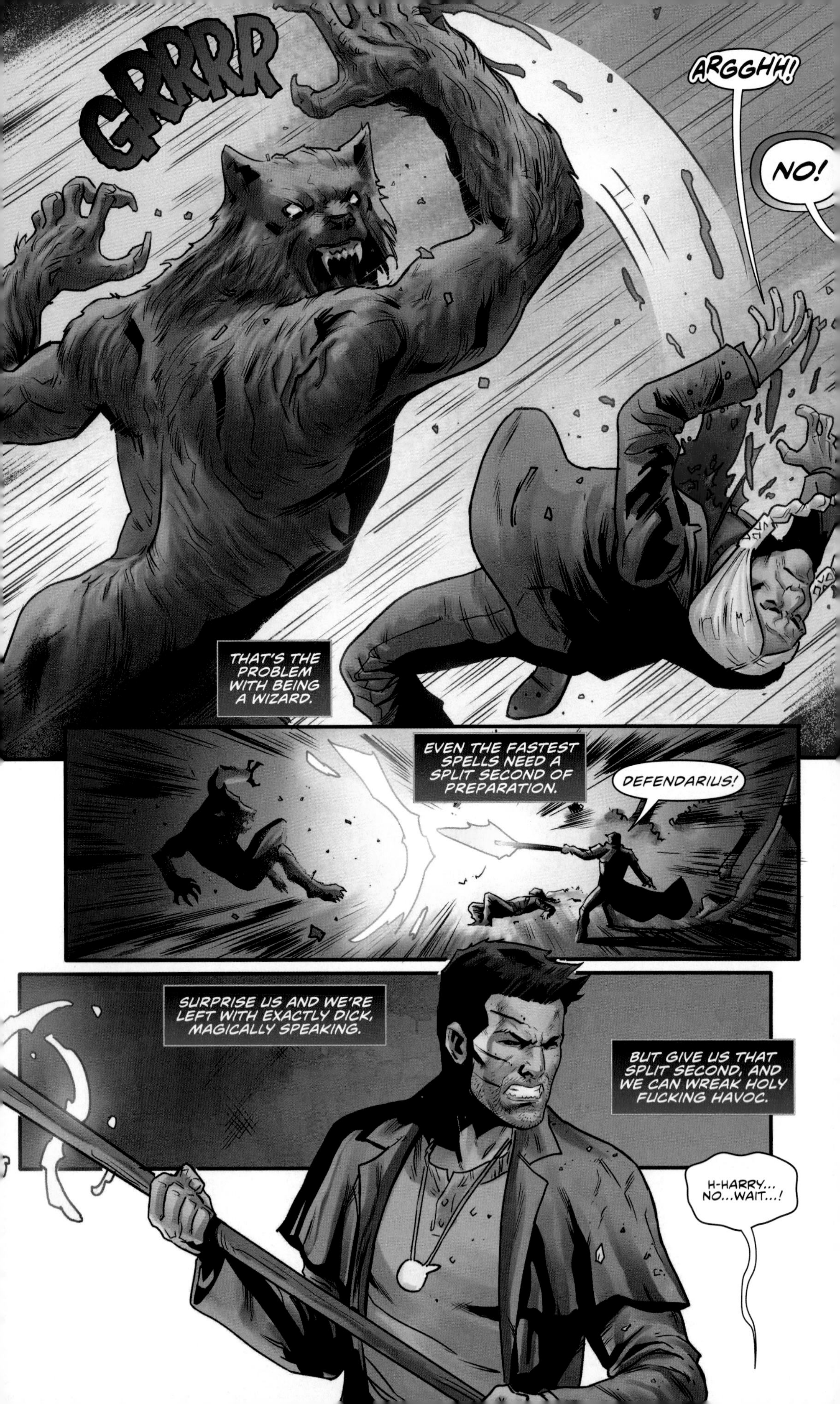
GRRRR
ARGGHH!
NO!
THAT'S THE PROBLEM WITH BEING A WIZARD.
EVEN THE FASTEST SPELLS NEED A SPLIT SECOND OF PREPARATION.
DEFENDARIUS!
SURPRISE US AND WE'RE LEFT WITH EXACTLY DICK, MAGICALLY SPEAKING.
BUT GIVE US THAT SPLIT SECOND, AND WE CAN WREAK HOLY FUCKING HAVOC.
H-HARRY... NO...WAIT...!

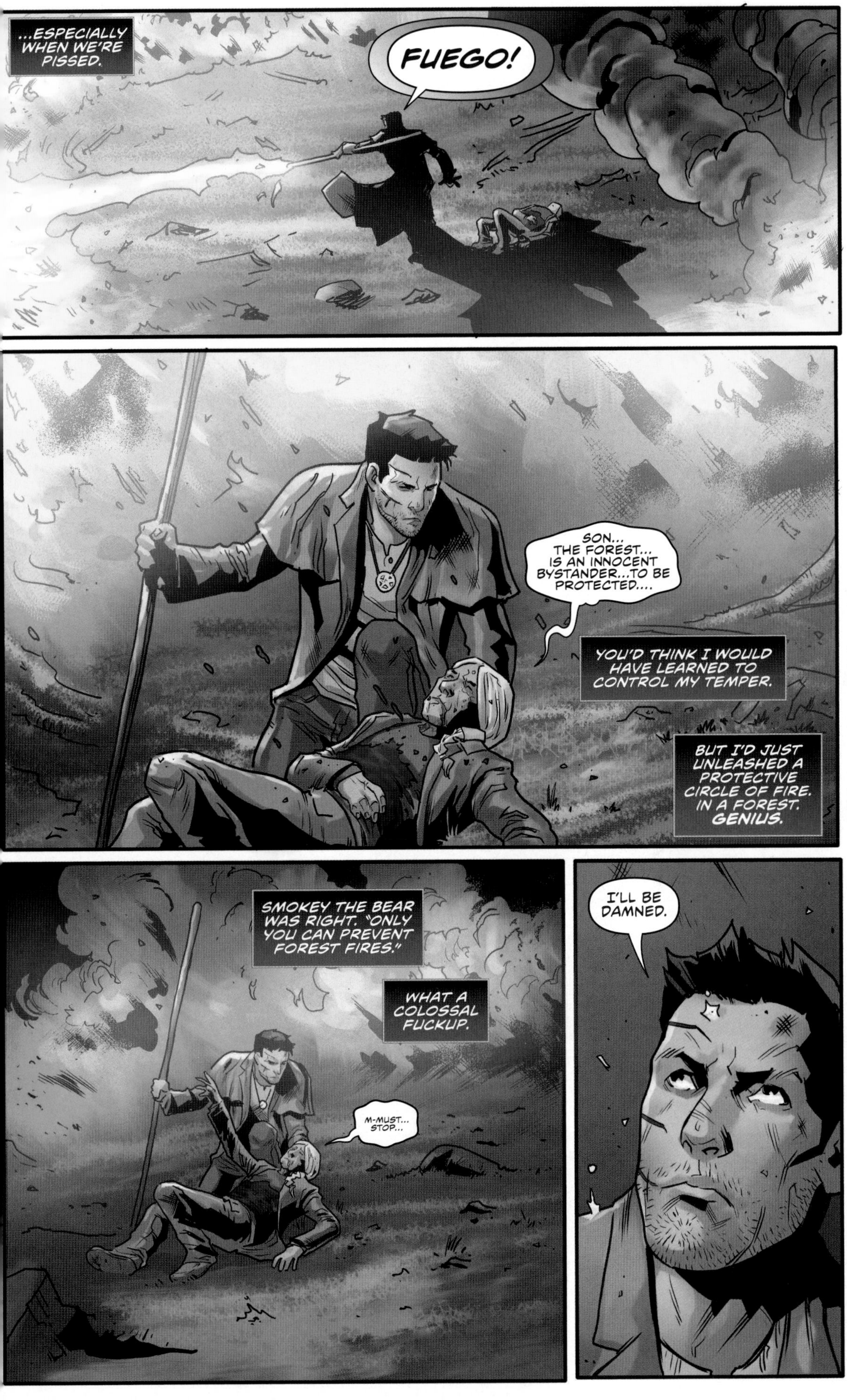
...ESPECIALLY WHEN WE'RE PISSED.
FUEGO!
SON... THE FOREST... IS AN INNOCENT BYSTANDER...TO BE PROTECTED....
YOU'D THINK I WOULD HAVE LEARNED TO CONTROL MY TEMPER.
BUT I'D JUST UNLEASHED A PROTECTIVE CIRCLE OF FIRE. IN A FOREST. GENIUS.
SMOKEY THE BEAR WAS RIGHT. "ONLY YOU CAN PREVENT FOREST FIRES."
WHAT A COLOSSAL FUCKUP.
M-MUST... STOP...
I'LL BE DAMNED.

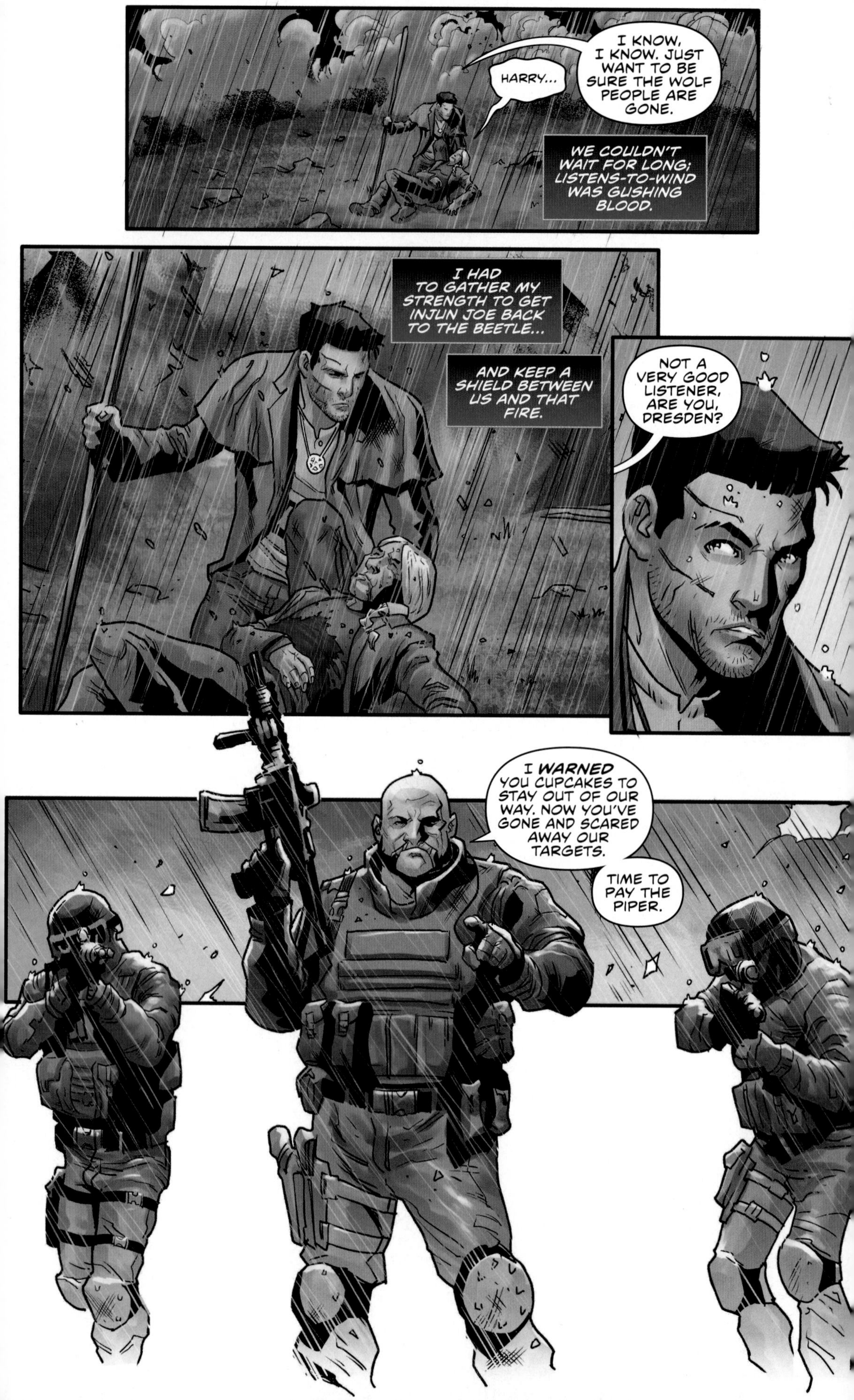
HARRY...
I KNOW, I KNOW. JUST WANT TO BE SURE THE WOLF PEOPLE ARE GONE.
WE COULDN'T WAIT FOR LONG; LISTENS-TO-WIND WAS GUSHING BLOOD.
I HAD TO GATHER MY STRENGTH TO GET INJUN JOE BACK TO THE BEETLE...
AND KEEP A SHIELD BETWEEN US AND THAT FIRE.
NOT A VERY GOOD LISTENER, ARE YOU, DRESDEN?
I WARNED YOU CUPCAKES TO STAY OUT OF OUR WAY. NOW YOU'VE GONE AND SCARED AWAY OUR TARGETS.
TIME TO PAY THE PIPER.

ISSUE FOUR COVER BY
DIEGO GALINDO

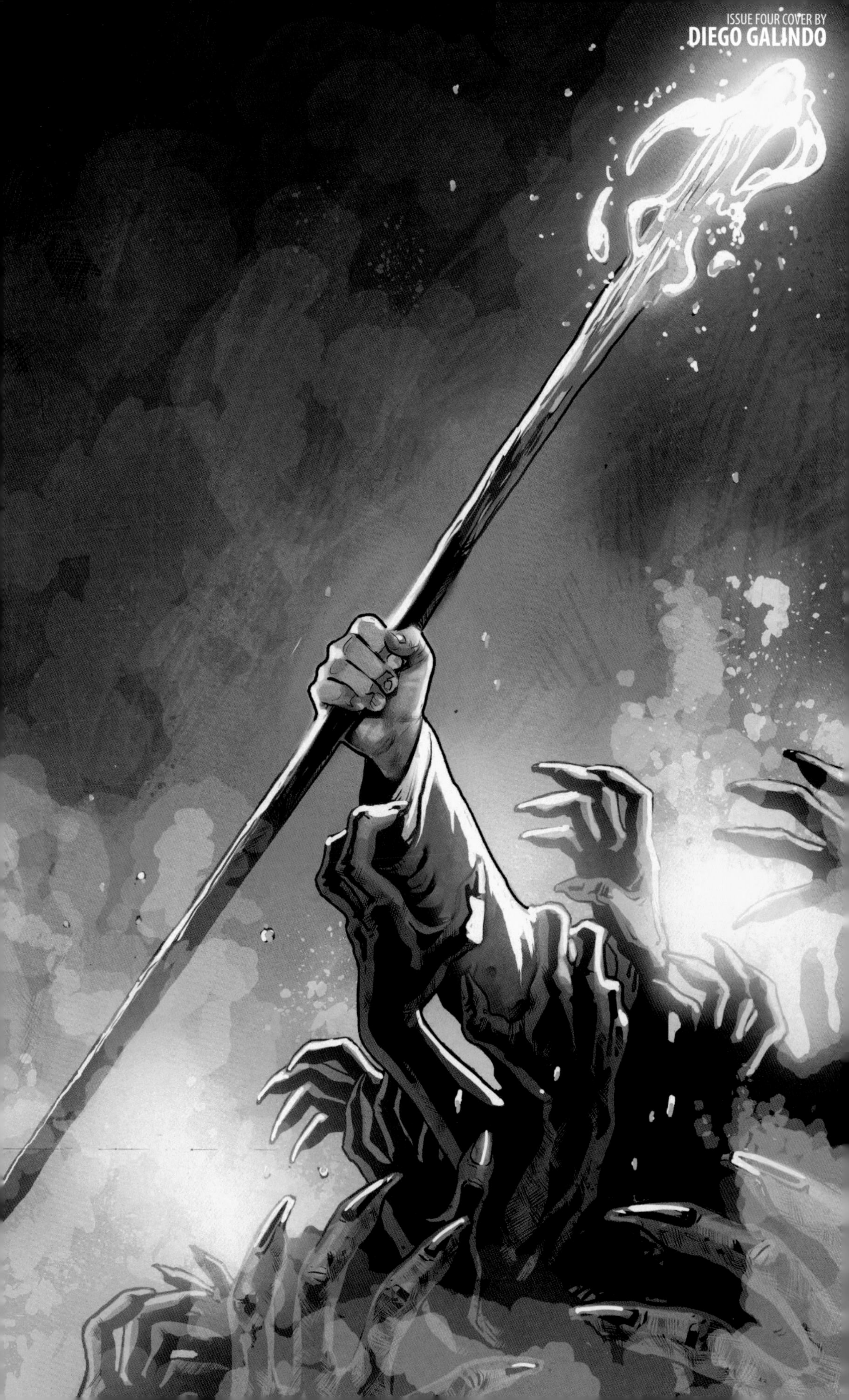

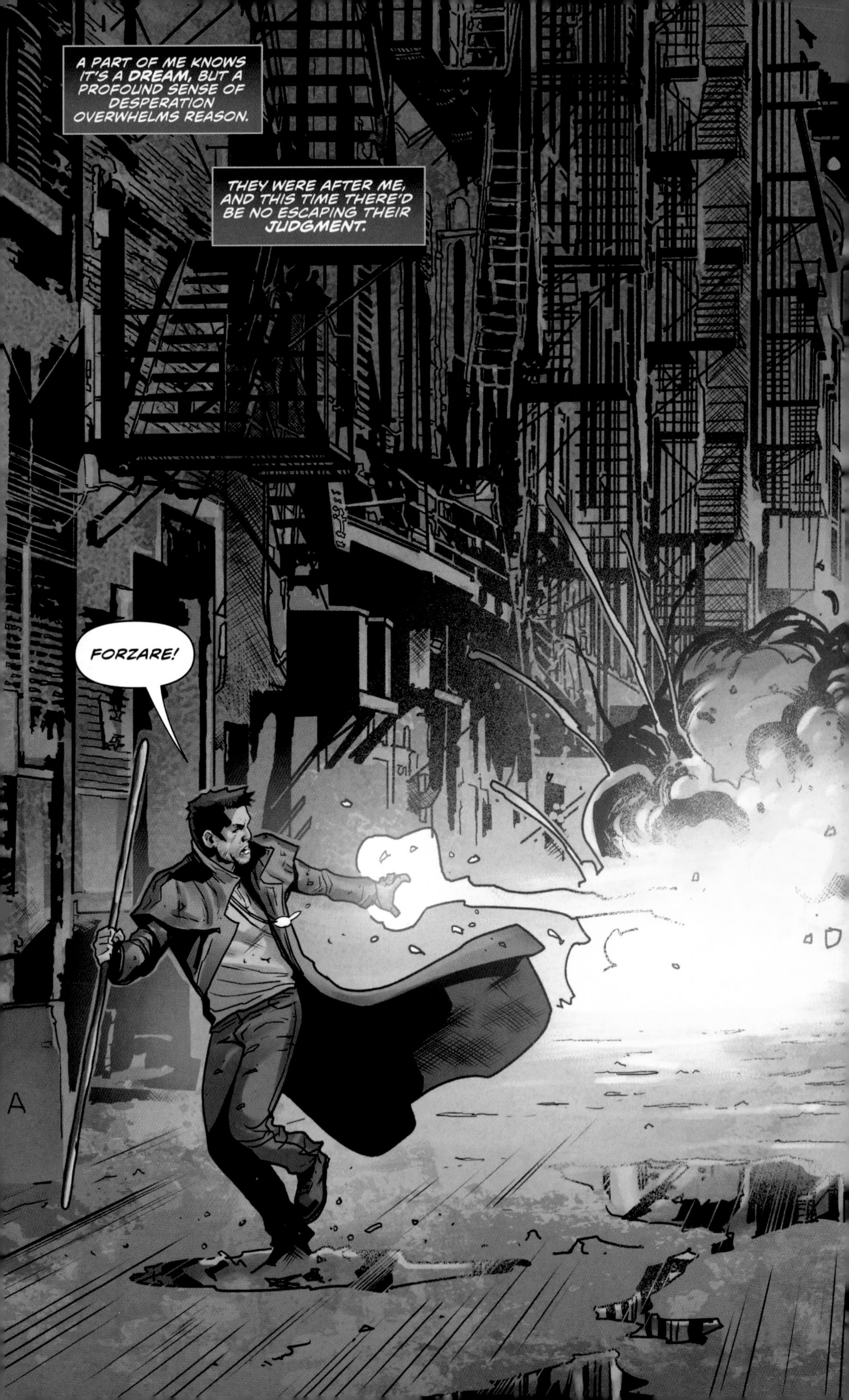
A PART OF ME KNOWS IT'S A DREAM, BUT A PROFOUND SENSE OF DESPERATION OVERWHELMS REASON.
THEY WERE AFTER ME, AND THIS TIME THERE'D BE NO ESCAPING THEIR JUDGMENT.
FORZARE!

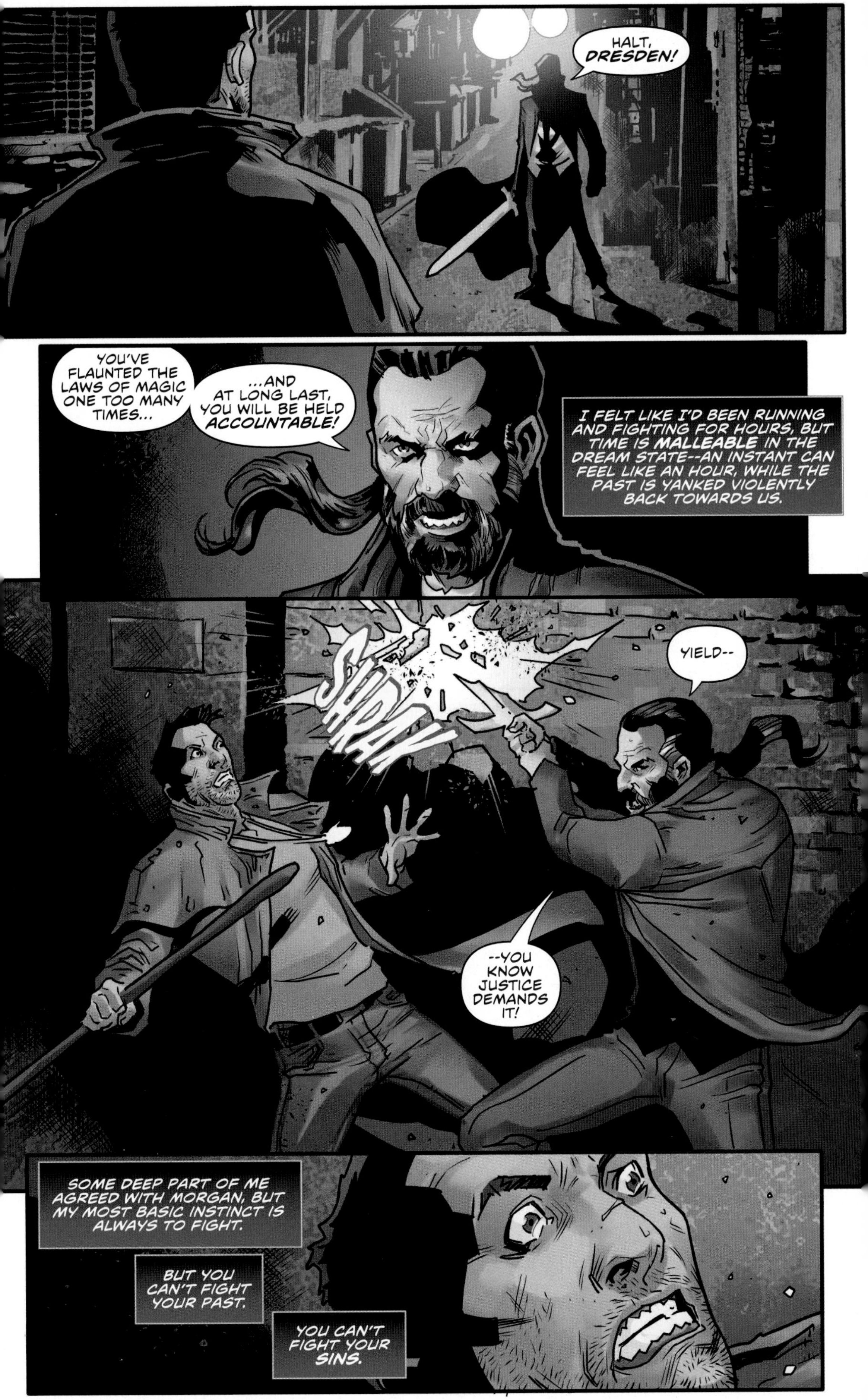
HALT, DRESDEN!
YOU'VE FLAUNTED THE LAWS OF MAGIC ONE TOO MANY TIMES...
...AND AT LONG LAST, YOU WILL BE HELD ACCOUNTABLE!
I FELT LIKE I'D BEEN RUNNING AND FIGHTING FOR HOURS, BUT TIME IS MALLEABLE IN THE DREAM STATE--AN INSTANT CAN FEEL LIKE AN HOUR, WHILE THE PAST IS YANKED VIOLENTLY BACK TOWARDS US.
SHRAK
YIELD--
--YOU KNOW JUSTICE DEMANDS IT!
SOME DEEP PART OF ME AGREED WITH MORGAN, BUT MY MOST BASIC INSTINCT IS ALWAYS TO FIGHT.
BUT YOU CAN'T FIGHT YOUR PAST.
YOU CAN'T FIGHT YOUR SINS.

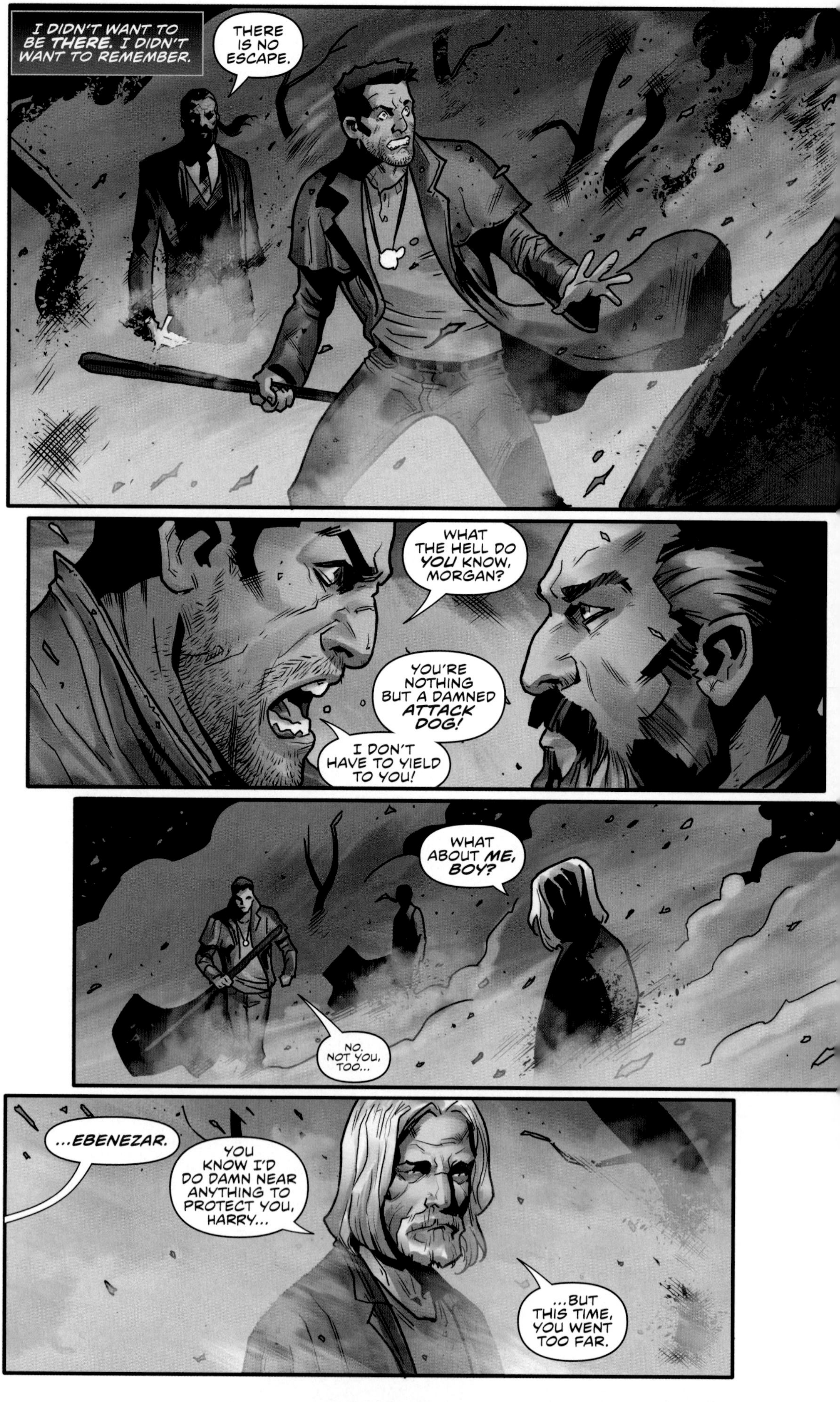

I DIDN'T WANT TO BE THERE. I DIDN'T WANT TO REMEMBER.
THERE IS NO ESCAPE.
WHAT THE HELL DO YOU KNOW, MORGAN?
YOU'RE NOTHING BUT A DAMNED ATTACK DOG!
I DON'T HAVE TO YIELD TO YOU!
WHAT ABOUT ME, BOY?
NO. NOT YOU, TOO...
...EBENEZAR.
YOU KNOW I'D DO DAMN NEAR ANYTHING TO PROTECT YOU, HARRY...
...BUT THIS TIME, YOU WENT TOO FAR.

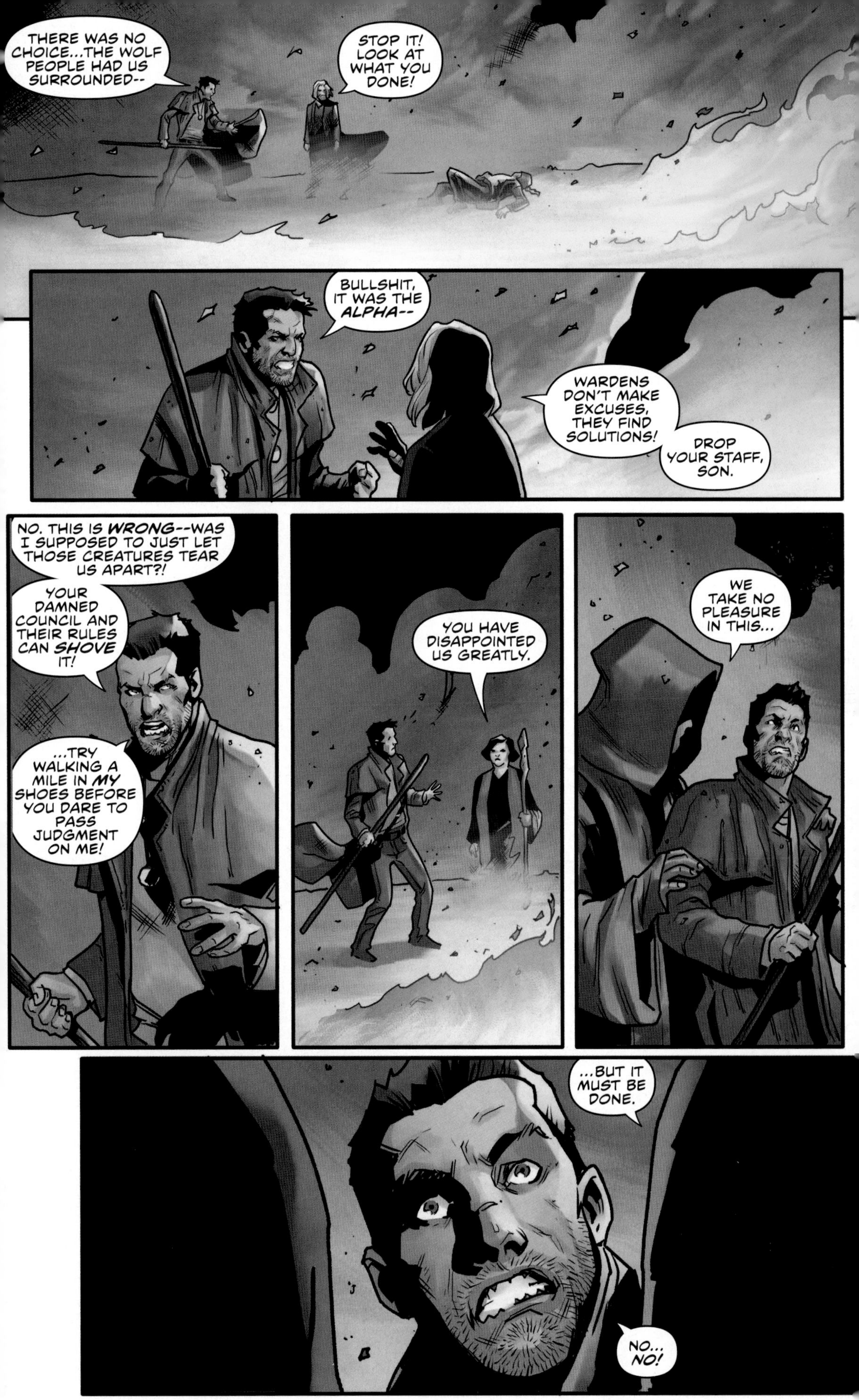
THERE WAS NO CHOICE...THE WOLF PEOPLE HAD US SURROUNDED--
STOP IT! LOOK AT WHAT YOU DONE!
BULLSHIT, IT WAS THE ALPHA--
WARDENS DON'T MAKE EXCUSES, THEY FIND SOLUTIONS!
DROP YOUR STAFF, SON.
NO. THIS IS WRONG--WAS I SUPPOSED TO JUST LET THOSE CREATURES TEAR US APART?!
YOUR DAMNED COUNCIL AND THEIR RULES CAN SHOVE IT!
...TRY WALKING A MILE IN MY SHOES BEFORE YOU DARE TO PASS JUDGMENT ON ME!
YOU HAVE DISAPPOINTED US GREATLY.
WE TAKE NO PLEASURE IN THIS...
...BUT IT MUST BE DONE.
NO... NO!

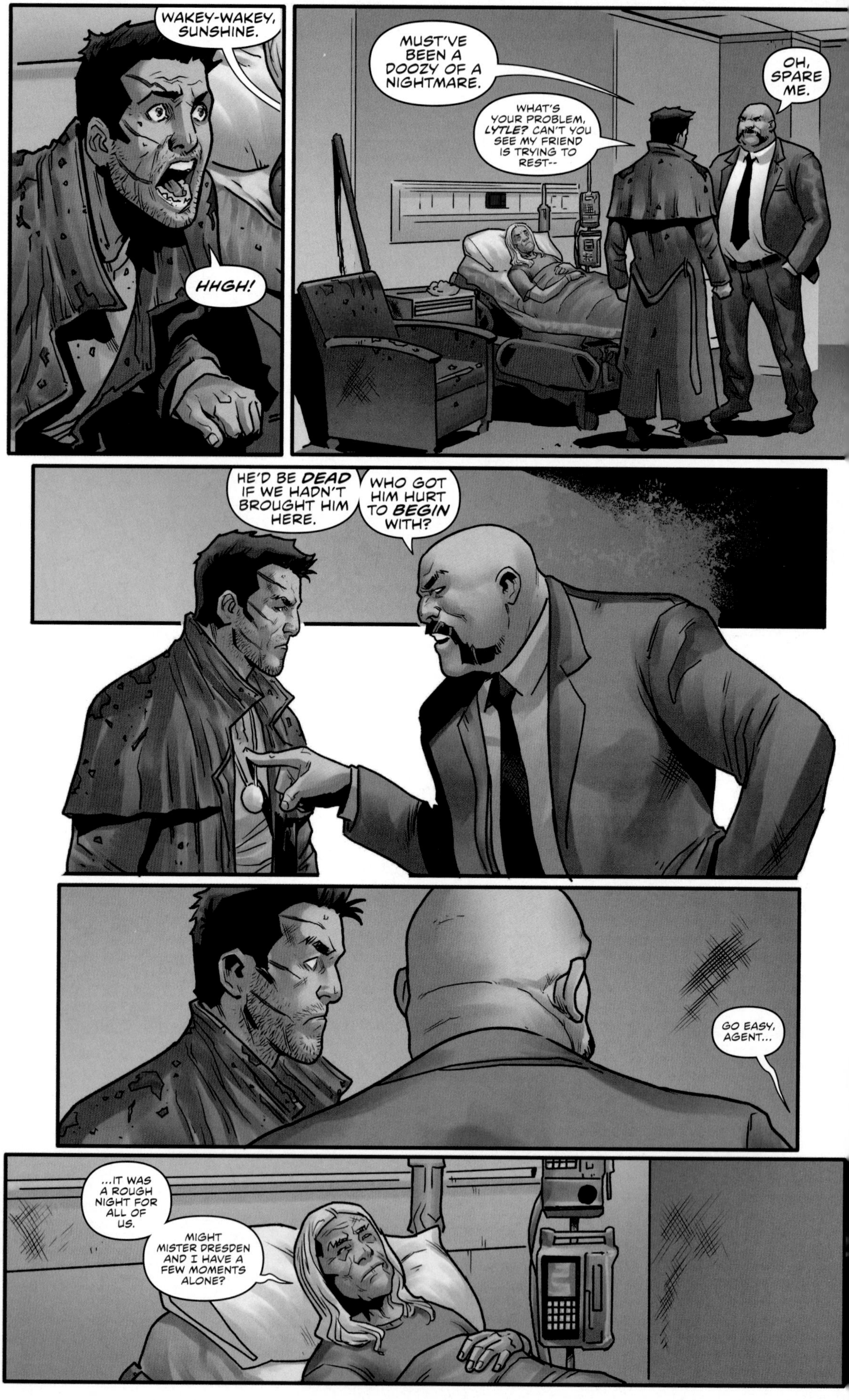
WAKEY-WAKEY, SUNSHINE.
HHGH!
MUST'VE BEEN A DOOZY OF A NIGHTMARE.
WHAT'S YOUR PROBLEM, LYTLE? CAN'T YOU SEE MY FRIEND IS TRYING TO REST--
OH, SPARE ME.
HE'D BE DEAD IF WE HADN'T BROUGHT HIM HERE.
WHO GOT HIM HURT TO BEGIN WITH?
GO EASY, AGENT...
...IT WAS A ROUGH NIGHT FOR ALL OF US.
MIGHT MISTER DRESDEN AND I HAVE A FEW MOMENTS ALONE?

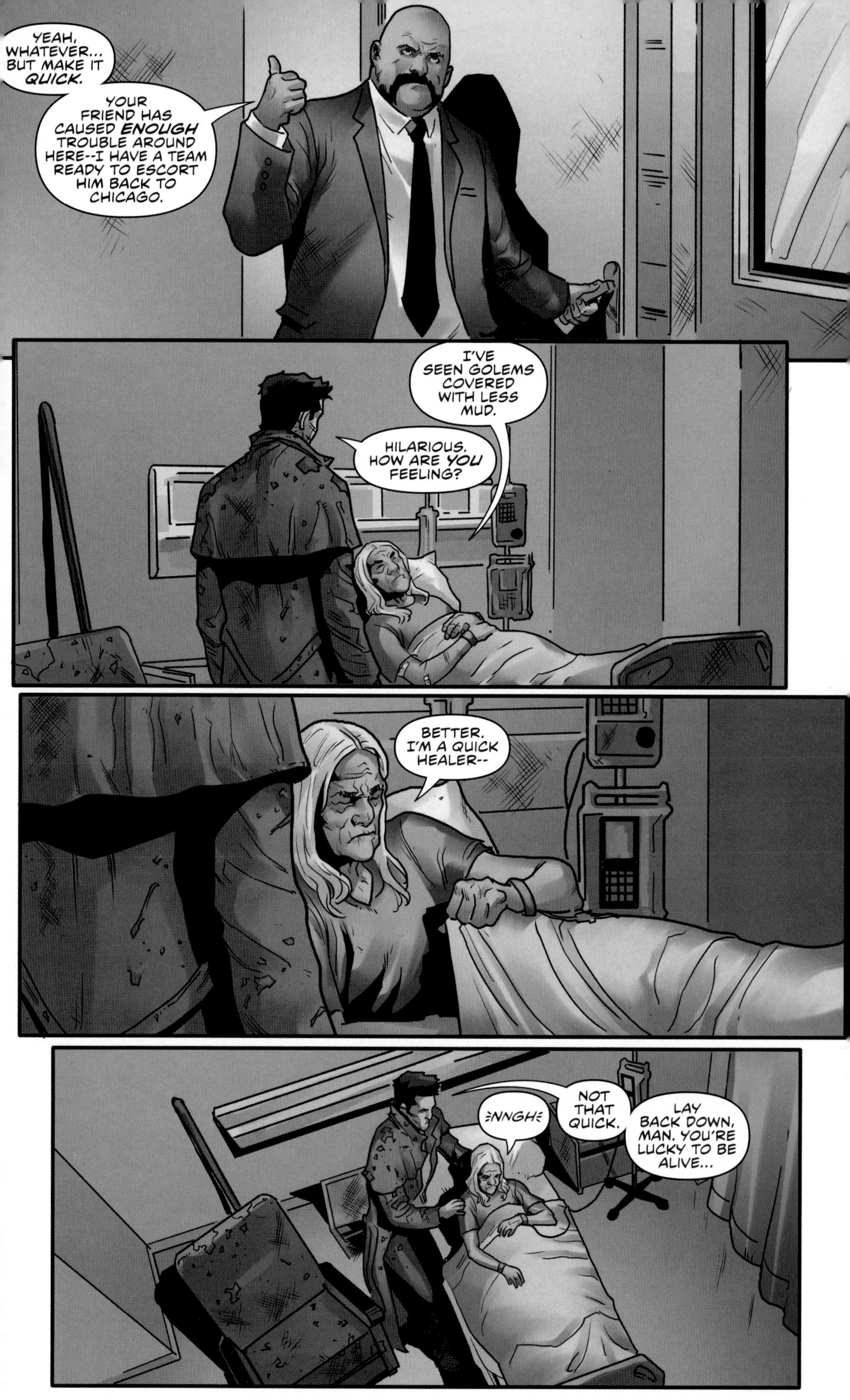
YEAH, WHATEVER... BUT MAKE IT QUICK.
YOUR FRIEND HAS CAUSED ENOUGH TROUBLE AROUND HERE--I HAVE A TEAM READY TO ESCORT HIM BACK TO CHICAGO.
I'VE SEEN GOLEMS COVERED WITH LESS MUD.
HILARIOUS. HOW ARE YOU FEELING?
BETTER. I'M A QUICK HEALER--
NNGH
NOT THAT QUICK.
LAY BACK DOWN, MAN. YOU'RE LUCKY TO BE ALIVE...

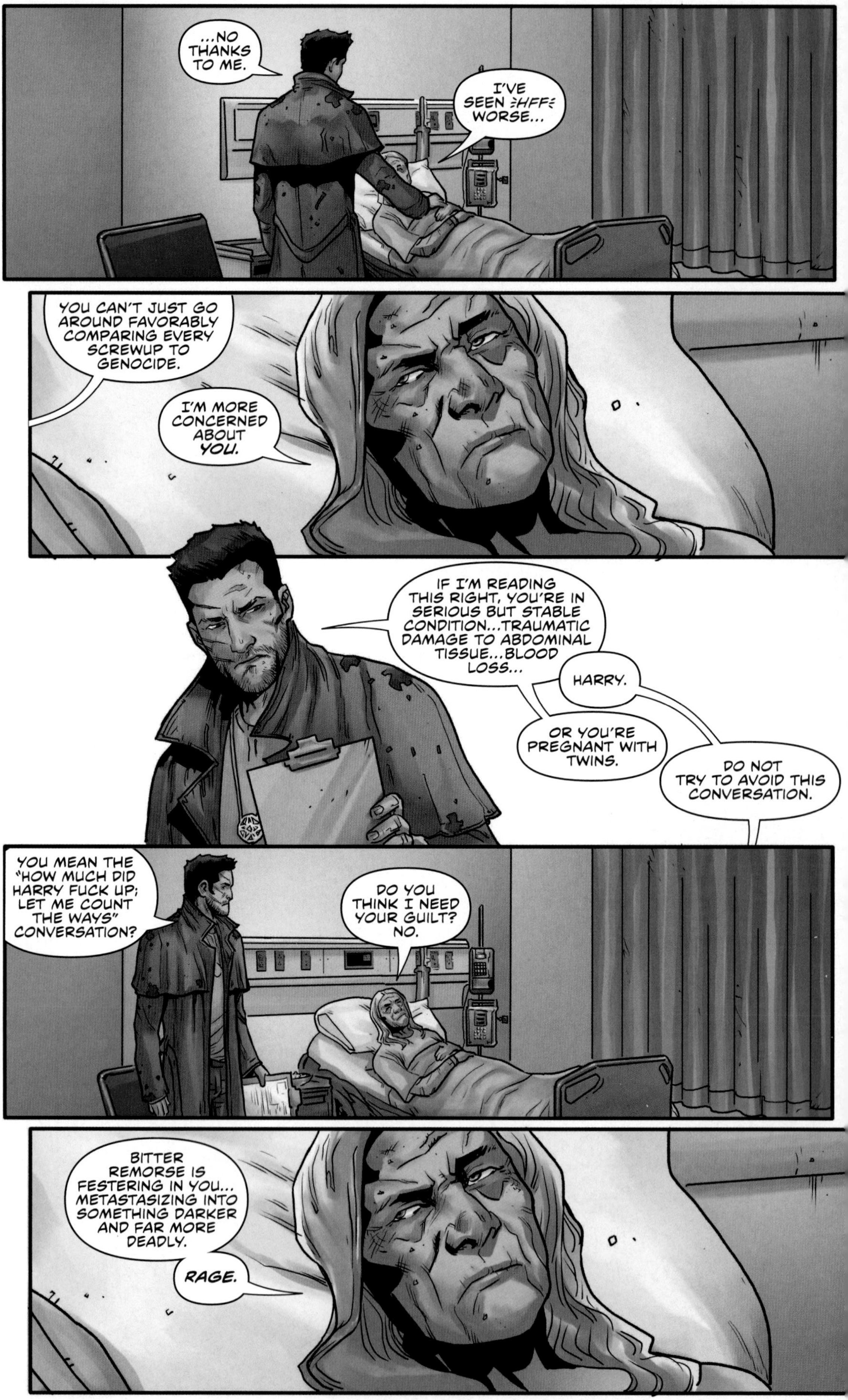
...NO THANKS TO ME.
I'VE SEEN =HFF= WORSE...
YOU CAN'T JUST GO AROUND FAVORABLY COMPARING EVERY SCREWUP TO GENOCIDE.
I'M MORE CONCERNED ABOUT *YOU.*
IF I'M READING THIS RIGHT, YOU'RE IN SERIOUS BUT STABLE CONDITION...TRAUMATIC DAMAGE TO ABDOMINAL TISSUE...BLOOD LOSS...
OR YOU'RE PREGNANT WITH TWINS.
HARRY.
DO NOT TRY TO AVOID THIS CONVERSATION.
YOU MEAN THE "HOW MUCH DID HARRY FUCK UP; LET ME COUNT THE WAYS" CONVERSATION?
DO YOU THINK I NEED YOUR GUILT? NO.
BITTER REMORSE IS FESTERING IN YOU... METASTASIZING INTO SOMETHING DARKER AND FAR MORE DEADLY.
RAGE.

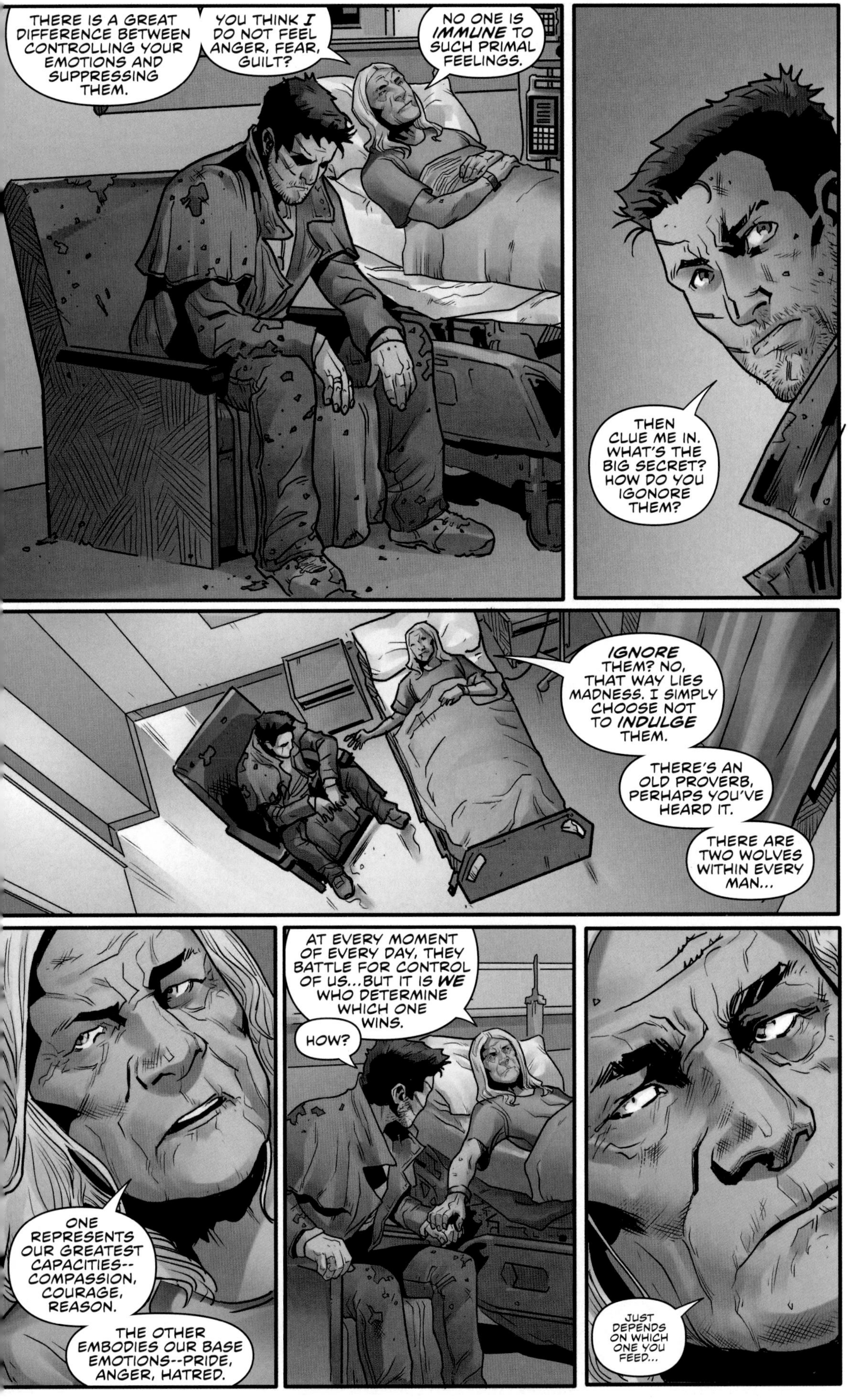
THERE IS A GREAT DIFFERENCE BETWEEN CONTROLLING YOUR EMOTIONS AND SUPPRESSING THEM.
YOU THINK *I* DO NOT FEEL ANGER, FEAR, GUILT?
NO ONE IS *IMMUNE* TO SUCH PRIMAL FEELINGS.
THEN CLUE ME IN. WHAT'S THE BIG SECRET? HOW DO YOU IGNORE THEM?
IGNORE THEM? NO, THAT WAY LIES MADNESS. I SIMPLY CHOOSE NOT TO *INDULGE* THEM.
THERE'S AN OLD PROVERB, PERHAPS YOU'VE HEARD IT.
THERE ARE TWO WOLVES WITHIN EVERY MAN...
ONE REPRESENTS OUR GREATEST CAPACITIES-- COMPASSION, COURAGE, REASON.
THE OTHER EMBODIES OUR BASE EMOTIONS--PRIDE, ANGER, HATRED.
AT EVERY MOMENT OF EVERY DAY, THEY BATTLE FOR CONTROL OF US...BUT IT IS *WE* WHO DETERMINE WHICH ONE WINS.
HOW?
JUST DEPENDS ON WHICH ONE YOU FEED...

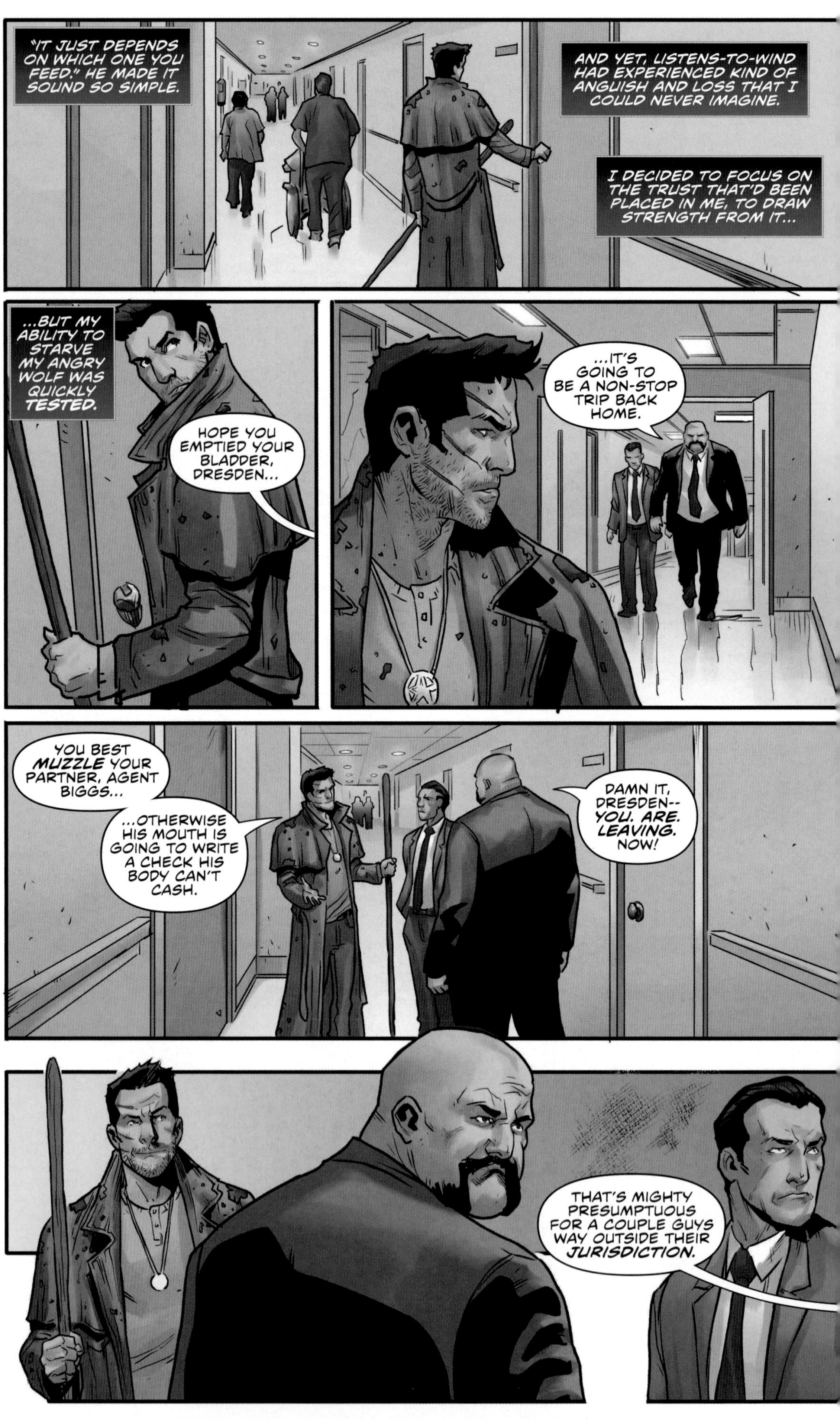
"IT JUST DEPENDS ON WHICH ONE YOU FEED." HE MADE IT SOUND SO SIMPLE.
AND YET, LISTENS-TO-WIND HAD EXPERIENCED KIND OF ANGUISH AND LOSS THAT I COULD NEVER IMAGINE.
I DECIDED TO FOCUS ON THE TRUST THAT'D BEEN PLACED IN ME, TO DRAW STRENGTH FROM IT...
...BUT MY ABILITY TO STARVE MY ANGRY WOLF WAS QUICKLY TESTED.
HOPE YOU EMPTIED YOUR BLADDER, DRESDEN...
...IT'S GOING TO BE A NON-STOP TRIP BACK HOME.
YOU BEST MUZZLE YOUR PARTNER, AGENT BIGGS...
...OTHERWISE HIS MOUTH IS GOING TO WRITE A CHECK HIS BODY CAN'T CASH.
DAMN IT, DRESDEN-- YOU. ARE. LEAVING. NOW!
THAT'S MIGHTY PRESUMPTUOUS FOR A COUPLE GUYS WAY OUTSIDE THEIR JURISDICTION.

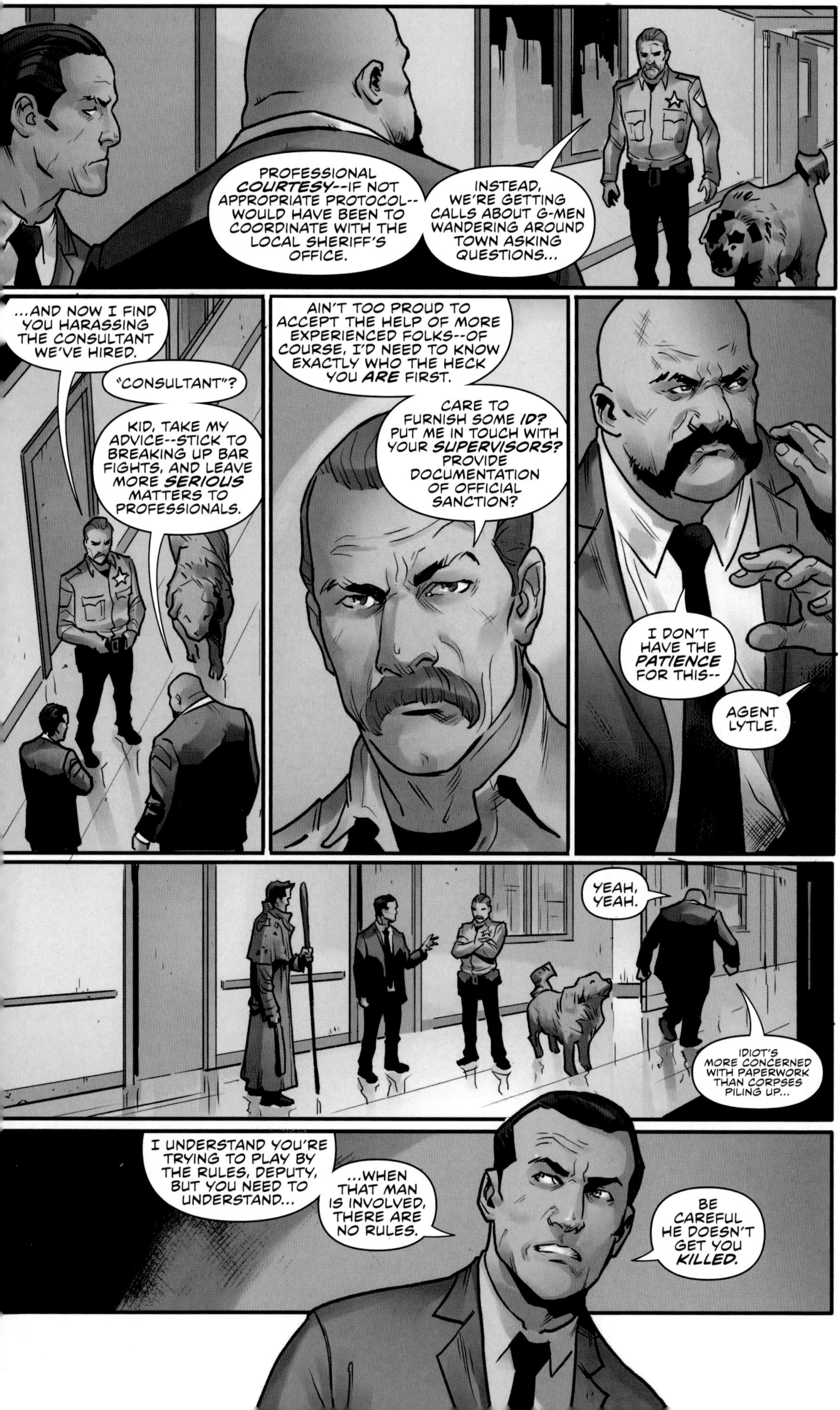
PROFESSIONAL COURTESY--IF NOT APPROPRIATE PROTOCOL--WOULD HAVE BEEN TO COORDINATE WITH THE LOCAL SHERIFF'S OFFICE.
INSTEAD, WE'RE GETTING CALLS ABOUT G-MEN WANDERING AROUND TOWN ASKING QUESTIONS...
...AND NOW I FIND YOU HARASSING THE CONSULTANT WE'VE HIRED.
"CONSULTANT"?
KID, TAKE MY ADVICE--STICK TO BREAKING UP BAR FIGHTS, AND LEAVE MORE SERIOUS MATTERS TO PROFESSIONALS.
AIN'T TOO PROUD TO ACCEPT THE HELP OF MORE EXPERIENCED FOLKS--OF COURSE, I'D NEED TO KNOW EXACTLY WHO THE HECK YOU ARE FIRST.
CARE TO FURNISH SOME ID? PUT ME IN TOUCH WITH YOUR SUPERVISORS? PROVIDE DOCUMENTATION OF OFFICIAL SANCTION?
I DON'T HAVE THE PATIENCE FOR THIS--
AGENT LYTLE.
YEAH, YEAH.
IDIOT'S MORE CONCERNED WITH PAPERWORK THAN CORPSES PILING UP...
I UNDERSTAND YOU'RE TRYING TO PLAY BY THE RULES, DEPUTY, BUT YOU NEED TO UNDERSTAND...
...WHEN THAT MAN IS INVOLVED, THERE ARE NO RULES.
BE CAREFUL HE DOESN'T GET YOU KILLED.

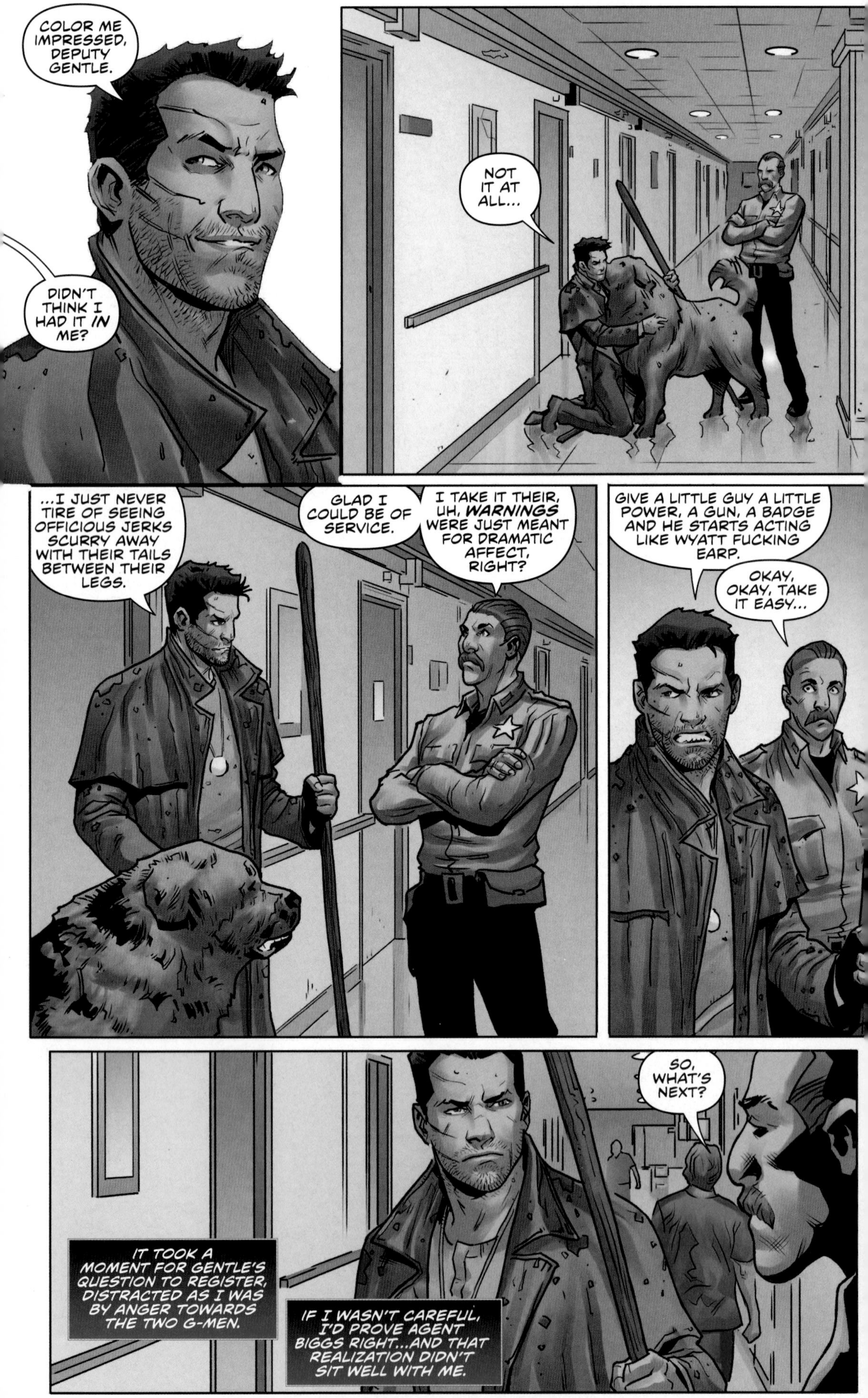
COLOR ME IMPRESSED, DEPUTY GENTLE.
DIDN'T THINK I HAD IT IN ME?
NOT IT AT ALL...
...I JUST NEVER TIRE OF SEEING OFFICIOUS JERKS SCURRY AWAY WITH THEIR TAILS BETWEEN THEIR LEGS.
GLAD I COULD BE OF SERVICE.
I TAKE IT THEIR, UH, WARNINGS WERE JUST MEANT FOR DRAMATIC AFFECT, RIGHT?
GIVE A LITTLE GUY A LITTLE POWER, A GUN, A BADGE AND HE STARTS ACTING LIKE WYATT FUCKING EARP.
OKAY, OKAY, TAKE IT EASY...
SO, WHAT'S NEXT?
IT TOOK A MOMENT FOR GENTLE'S QUESTION TO REGISTER, DISTRACTED AS I WAS BY ANGER TOWARDS THE TWO G-MEN.
IF I WASN'T CAREFUL, I'D PROVE AGENT BIGGS RIGHT...AND THAT REALIZATION DIDN'T SIT WELL WITH ME.

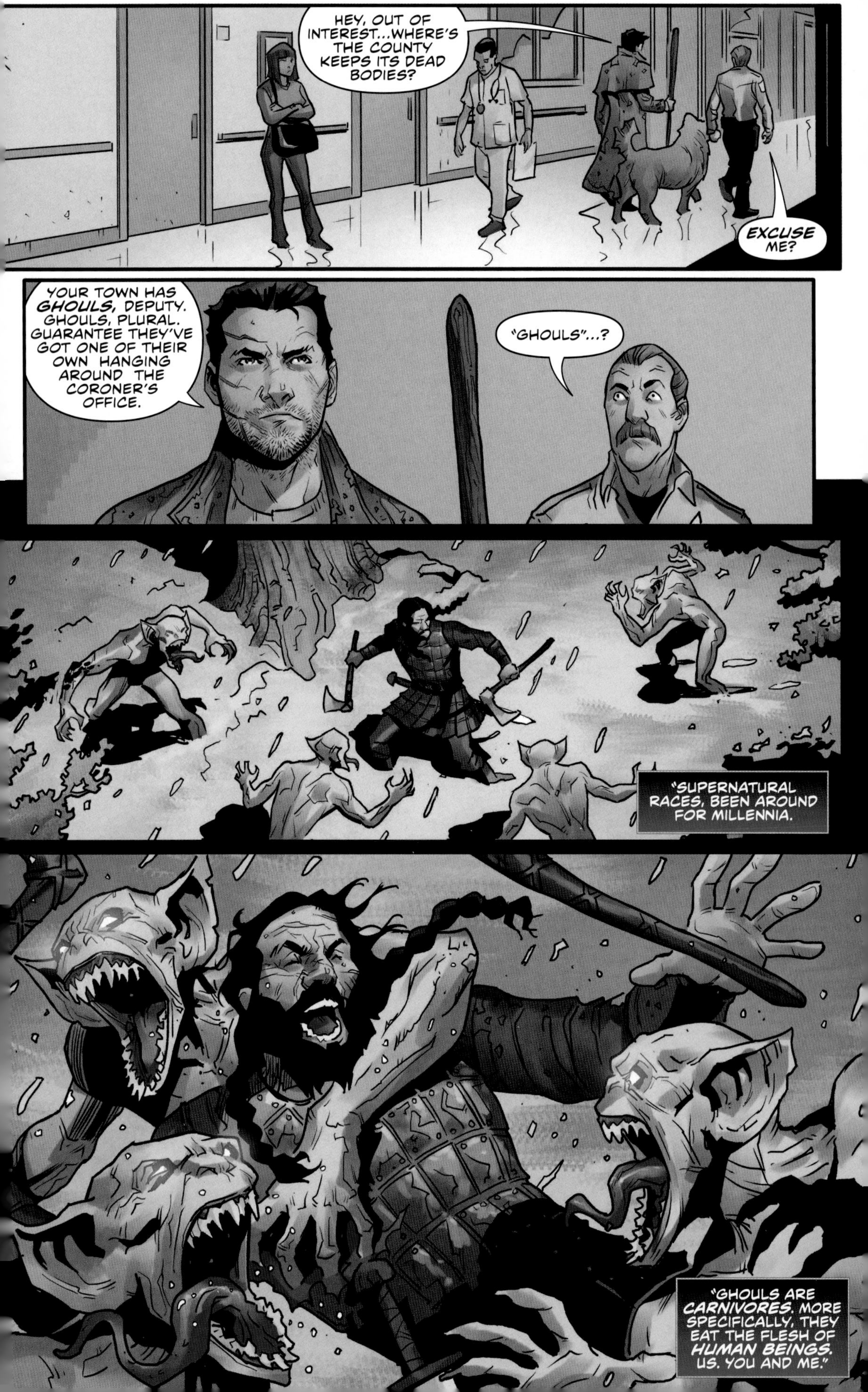
HEY, OUT OF INTEREST...WHERE'S THE COUNTY KEEPS ITS DEAD BODIES?
EXCUSE ME?
YOUR TOWN HAS GHOULS, DEPUTY. GHOULS, PLURAL. GUARANTEE THEY'VE GOT ONE OF THEIR OWN HANGING AROUND THE CORONER'S OFFICE.
"GHOULS"...?
"SUPERNATURAL RACES, BEEN AROUND FOR MILLENNIA.
"GHOULS ARE CARNIVORES. MORE SPECIFICALLY, THEY EAT THE FLESH OF HUMAN BEINGS. US. YOU AND ME."

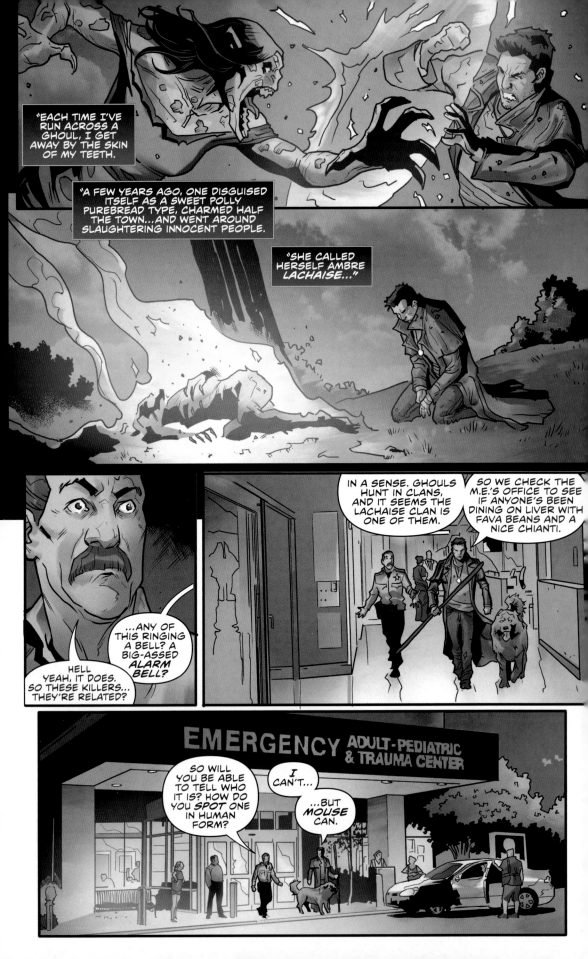

"EACH TIME I'VE RUN ACROSS A GHOUL, I GET AWAY BY THE SKIN OF MY TEETH.

"A FEW YEARS AGO, ONE DISGUISED ITSELF AS A SWEET POLLY PUREBREAD TYPE, CHARMED HALF THE TOWN...AND WENT AROUND SLAUGHTERING INNOCENT PEOPLE.

"SHE CALLED HERSELF AMBRE LACHAISE..."

...ANY OF THIS RINGING A BELL? A BIG-ASSED *ALARM BELL?*

HELL YEAH, IT DOES. SO THESE KILLERS... THEY'RE RELATED?

IN A SENSE. GHOULS HUNT IN CLANS, AND IT SEEMS THE LACHAISE CLAN IS ONE OF THEM.

SO WE CHECK THE M.E.'S OFFICE TO SEE IF ANYONE'S BEEN DINING ON LIVER WITH FAVA BEANS AND A NICE CHIANTI.

EMERGENCY ADULT-PEDIATRIC & TRAUMA CENTER

SO WILL YOU BE ABLE TO TELL WHO IT IS? HOW DO YOU *SPOT* ONE IN HUMAN FORM?

I CAN'T...

...BUT *MOUSE* CAN.

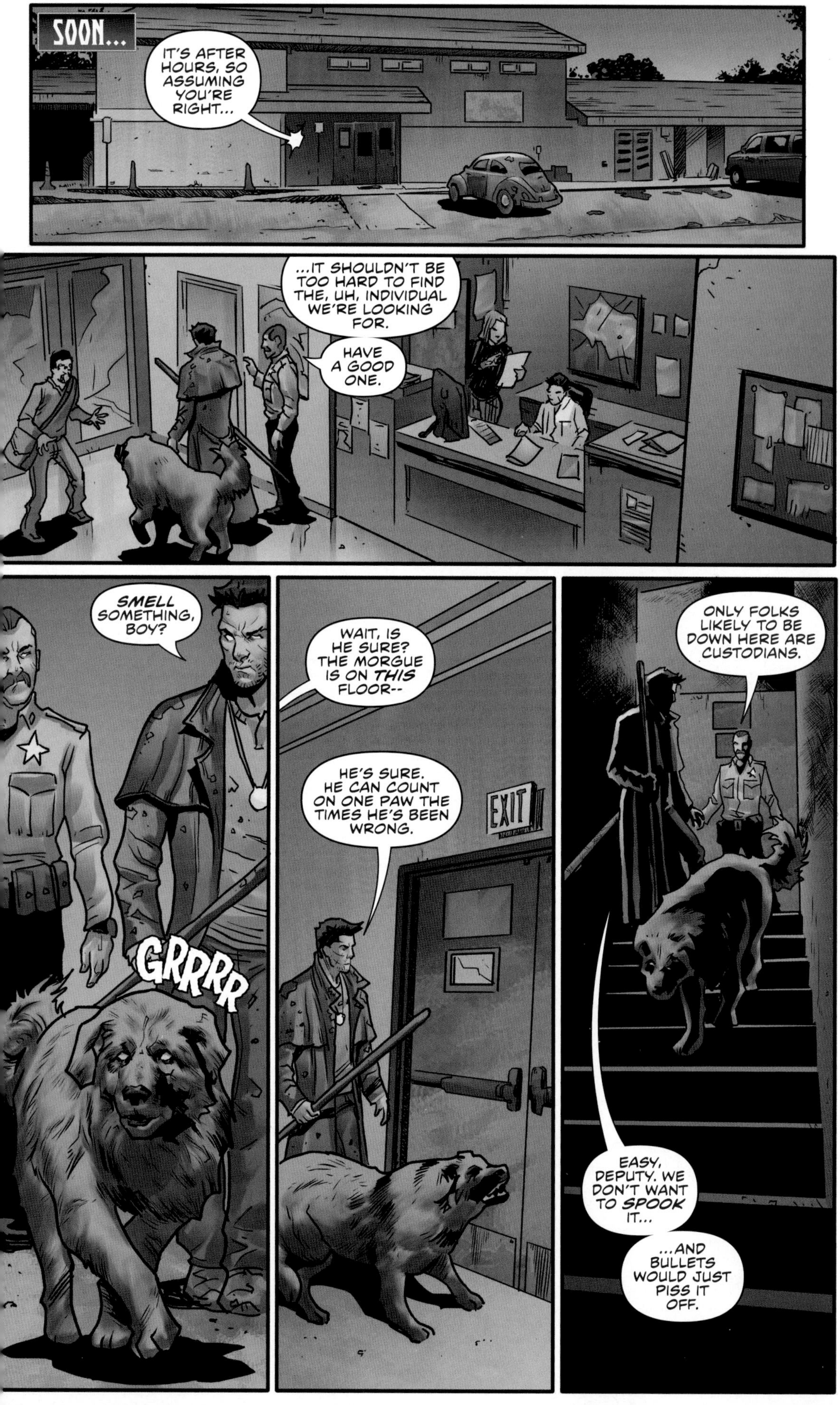
SOON...
IT'S AFTER HOURS, SO ASSUMING YOU'RE RIGHT...
...IT SHOULDN'T BE TOO HARD TO FIND THE, UH, INDIVIDUAL WE'RE LOOKING FOR.
HAVE A GOOD ONE.
SMELL SOMETHING, BOY?
GRRRR
WAIT, IS HE SURE? THE MORGUE IS ON THIS FLOOR--
HE'S SURE. HE CAN COUNT ON ONE PAW THE TIMES HE'S BEEN WRONG.
EXIT
ONLY FOLKS LIKELY TO BE DOWN HERE ARE CUSTODIANS.
EASY, DEPUTY. WE DON'T WANT TO SPOOK IT...
...AND BULLETS WOULD JUST PISS IT OFF.

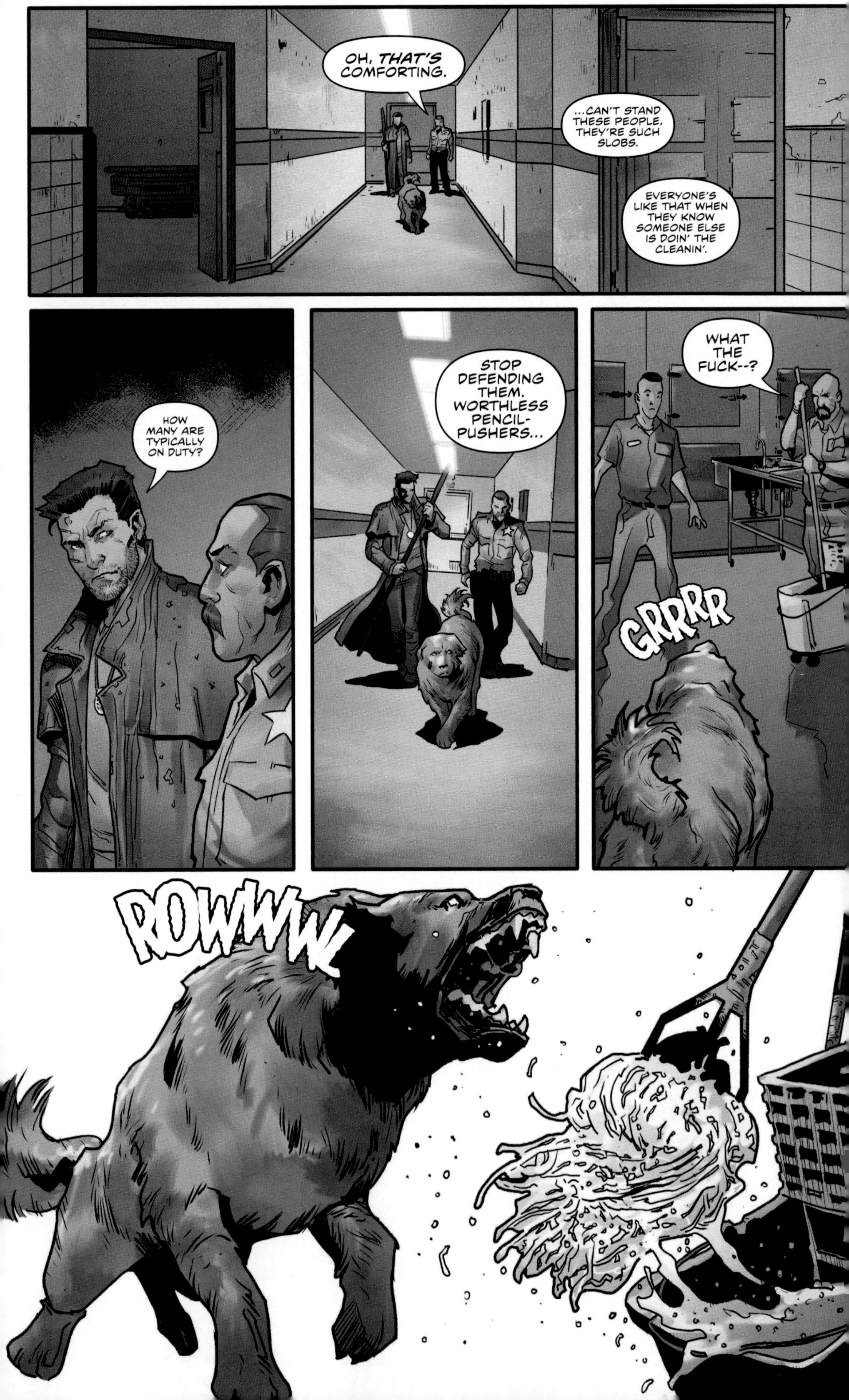

OH, THAT'S COMFORTING.
...CAN'T STAND THESE PEOPLE, THEY'RE SUCH SLOBS.
EVERYONE'S LIKE THAT WHEN THEY KNOW SOMEONE ELSE IS DOIN' THE CLEANIN'.
HOW MANY ARE TYPICALLY ON DUTY?
STOP DEFENDING THEM. WORTHLESS PENCIL-PUSHERS...
WHAT THE FUCK--?
GRRRR
ROWWW

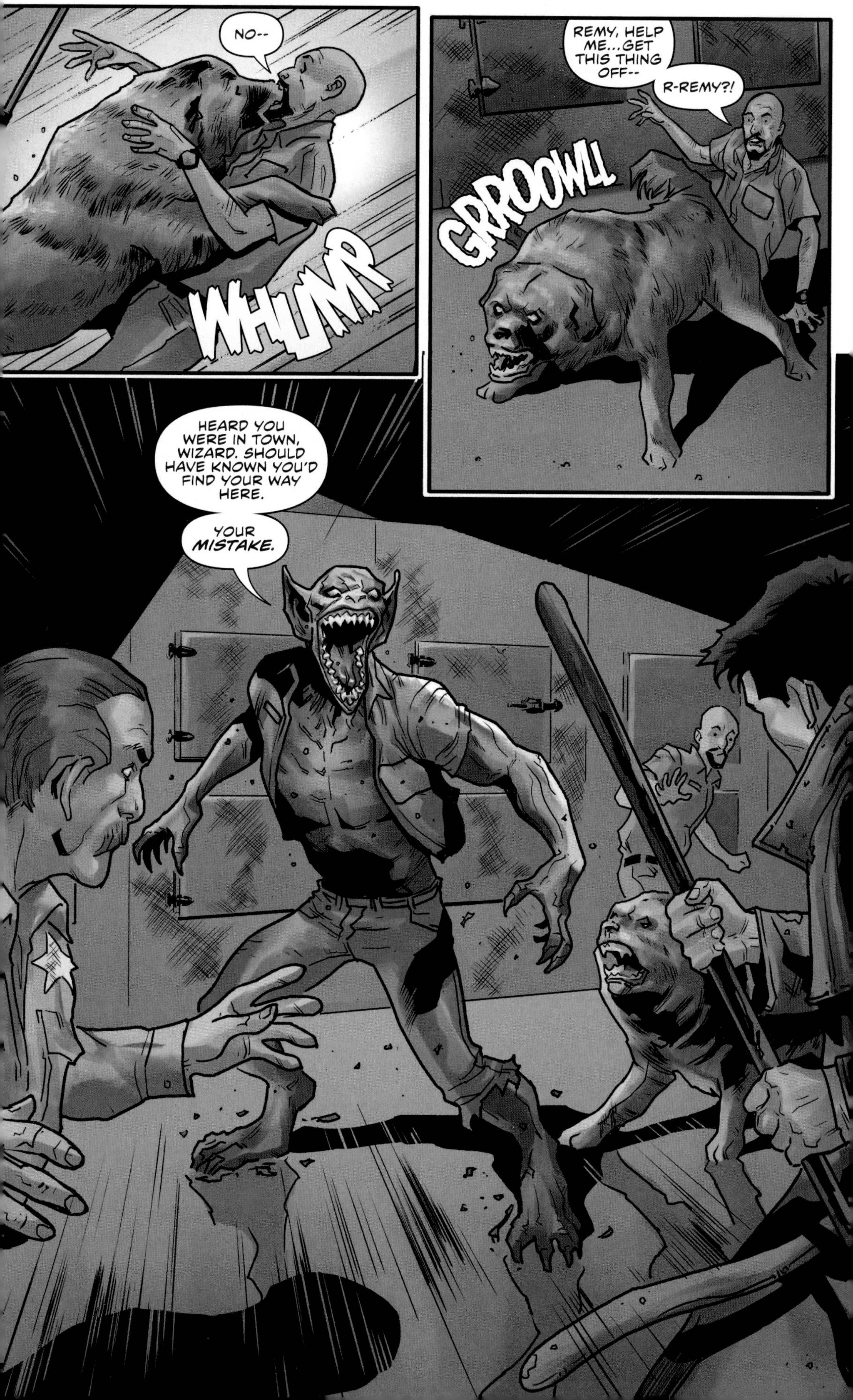
NO--
WHUMP
REMY, HELP ME...GET THIS THING OFF--
R-REMY?!
GRROOWLL
HEARD YOU WERE IN TOWN, WIZARD. SHOULD HAVE KNOWN YOU'D FIND YOUR WAY HERE.
YOUR MISTAKE.

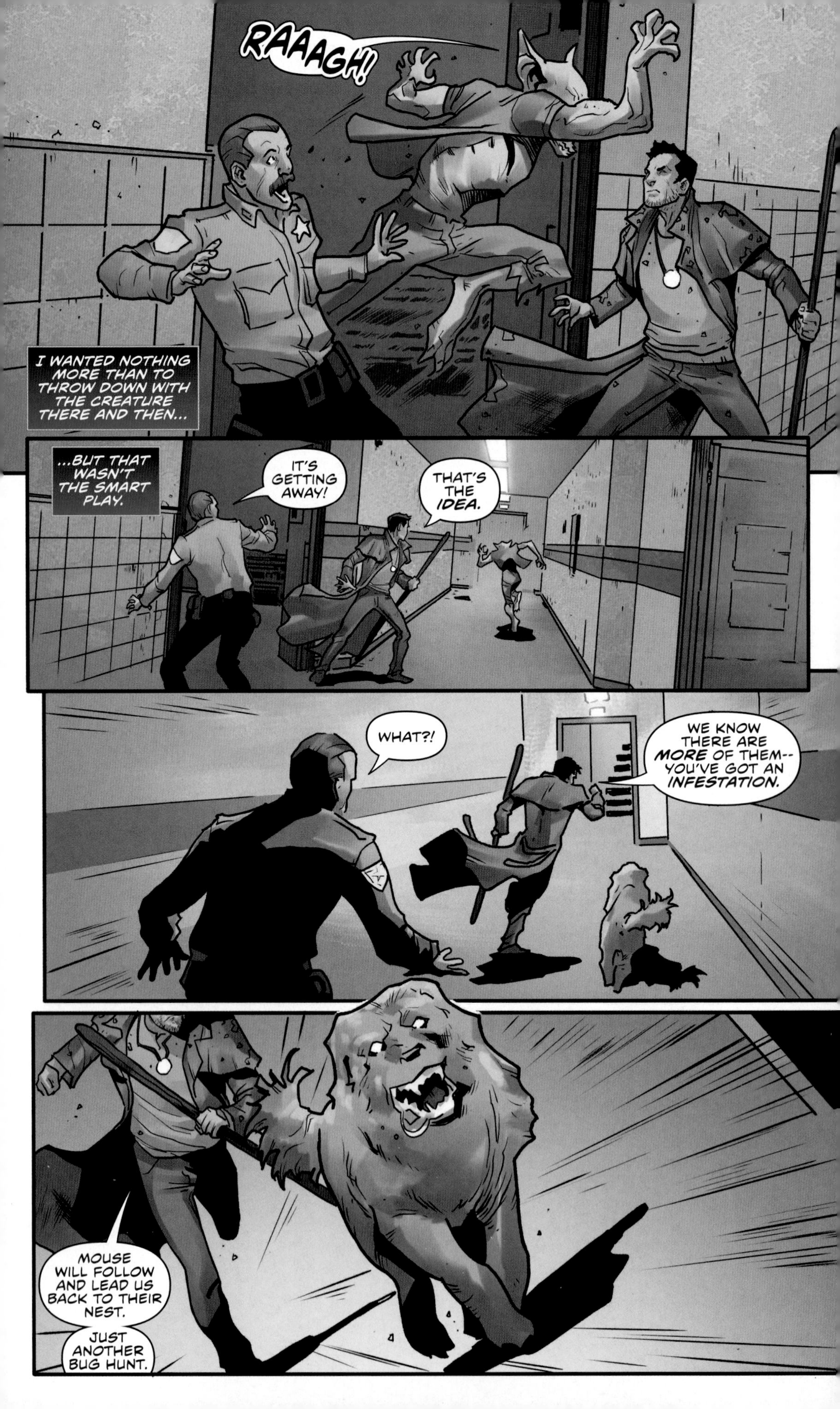
RAAAGH!
I WANTED NOTHING MORE THAN TO THROW DOWN WITH THE CREATURE THERE AND THEN...
...BUT THAT WASN'T THE SMART PLAY.
IT'S GETTING AWAY!
THAT'S THE IDEA.
WHAT?!
WE KNOW THERE ARE MORE OF THEM-- YOU'VE GOT AN INFESTATION.
MOUSE WILL FOLLOW AND LEAD US BACK TO THEIR NEST.
JUST ANOTHER BUG HUNT.

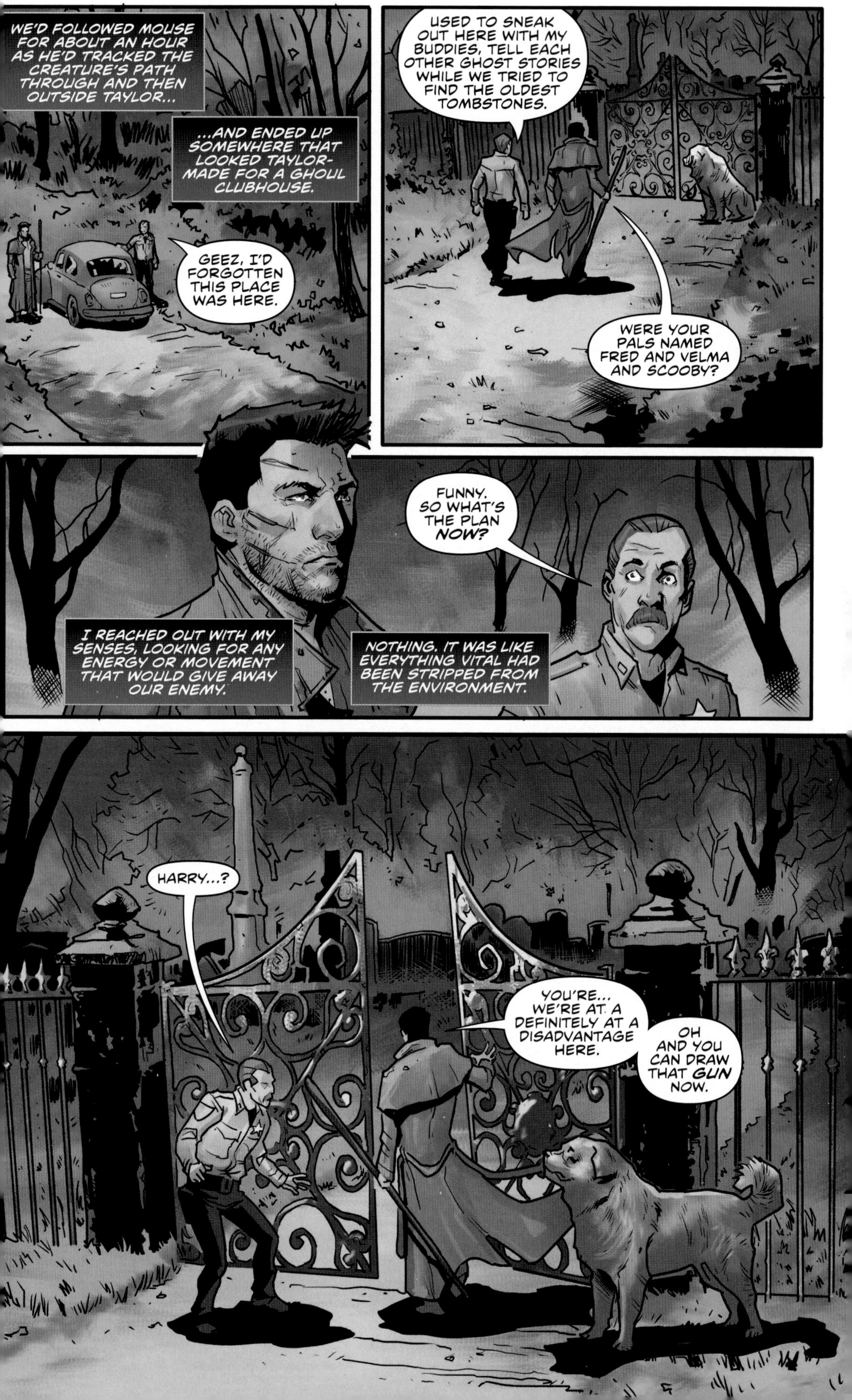
WE'D FOLLOWED MOUSE FOR ABOUT AN HOUR AS HE'D TRACKED THE CREATURE'S PATH THROUGH AND THEN OUTSIDE TAYLOR...
...AND ENDED UP SOMEWHERE THAT LOOKED TAYLOR-MADE FOR A GHOUL CLUBHOUSE.
GEEZ, I'D FORGOTTEN THIS PLACE WAS HERE.
USED TO SNEAK OUT HERE WITH MY BUDDIES, TELL EACH OTHER GHOST STORIES WHILE WE TRIED TO FIND THE OLDEST TOMBSTONES.
WERE YOUR PALS NAMED FRED AND VELMA AND SCOOBY?
FUNNY. SO WHAT'S THE PLAN NOW?
I REACHED OUT WITH MY SENSES, LOOKING FOR ANY ENERGY OR MOVEMENT THAT WOULD GIVE AWAY OUR ENEMY.
NOTHING. IT WAS LIKE EVERYTHING VITAL HAD BEEN STRIPPED FROM THE ENVIRONMENT.
HARRY...?
YOU'RE... WE'RE AT A DEFINITELY AT A DISADVANTAGE HERE.
OH AND YOU CAN DRAW THAT GUN NOW.

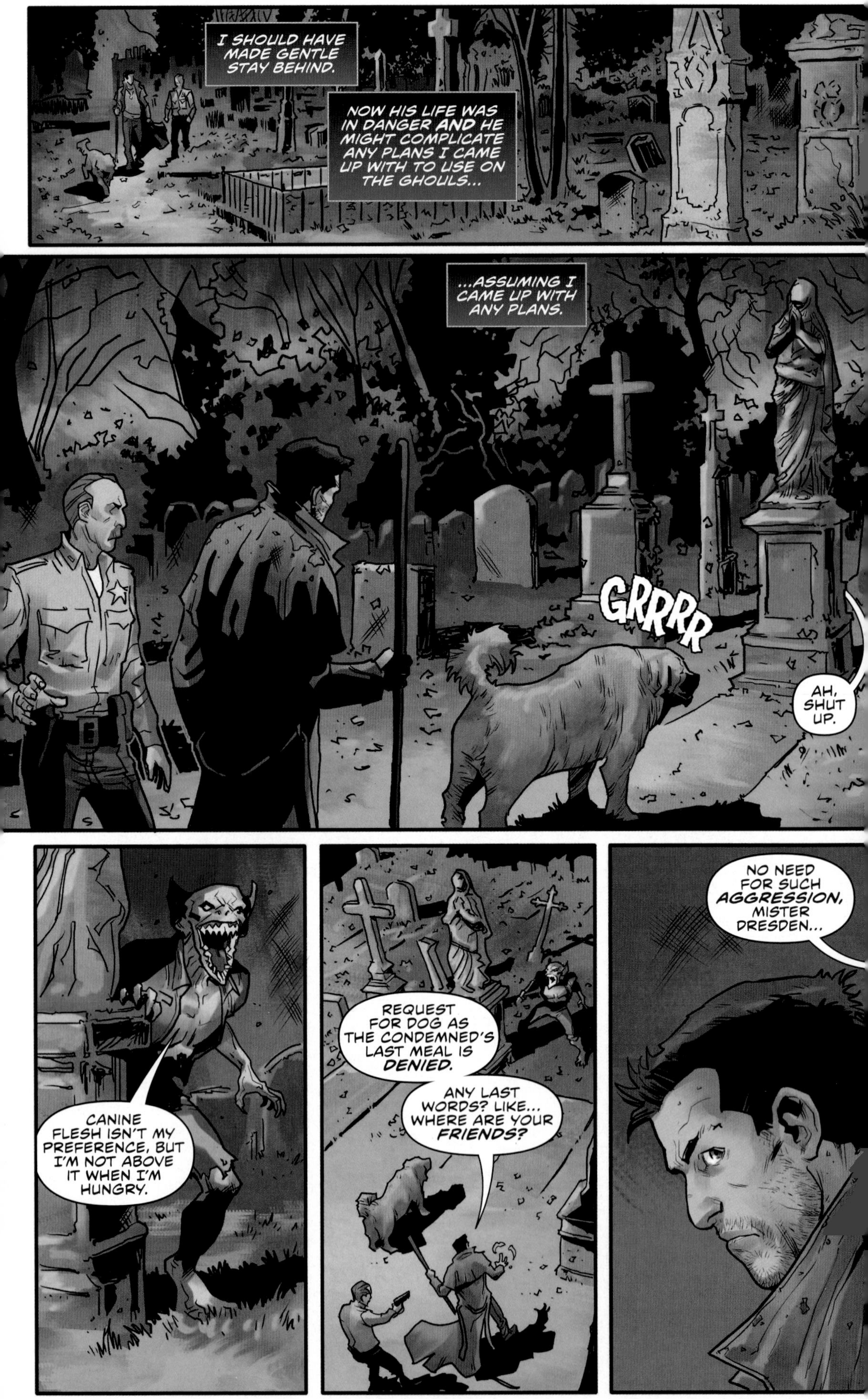
I SHOULD HAVE MADE GENTLE STAY BEHIND.
NOW HIS LIFE WAS IN DANGER **AND** HE MIGHT COMPLICATE ANY PLANS I CAME UP WITH TO USE ON THE GHOULS...
...ASSUMING I CAME UP WITH ANY PLANS.
GRRRR
AH, SHUT UP.
CANINE FLESH ISN'T MY PREFERENCE, BUT I'M NOT ABOVE IT WHEN I'M HUNGRY.
REQUEST FOR DOG AS THE CONDEMNED'S LAST MEAL IS ***DENIED.***
ANY LAST WORDS? LIKE... WHERE ARE YOUR ***FRIENDS?***
NO NEED FOR SUCH ***AGGRESSION,*** MISTER DRESDEN...

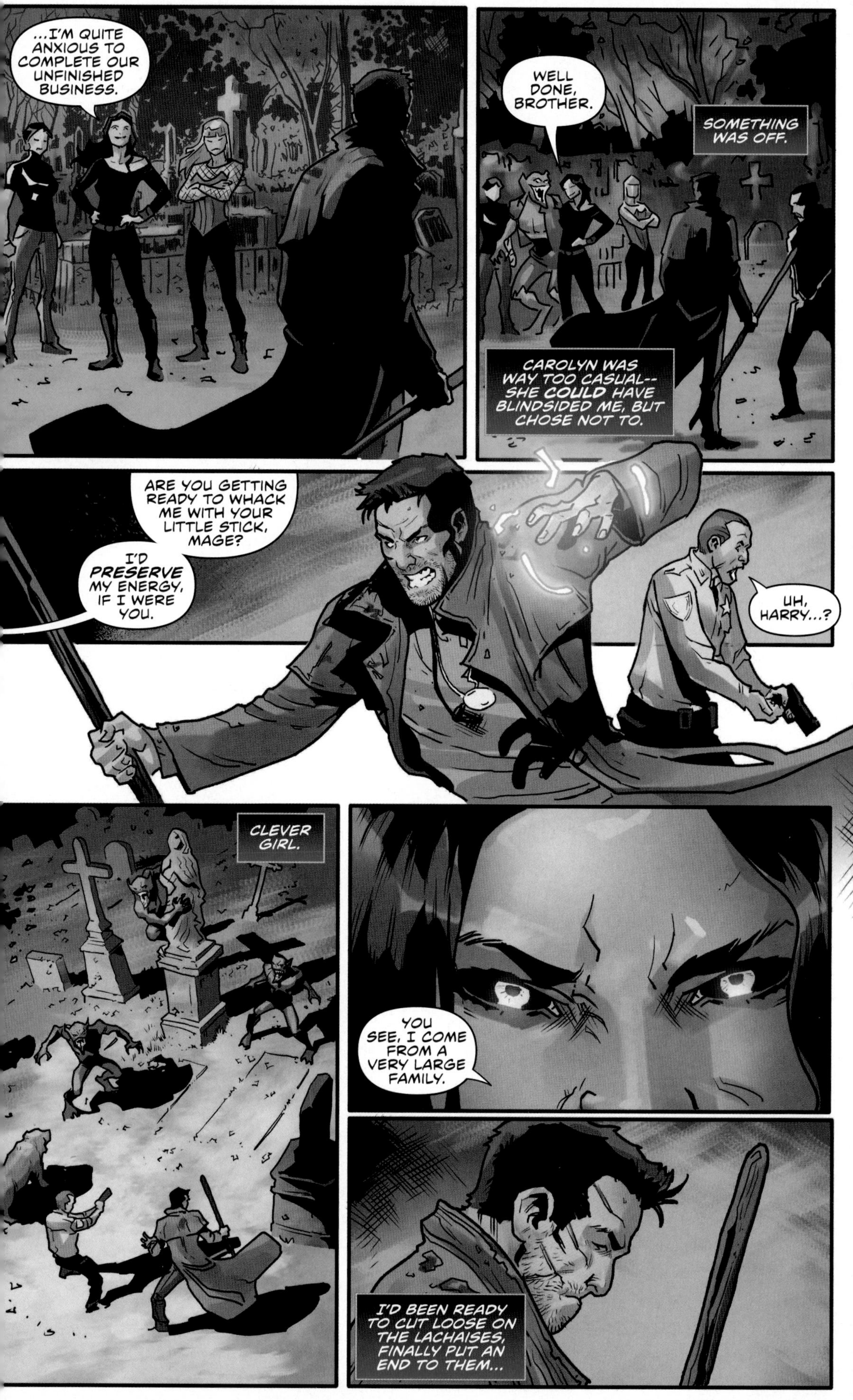
...I'M QUITE ANXIOUS TO COMPLETE OUR UNFINISHED BUSINESS.
WELL DONE, BROTHER.
SOMETHING WAS OFF.
CAROLYN WAS WAY TOO CASUAL-- SHE COULD HAVE BLINDSIDED ME, BUT CHOSE NOT TO.
ARE YOU GETTING READY TO WHACK ME WITH YOUR LITTLE STICK, MAGE?
I'D PRESERVE MY ENERGY, IF I WERE YOU.
UH, HARRY...?
CLEVER GIRL.
YOU SEE, I COME FROM A VERY LARGE FAMILY.
I'D BEEN READY TO CUT LOOSE ON THE LACHAISES, FINALLY PUT AN END TO THEM...

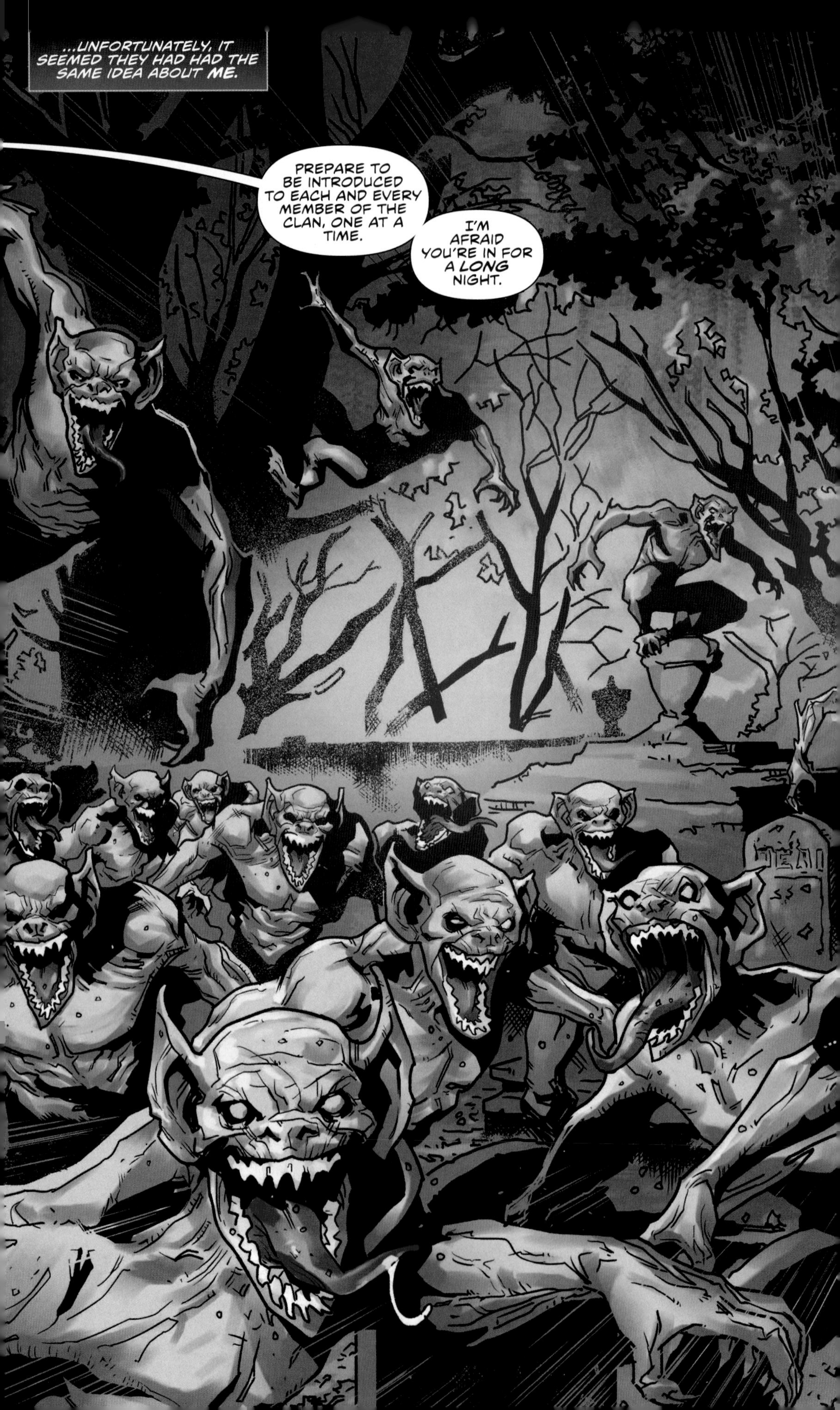
...UNFORTUNATELY, IT SEEMED THEY HAD HAD THE SAME IDEA ABOUT ME.
PREPARE TO BE INTRODUCED TO EACH AND EVERY MEMBER OF THE CLAN, ONE AT A TIME.
I'M AFRAID YOU'RE IN FOR A LONG NIGHT.

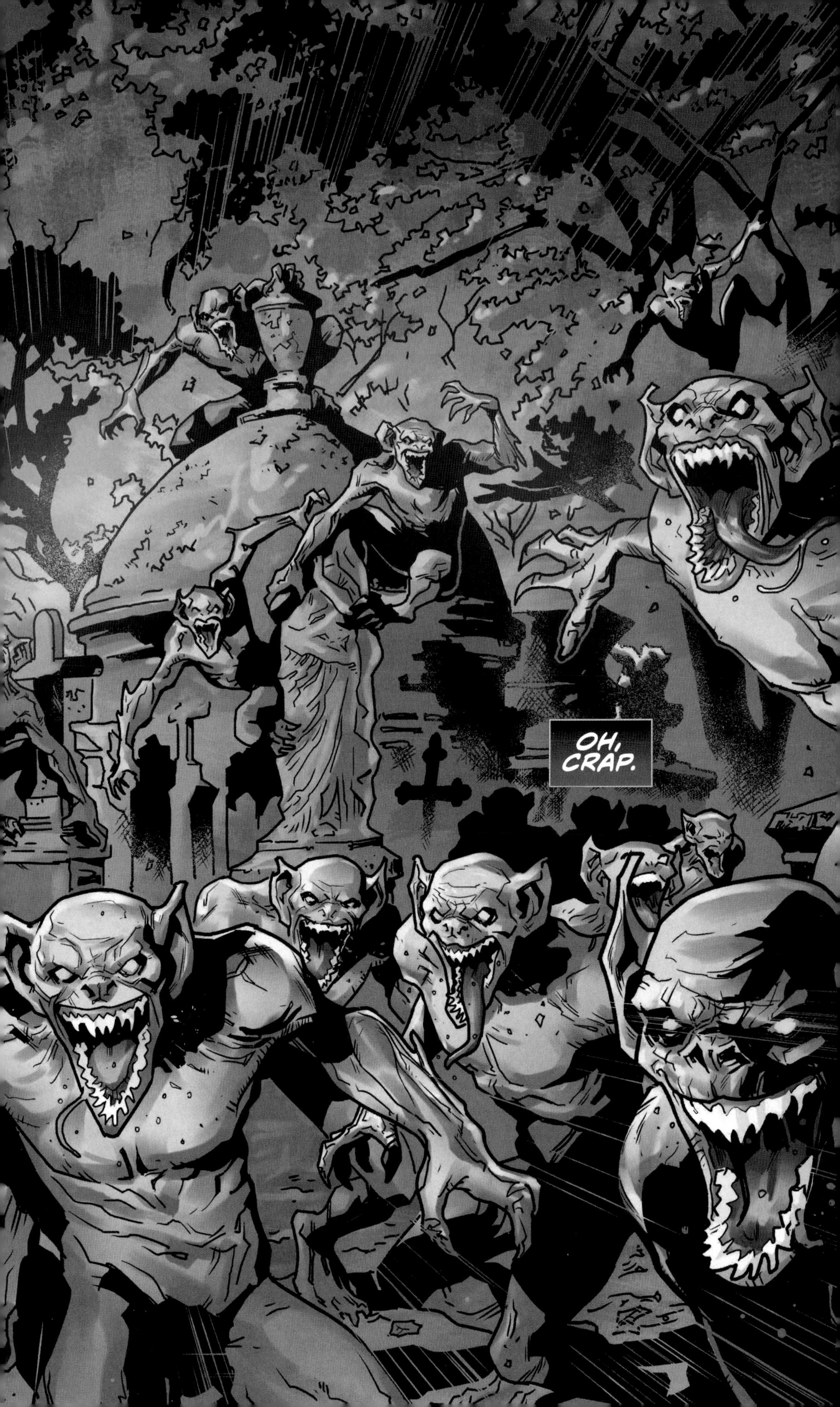
OH, CRAP.

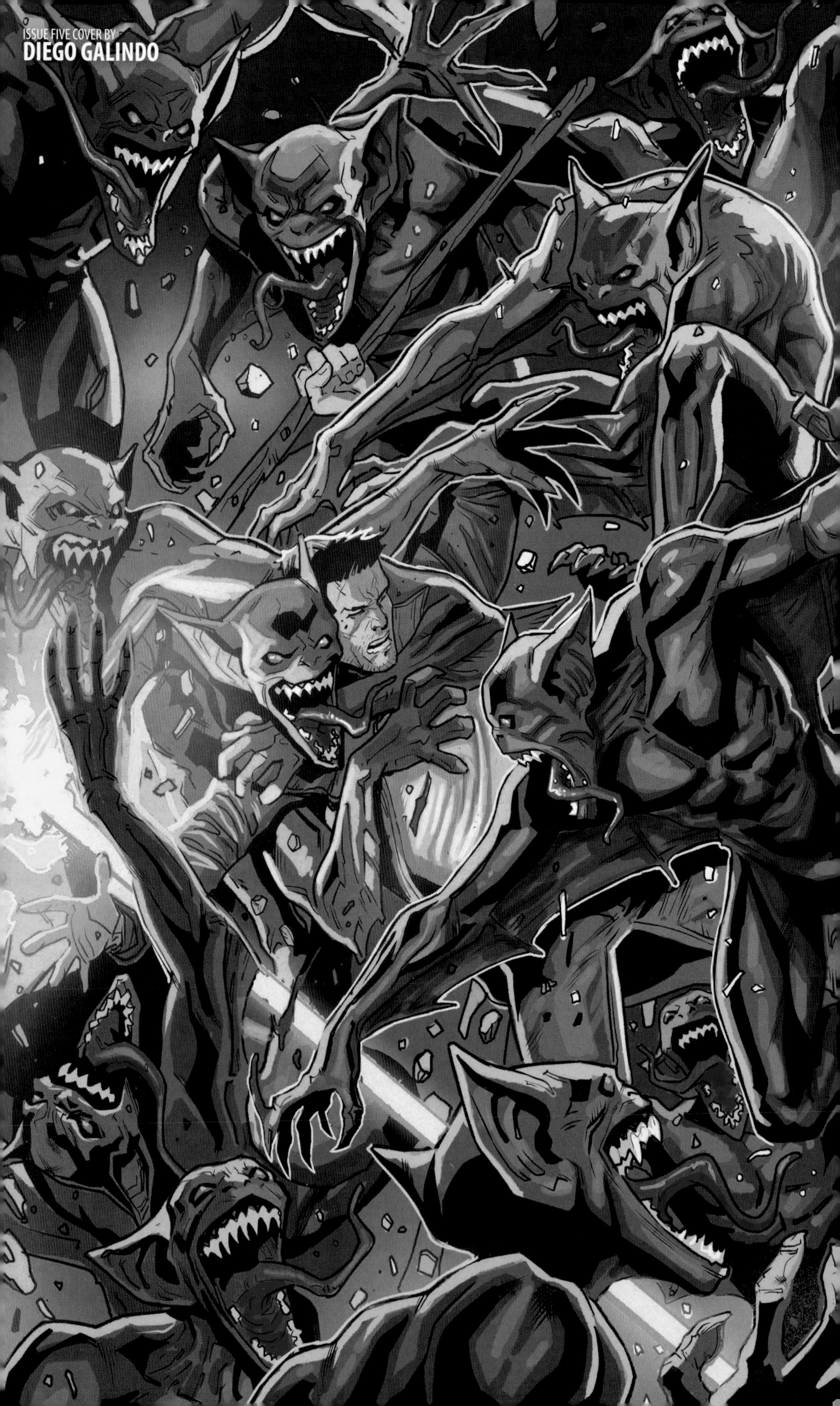

ISSUE FIVE COVER BY
DIEGO GALINDO

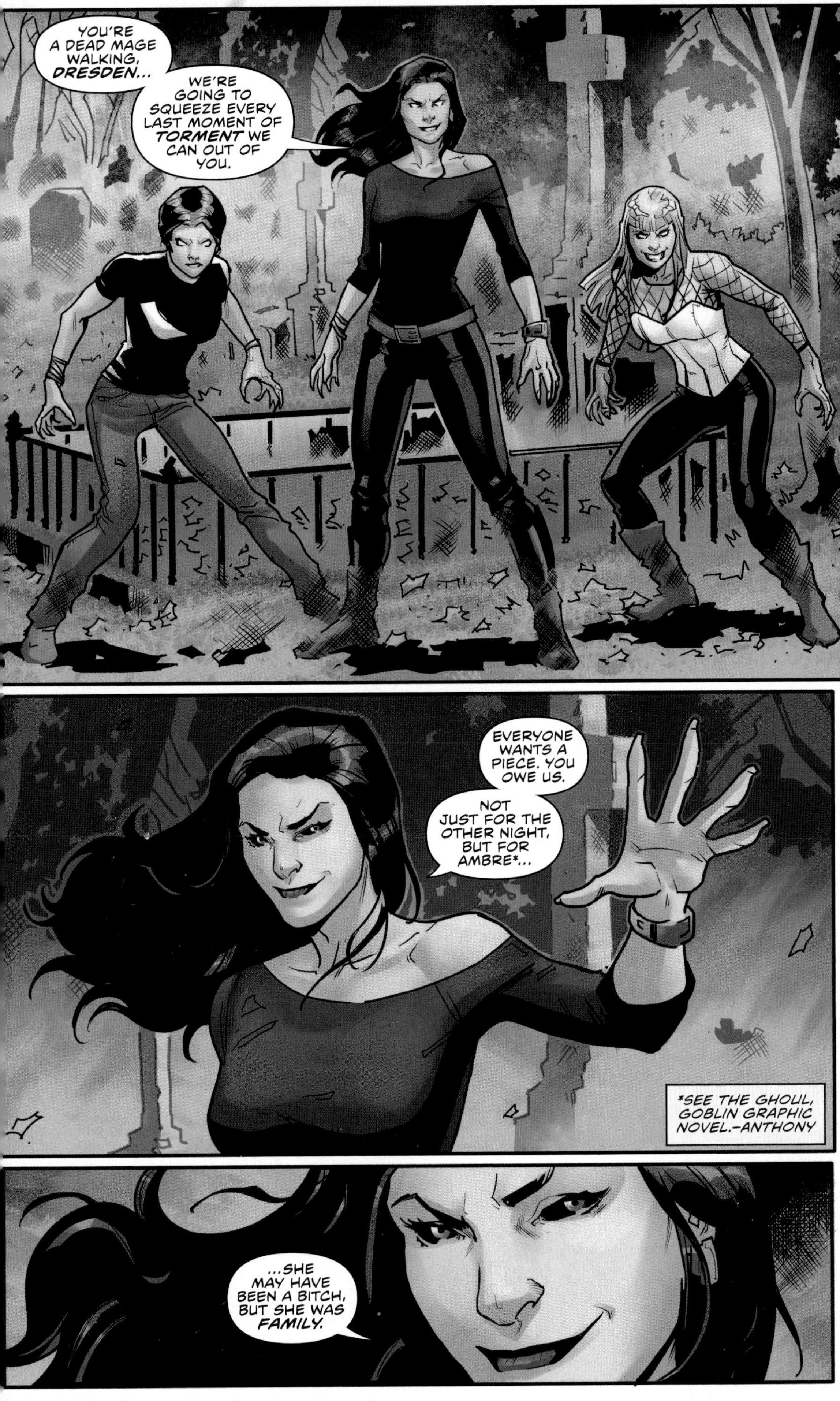

YOU'RE A DEAD MAGE WALKING, DRESDEN...
WE'RE GOING TO SQUEEZE EVERY LAST MOMENT OF TORMENT WE CAN OUT OF YOU.
EVERYONE WANTS A PIECE. YOU OWE US.
NOT JUST FOR THE OTHER NIGHT, BUT FOR AMBRE*...
*SEE THE GHOUL, GOBLIN GRAPHIC NOVEL.-ANTHONY
...SHE MAY HAVE BEEN A BITCH, BUT SHE WAS FAMILY.

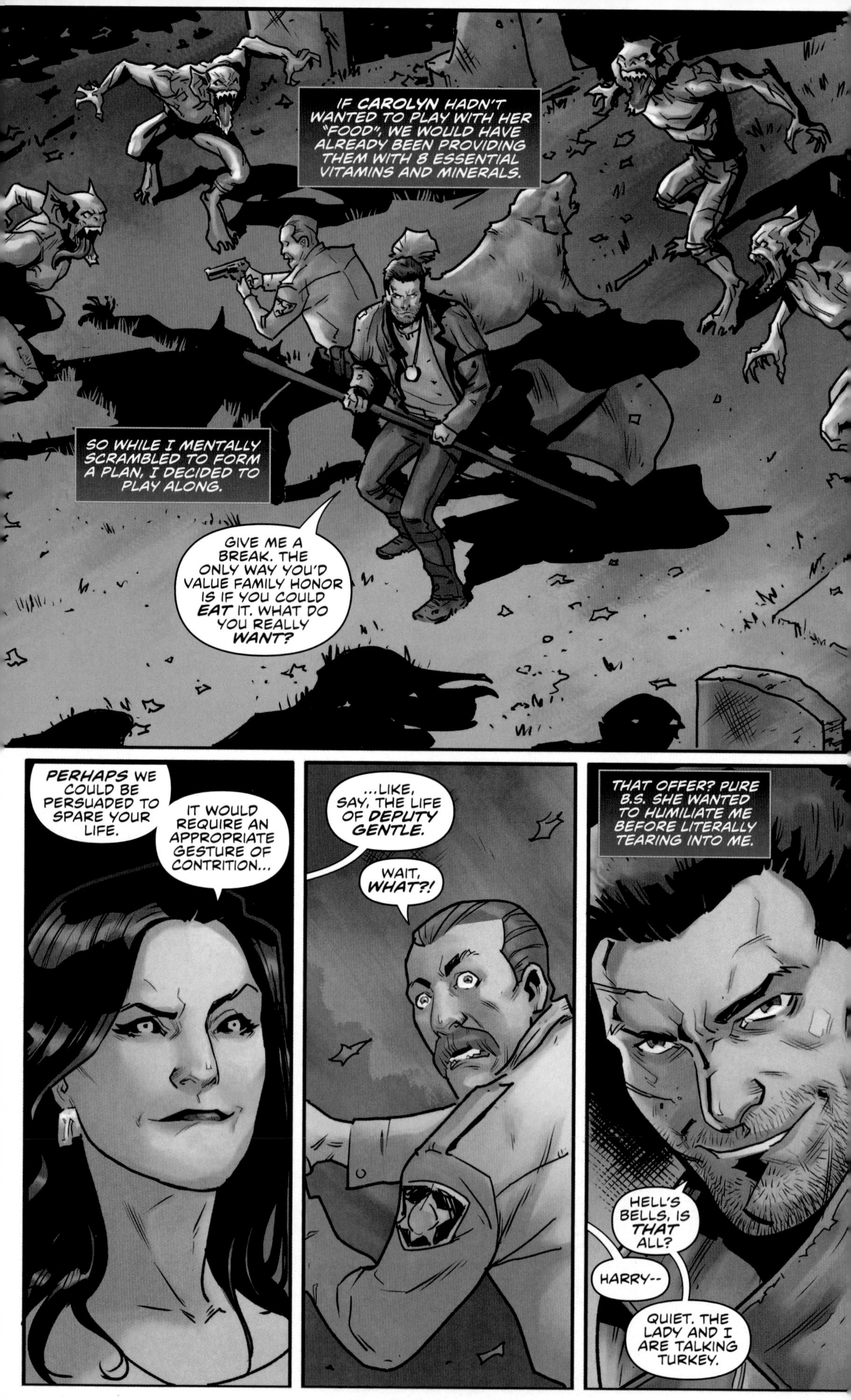
IF CAROLYN HADN'T WANTED TO PLAY WITH HER "FOOD", WE WOULD HAVE ALREADY BEEN PROVIDING THEM WITH 8 ESSENTIAL VITAMINS AND MINERALS.
SO WHILE I MENTALLY SCRAMBLED TO FORM A PLAN, I DECIDED TO PLAY ALONG.
GIVE ME A BREAK. THE ONLY WAY YOU'D VALUE FAMILY HONOR IS IF YOU COULD EAT IT. WHAT DO YOU REALLY WANT?
PERHAPS WE COULD BE PERSUADED TO SPARE YOUR LIFE.
IT WOULD REQUIRE AN APPROPRIATE GESTURE OF CONTRITION...
...LIKE, SAY, THE LIFE OF DEPUTY GENTLE.
WAIT, WHAT?!
THAT OFFER? PURE B.S. SHE WANTED TO HUMILIATE ME BEFORE LITERALLY TEARING INTO ME.
HELL'S BELLS, IS THAT ALL?
HARRY--
QUIET. THE LADY AND I ARE TALKING TURKEY.

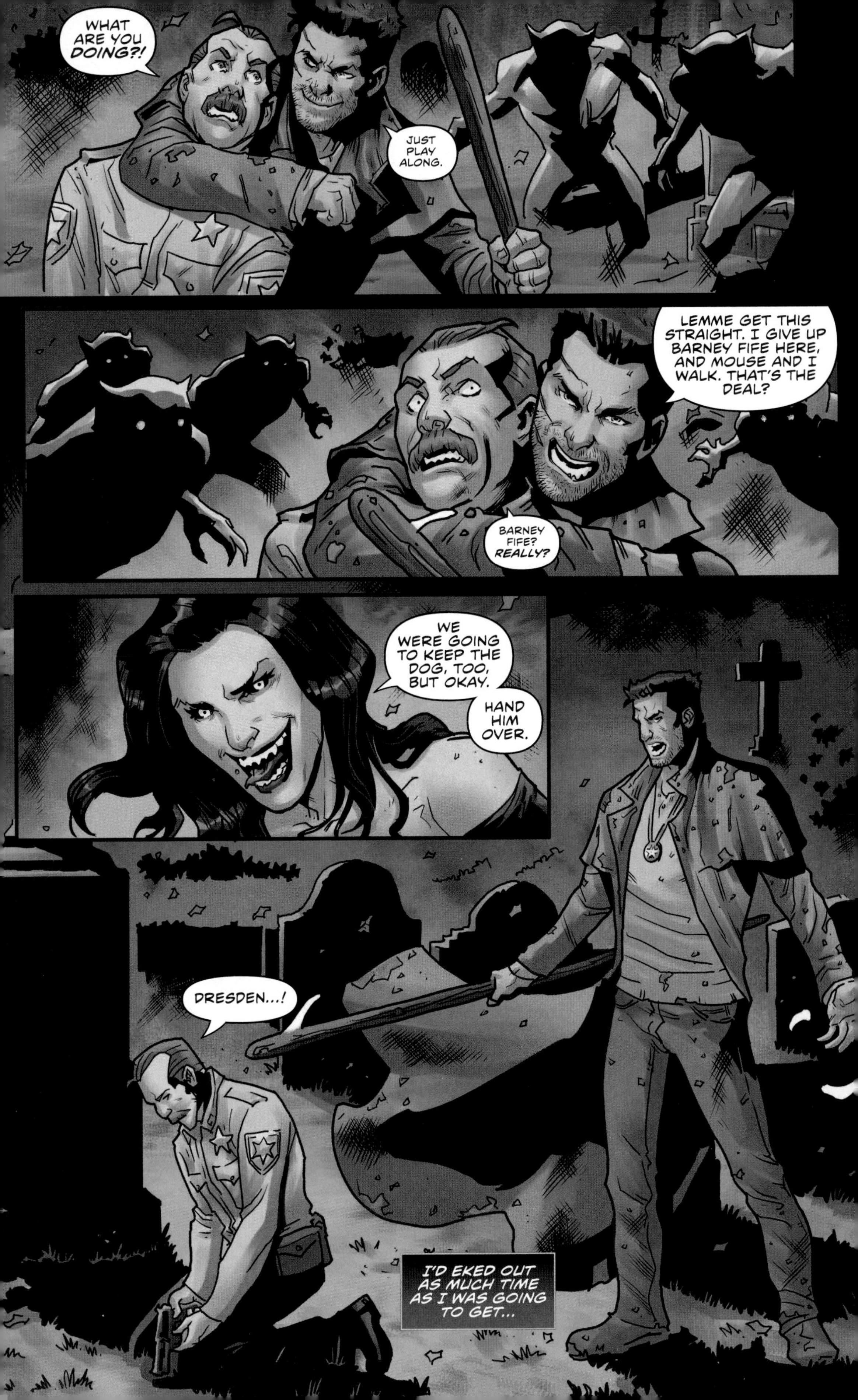
WHAT ARE YOU DOING?!
JUST PLAY ALONG.
LEMME GET THIS STRAIGHT. I GIVE UP BARNEY FIFE HERE, AND MOUSE AND I WALK. THAT'S THE DEAL?
BARNEY FIFE? REALLY?
WE WERE GOING TO KEEP THE DOG, TOO, BUT OKAY.
HAND HIM OVER.
DRESDEN...!
I'D EKED OUT AS MUCH TIME AS I WAS GOING TO GET...

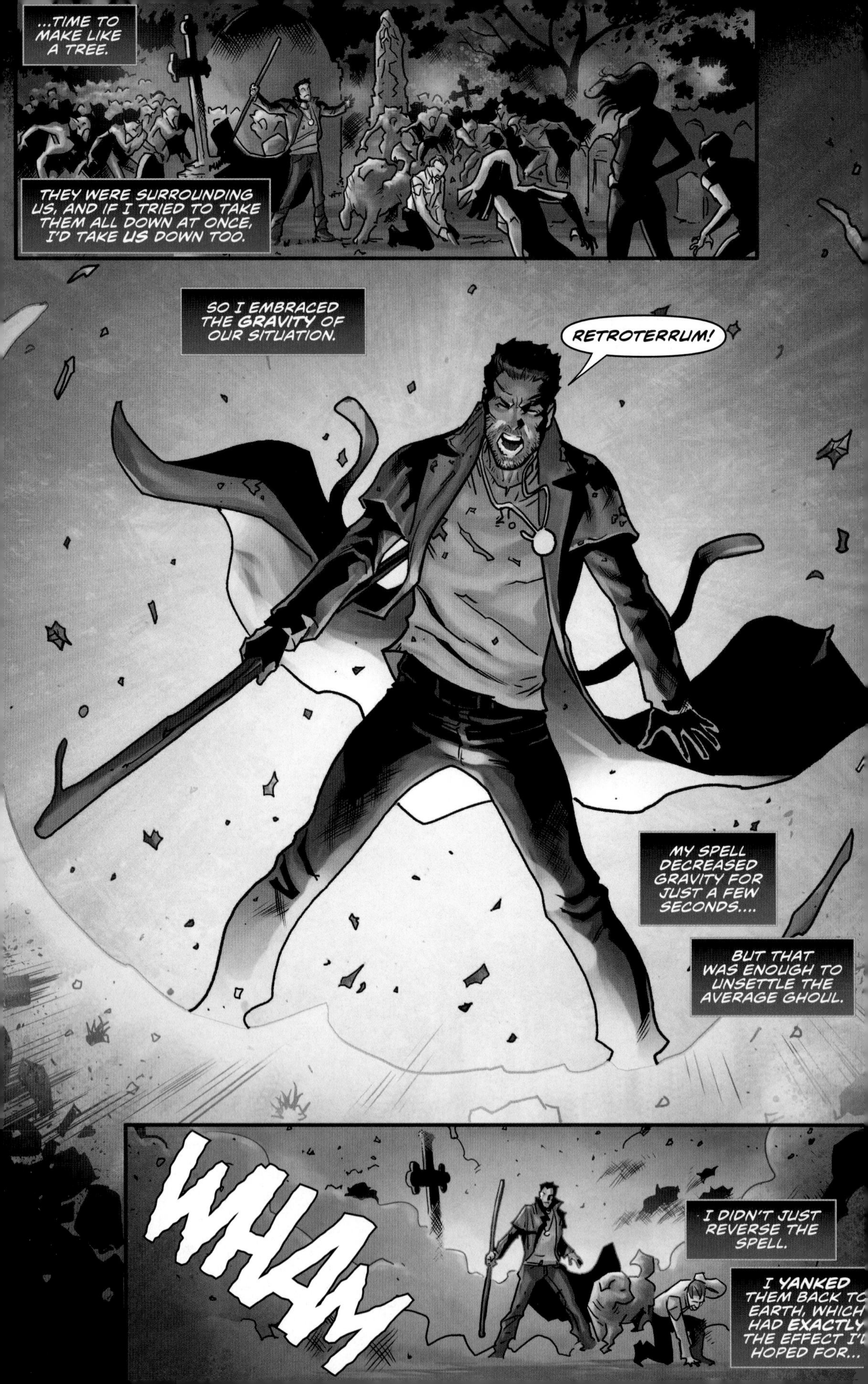
...TIME TO MAKE LIKE A TREE.
THEY WERE SURROUNDING US, AND IF I TRIED TO TAKE THEM ALL DOWN AT ONCE, I'D TAKE US DOWN TOO.
SO I EMBRACED THE GRAVITY OF OUR SITUATION.
RETROTERRUM!
MY SPELL DECREASED GRAVITY FOR JUST A FEW SECONDS....
BUT THAT WAS ENOUGH TO UNSETTLE THE AVERAGE GHOUL.
WHAM
I DIDN'T JUST REVERSE THE SPELL.
I YANKED THEM BACK TO EARTH, WHICH HAD EXACTLY THE EFFECT I'D HOPED FOR...

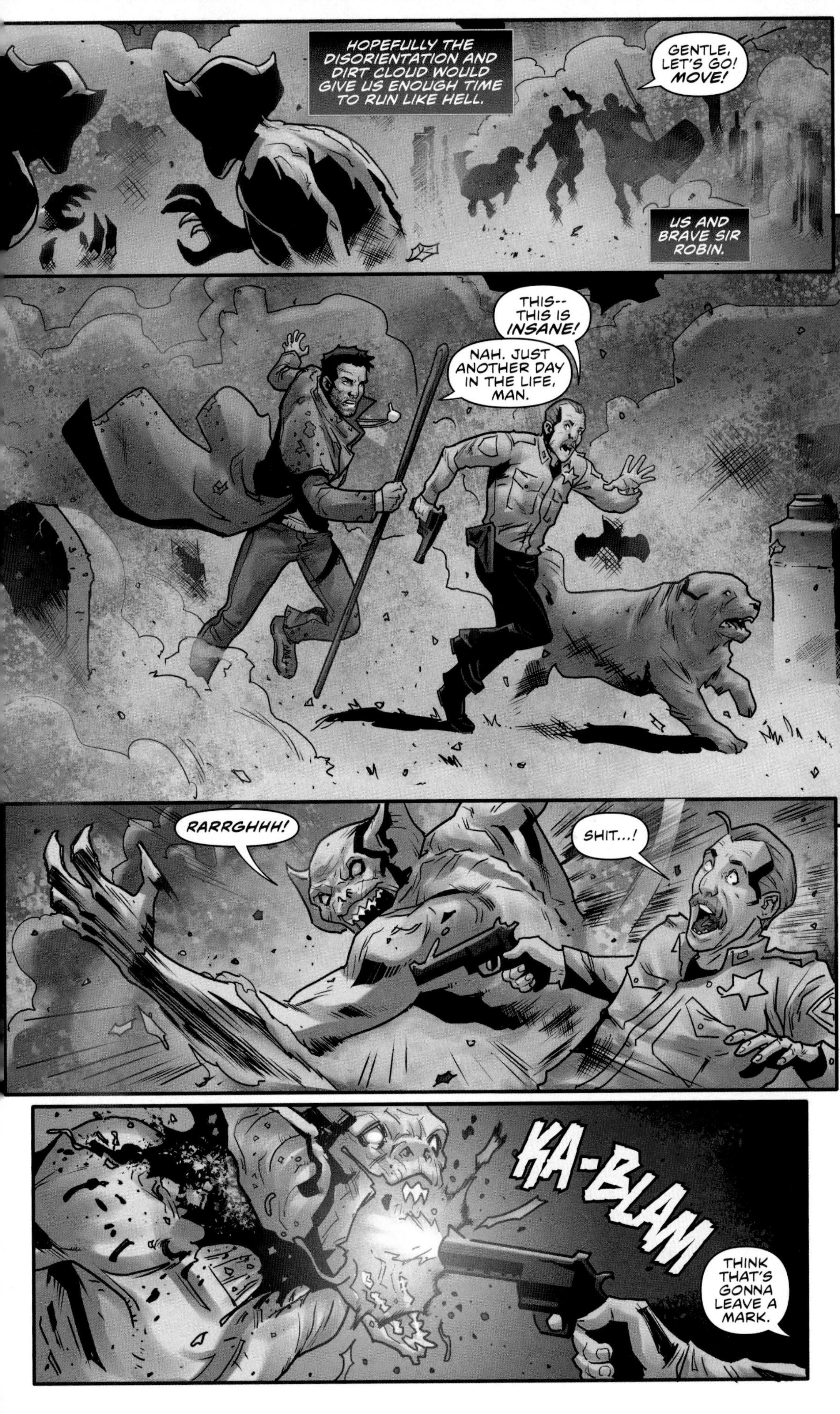
HOPEFULLY THE DISORIENTATION AND DIRT CLOUD WOULD GIVE US ENOUGH TIME TO RUN LIKE HELL.
GENTLE, LET'S GO! MOVE!
US AND BRAVE SIR ROBIN.
THIS-- THIS IS INSANE!
NAH. JUST ANOTHER DAY IN THE LIFE, MAN.
RARRGHHH!
SHIT...!
KA-BLAM
THINK THAT'S GONNA LEAVE A MARK.

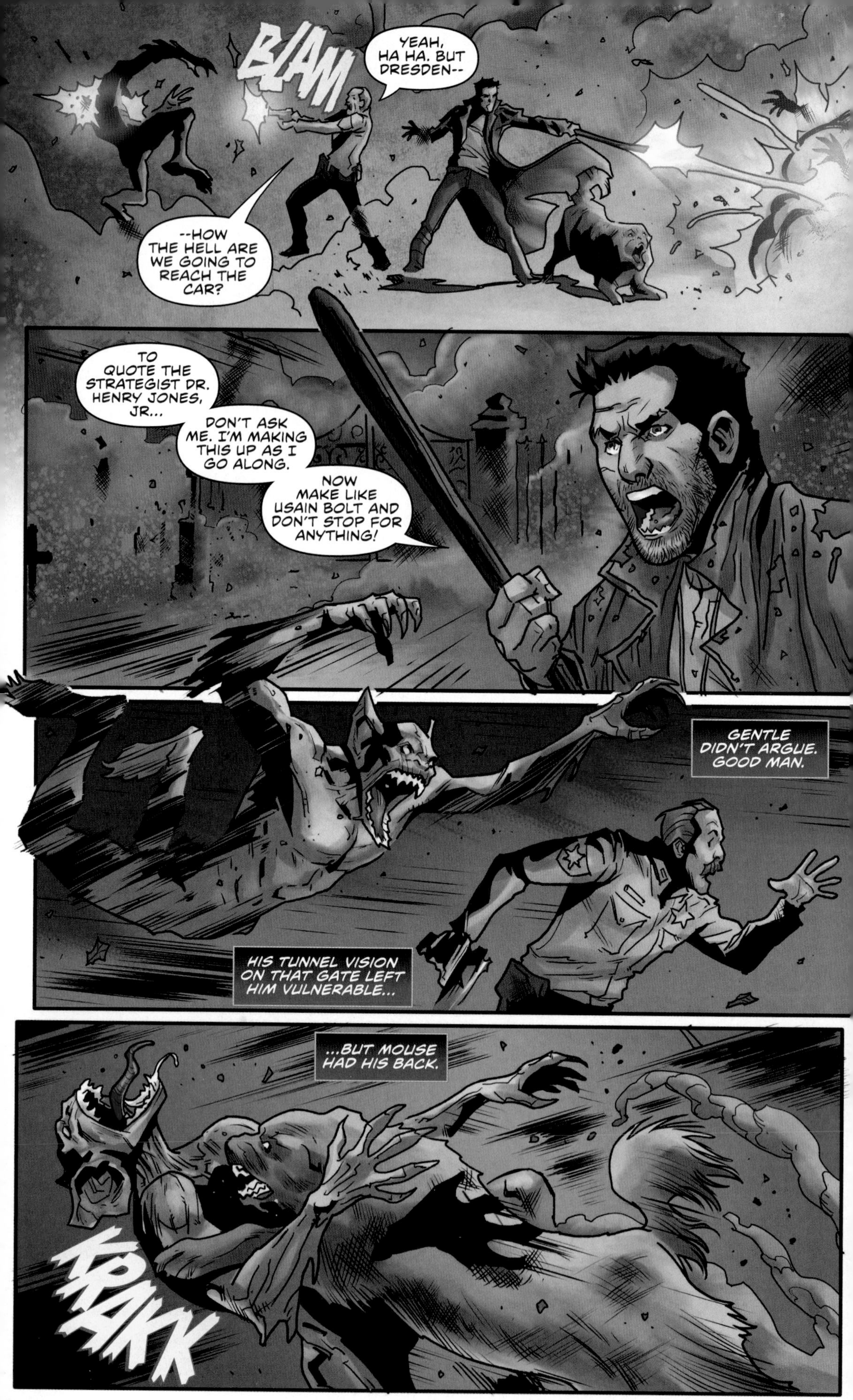

BLAM
YEAH, HA HA. BUT DRESDEN--
--HOW THE HELL ARE WE GOING TO REACH THE CAR?
TO QUOTE THE STRATEGIST DR. HENRY JONES, JR...
DON'T ASK ME. I'M MAKING THIS UP AS I GO ALONG.
NOW MAKE LIKE USAIN BOLT AND DON'T STOP FOR ANYTHING!
GENTLE DIDN'T ARGUE. GOOD MAN.
HIS TUNNEL VISION ON THAT GATE LEFT HIM VULNERABLE...
...BUT MOUSE HAD HIS BACK.
KRAKK

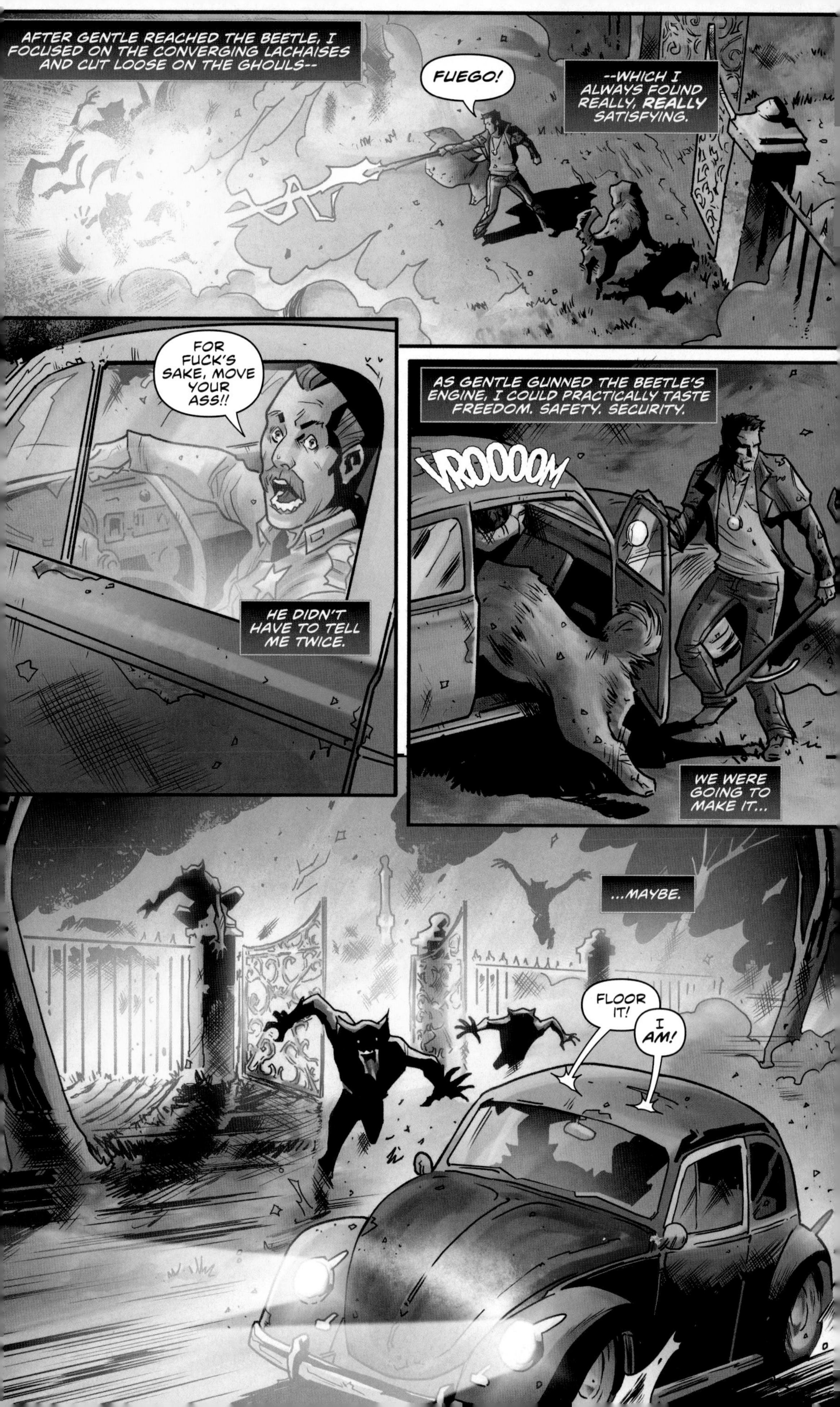
AFTER GENTLE REACHED THE BEETLE, I FOCUSED ON THE CONVERGING LACHAISES AND CUT LOOSE ON THE GHOULS--
FUEGO!
--WHICH I ALWAYS FOUND REALLY, REALLY SATISFYING.
FOR FUCK'S SAKE, MOVE YOUR ASS!!
HE DIDN'T HAVE TO TELL ME TWICE.
AS GENTLE GUNNED THE BEETLE'S ENGINE, I COULD PRACTICALLY TASTE FREEDOM. SAFETY. SECURITY.
VROOOOM
WE WERE GOING TO MAKE IT...
...MAYBE.
FLOOR IT!
I AM!

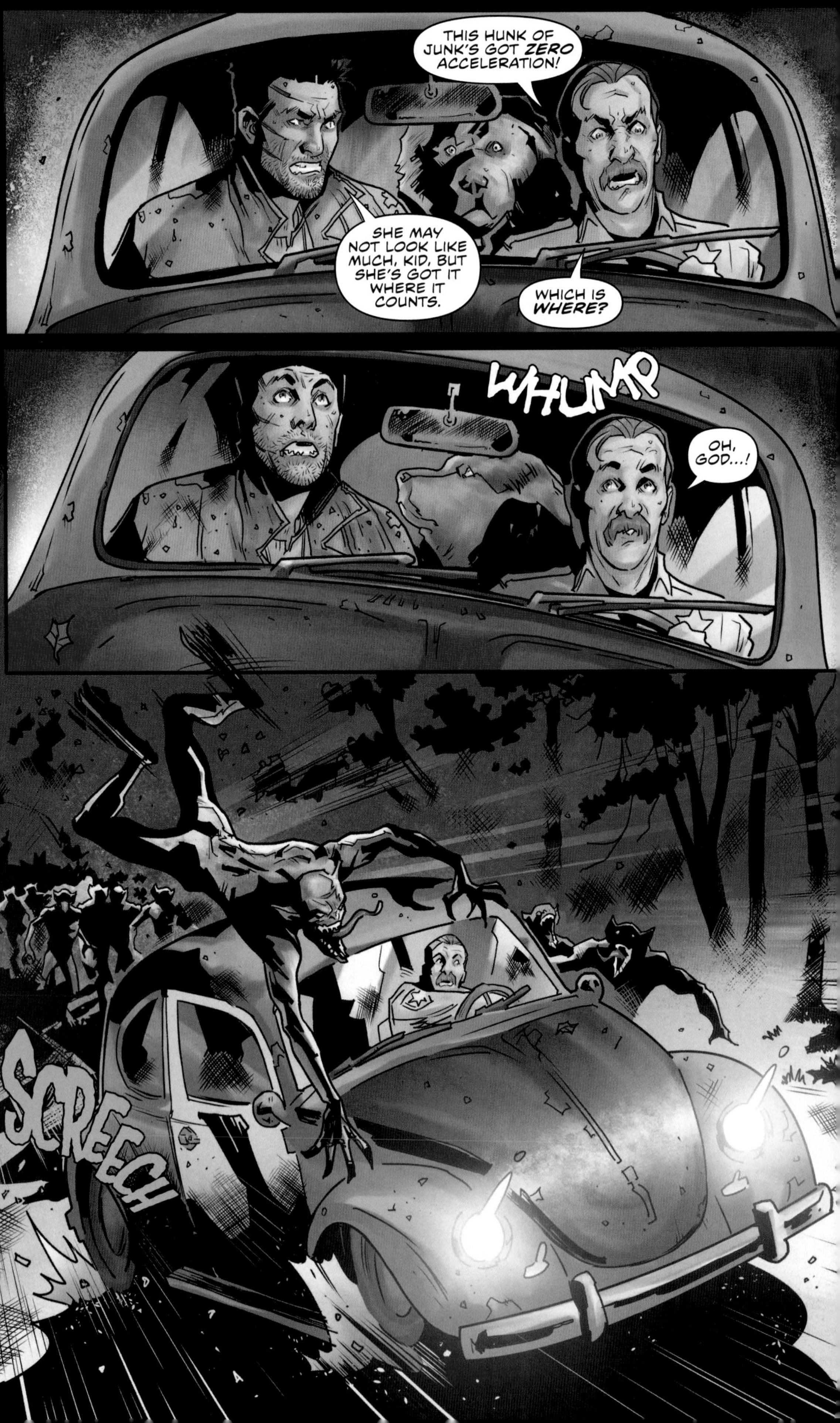
THIS HUNK OF JUNK'S GOT *ZERO* ACCELERATION!
SHE MAY NOT LOOK LIKE MUCH, KID, BUT SHE'S GOT IT WHERE IT COUNTS.
WHICH IS *WHERE?*
WHUMP
OH, GOD...!
SCREECH

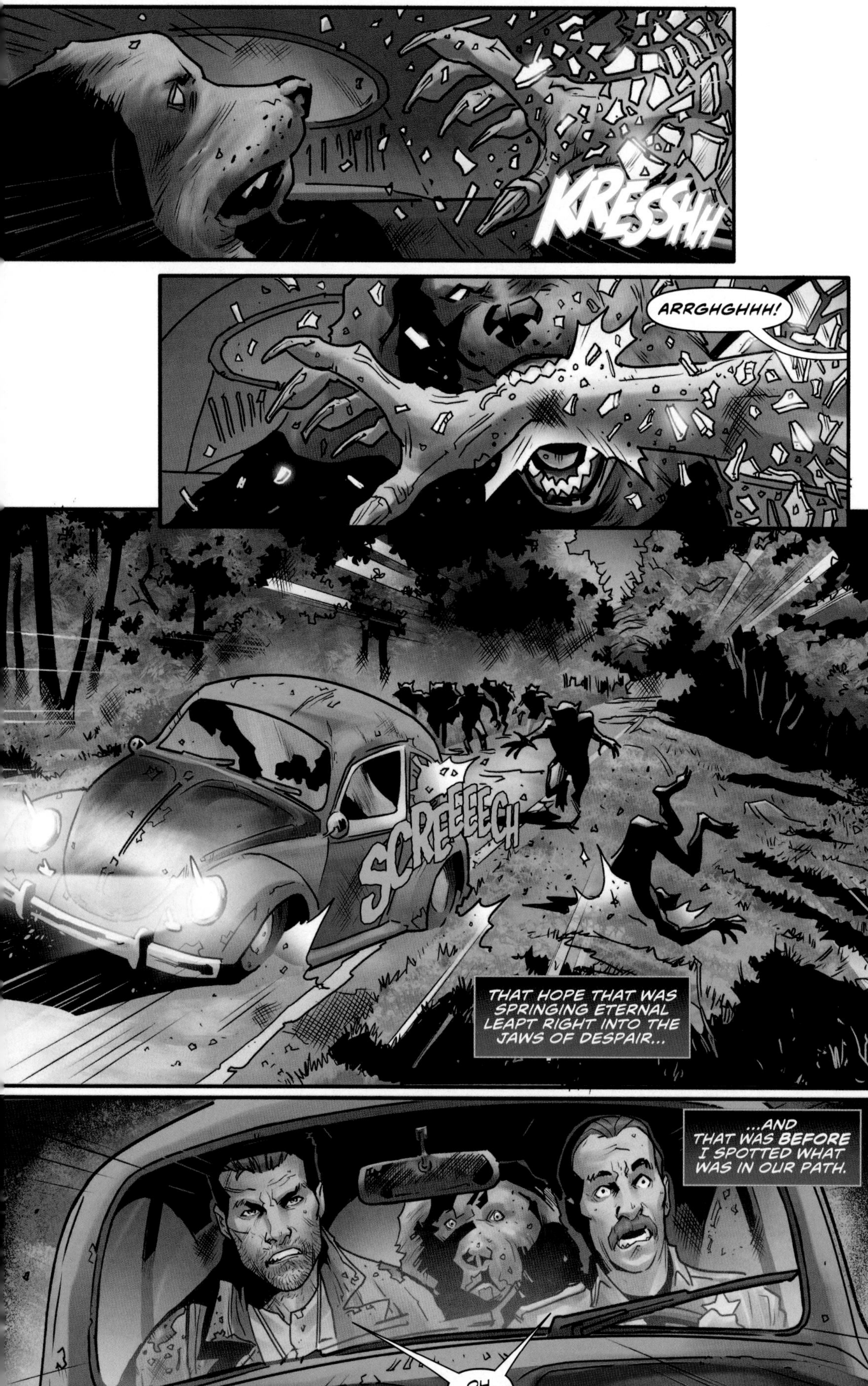
KRESSHH
ARRGHGHHH!
SCREEEECH
THAT HOPE THAT WAS SPRINGING ETERNAL LEAPT RIGHT INTO THE JAWS OF DESPAIR...
...AND THAT WAS BEFORE I SPOTTED WHAT WAS IN OUR PATH.
OH, CRAP.

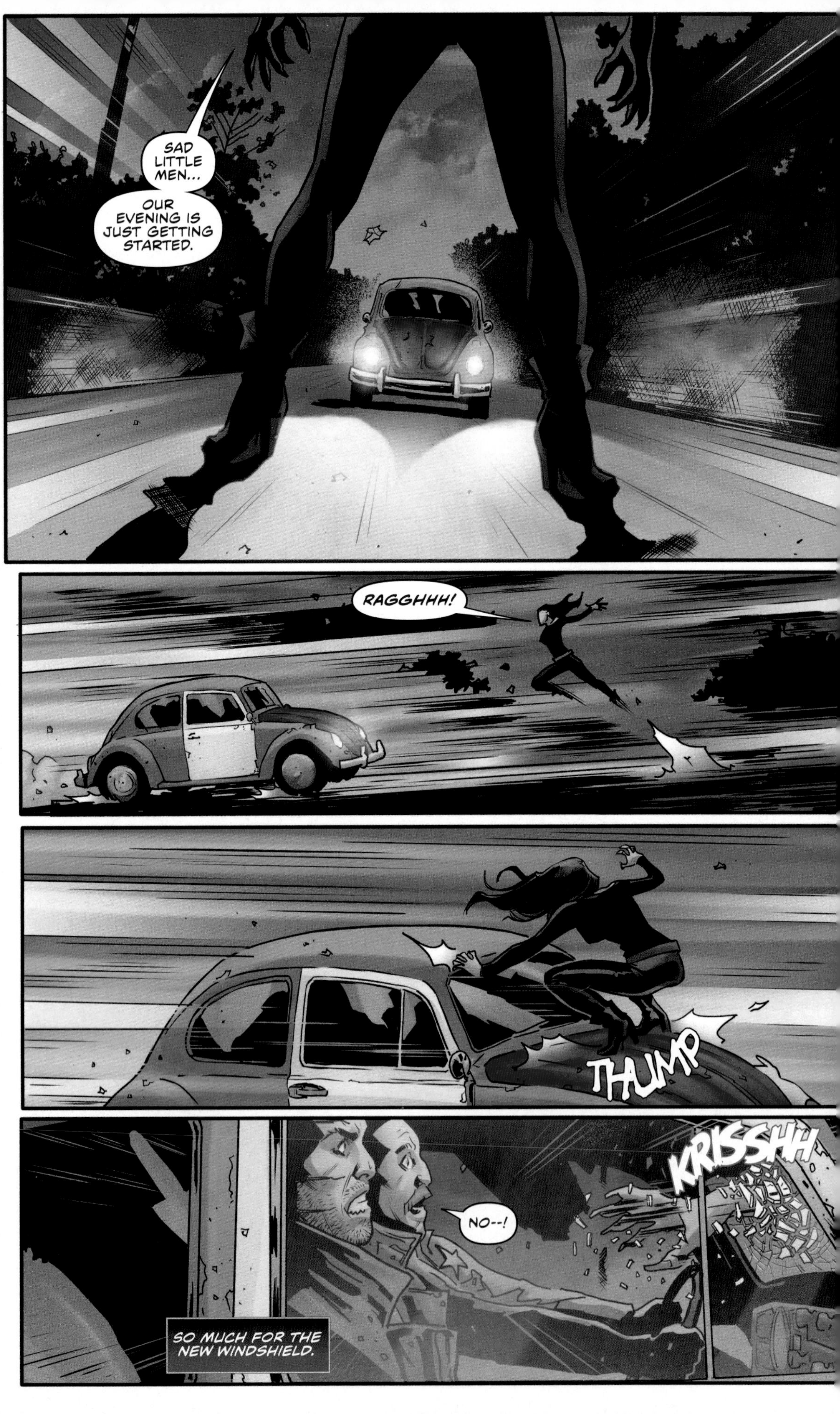
SAD LITTLE MEN...
OUR EVENING IS JUST GETTING STARTED.
RAGGHHH!
THUMP
KRISSHH
NO--!
SO MUCH FOR THE NEW WINDSHIELD.

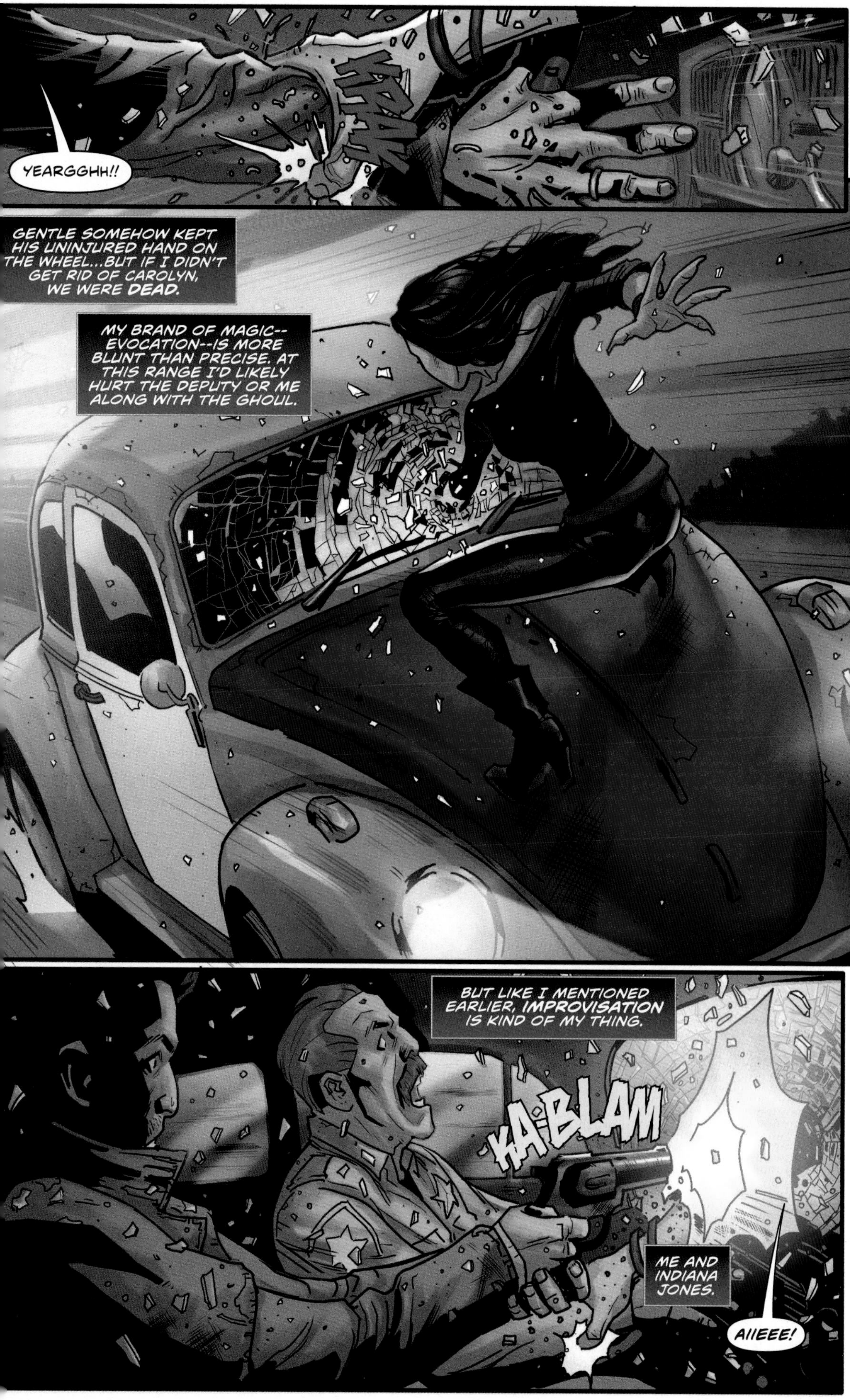

YEARGGHH!!
GENTLE SOMEHOW KEPT HIS UNINJURED HAND ON THE WHEEL...BUT IF I DIDN'T GET RID OF CAROLYN, WE WERE DEAD.
MY BRAND OF MAGIC--EVOCATION--IS MORE BLUNT THAN PRECISE. AT THIS RANGE I'D LIKELY HURT THE DEPUTY OR ME ALONG WITH THE GHOUL.
BUT LIKE I MENTIONED EARLIER, IMPROVISATION IS KIND OF MY THING.
KA-BLAM
ME AND INDIANA JONES.
AIIEEE!

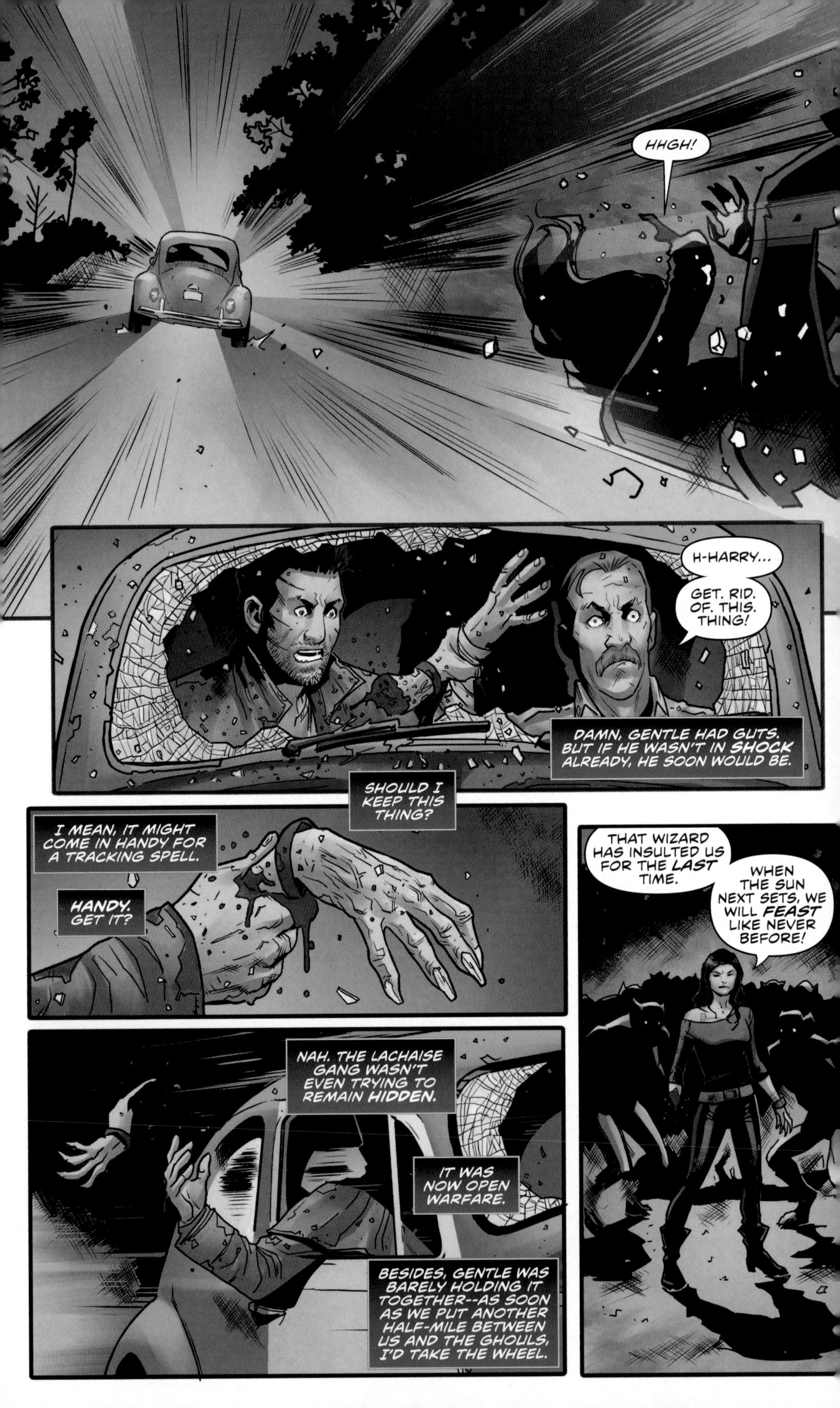

HHGH!
H-HARRY...
GET. RID. OF. THIS. THING!
DAMN, GENTLE HAD GUTS. BUT IF HE WASN'T IN SHOCK ALREADY, HE SOON WOULD BE.
SHOULD I KEEP THIS THING?
I MEAN, IT MIGHT COME IN HANDY FOR A TRACKING SPELL.
HANDY. GET IT?
NAH. THE LACHAISE GANG WASN'T EVEN TRYING TO REMAIN HIDDEN.
IT WAS NOW OPEN WARFARE.
BESIDES, GENTLE WAS BARELY HOLDING IT TOGETHER--AS SOON AS WE PUT ANOTHER HALF-MILE BETWEEN US AND THE GHOULS, I'D TAKE THE WHEEL.
THAT WIZARD HAS INSULTED US FOR THE LAST TIME.
WHEN THE SUN NEXT SETS, WE WILL FEAST LIKE NEVER BEFORE!

EMERGENCY ADULT-PEDIATRIC & TRAUMA CENTER

THERE WERE A SHIT TON OF GHOULS THERE.

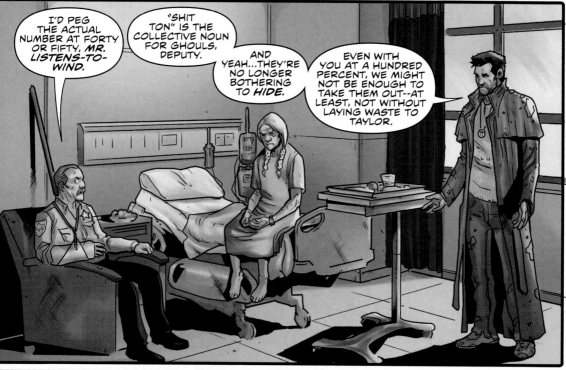

I'D PEG THE ACTUAL NUMBER AT FORTY OR FIFTY, *MR. LISTENS-TO-WIND.*

"SHIT TON" IS THE COLLECTIVE NOUN FOR GHOULS, DEPUTY.

AND YEAH...THEY'RE NO LONGER BOTHERING TO *HIDE.*

EVEN WITH YOU AT A HUNDRED PERCENT, WE MIGHT NOT BE ENOUGH TO TAKE THEM OUT--AT LEAST, NOT WITHOUT LAYING WASTE TO TAYLOR.

PEOPLE ARE GOING TO DIE.

HOW FAST CAN WE GET *THE COUNCIL* TO SEND REINFORCEMENTS?

NOT FAST ENOUGH.

FORTUNATELY, WE HAVE *ANOTHER* RECOURSE.

AGENTS BIGGS, LYTLE AND THEIR MEN.

NO FREAKING *WAY.*

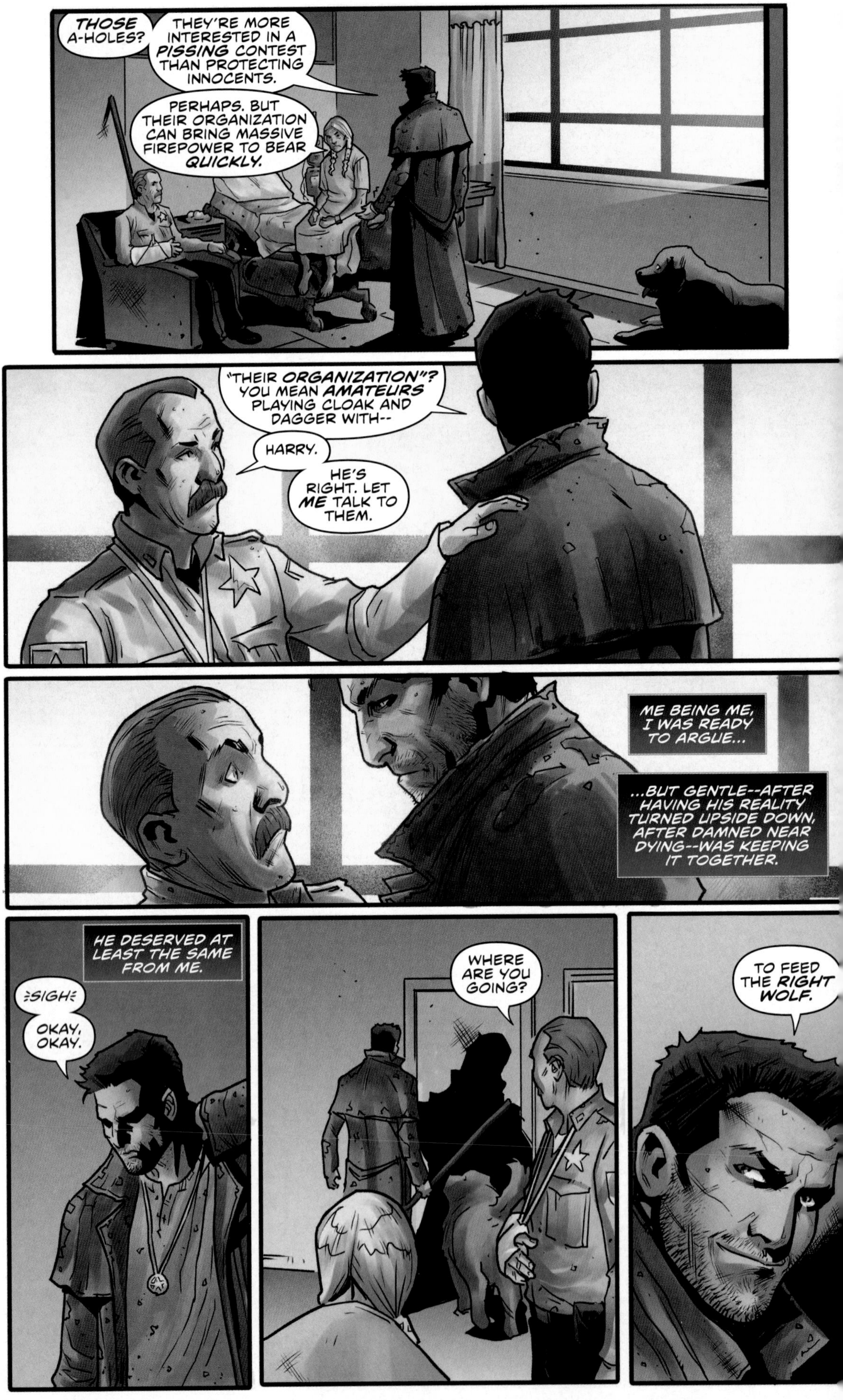
THOSE A-HOLES?
THEY'RE MORE INTERESTED IN A PISSING CONTEST THAN PROTECTING INNOCENTS.
PERHAPS. BUT THEIR ORGANIZATION CAN BRING MASSIVE FIREPOWER TO BEAR QUICKLY.
"THEIR ORGANIZATION"? YOU MEAN AMATEURS PLAYING CLOAK AND DAGGER WITH--
HARRY.
HE'S RIGHT. LET ME TALK TO THEM.
ME BEING ME, I WAS READY TO ARGUE...
...BUT GENTLE--AFTER HAVING HIS REALITY TURNED UPSIDE DOWN, AFTER DAMNED NEAR DYING--WAS KEEPING IT TOGETHER.
HE DESERVED AT LEAST THE SAME FROM ME.
SIGH
OKAY, OKAY.
WHERE ARE YOU GOING?
TO FEED THE RIGHT WOLF.

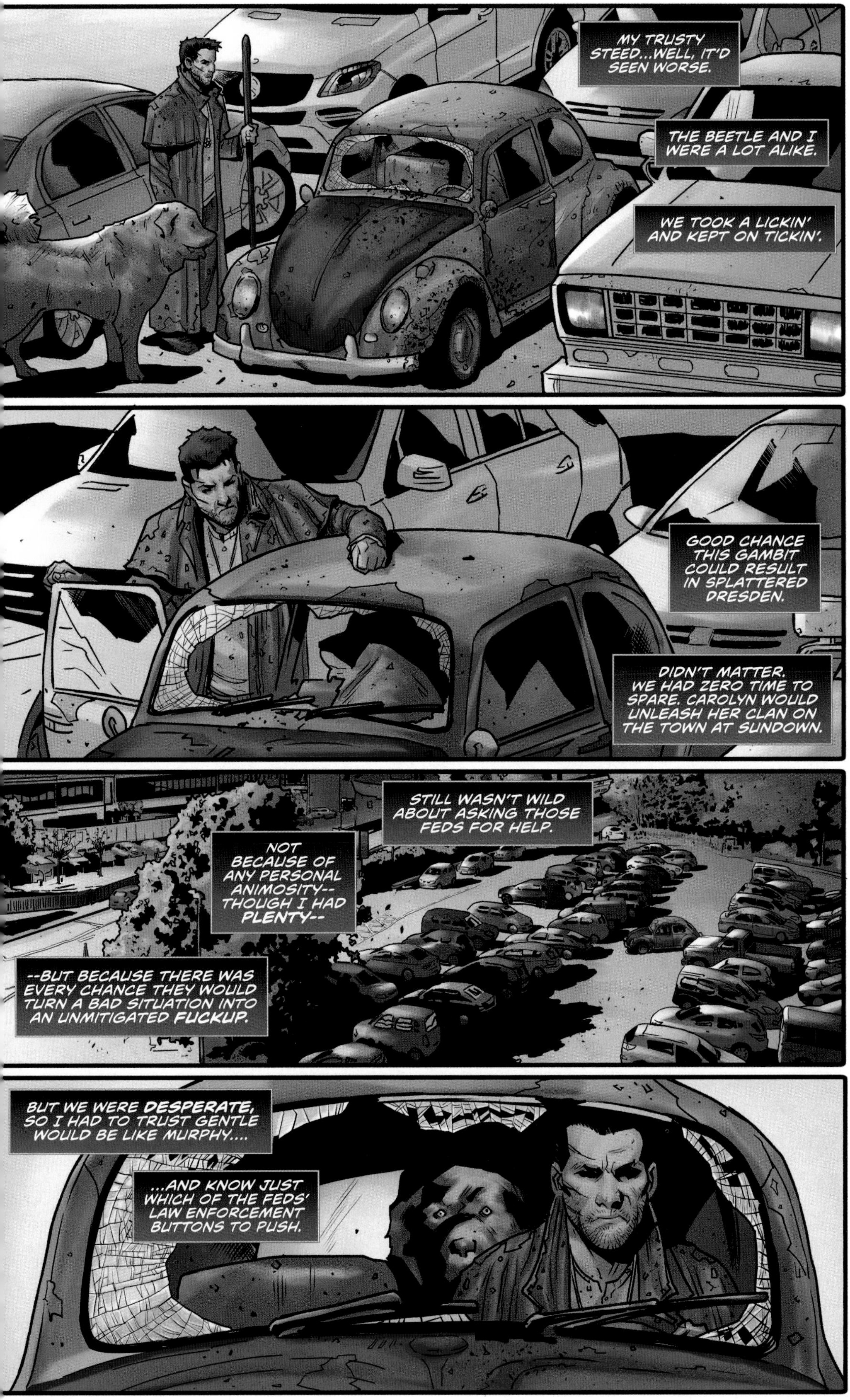
MY TRUSTY STEED...WELL, IT'D SEEN WORSE.
THE BEETLE AND I WERE A LOT ALIKE.
WE TOOK A LICKIN' AND KEPT ON TICKIN'.
GOOD CHANCE THIS GAMBIT COULD RESULT IN SPLATTERED DRESDEN.
DIDN'T MATTER. WE HAD ZERO TIME TO SPARE. CAROLYN WOULD UNLEASH HER CLAN ON THE TOWN AT SUNDOWN.
STILL WASN'T WILD ABOUT ASKING THOSE FEDS FOR HELP.
NOT BECAUSE OF ANY PERSONAL ANIMOSITY-- THOUGH I HAD **PLENTY**--
--BUT BECAUSE THERE WAS EVERY CHANCE THEY WOULD TURN A BAD SITUATION INTO AN UNMITIGATED **FUCKUP.**
BUT WE WERE **DESPERATE,** SO I HAD TO TRUST GENTLE WOULD BE LIKE MURPHY....
...AND KNOW JUST WHICH OF THE FEDS' LAW ENFORCEMENT BUTTONS TO PUSH.

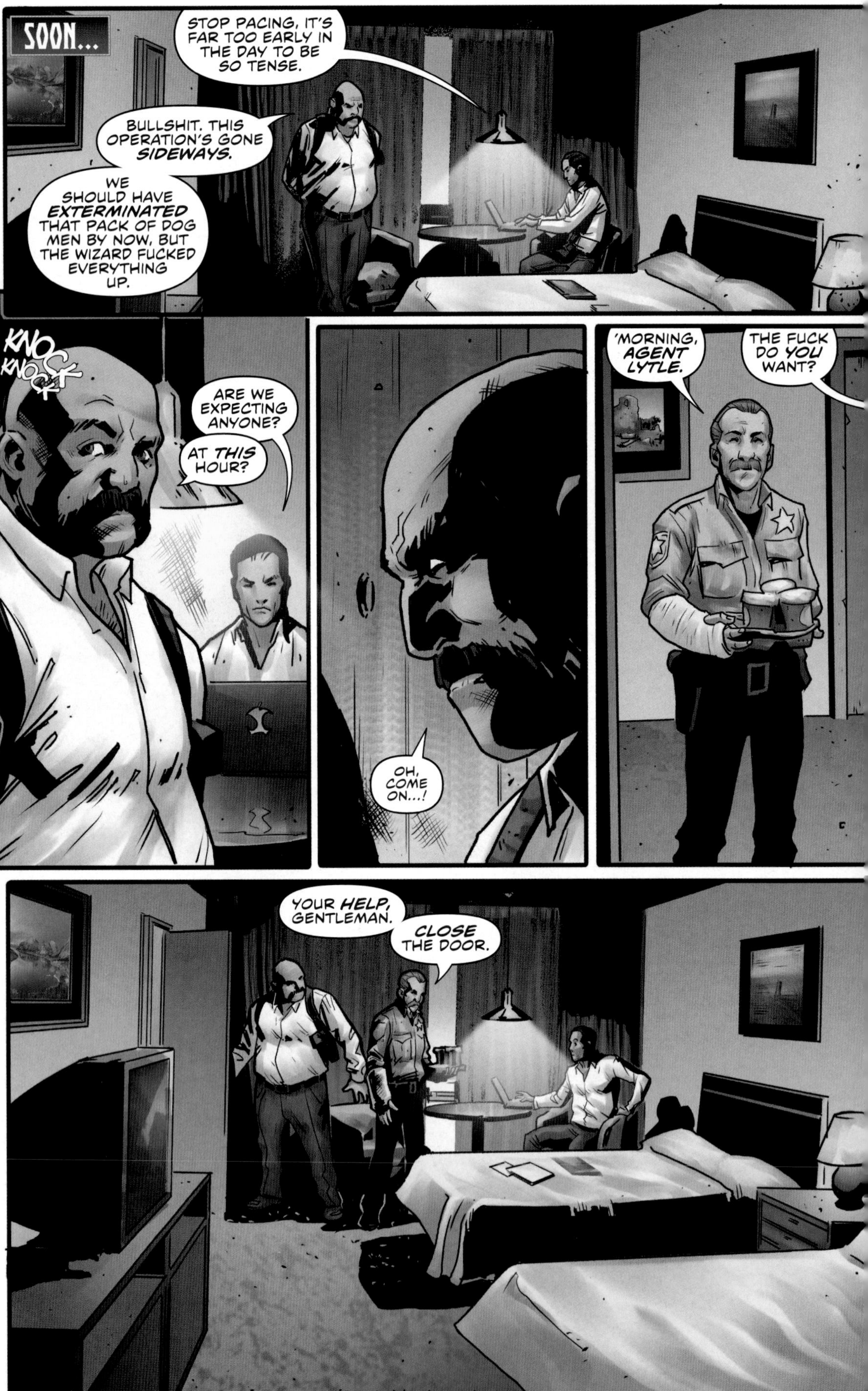
SOON...
STOP PACING, IT'S FAR TOO EARLY IN THE DAY TO BE SO TENSE.
BULLSHIT. THIS OPERATION'S GONE SIDEWAYS.
WE SHOULD HAVE EXTERMINATED THAT PACK OF DOG MEN BY NOW, BUT THE WIZARD FUCKED EVERYTHING UP.
KNOCK KNOCK
ARE WE EXPECTING ANYONE?
AT THIS HOUR?
OH, COME ON...!
'MORNING, AGENT LYTLE.
THE FUCK DO YOU WANT?
YOUR HELP, GENTLEMAN.
CLOSE THE DOOR.

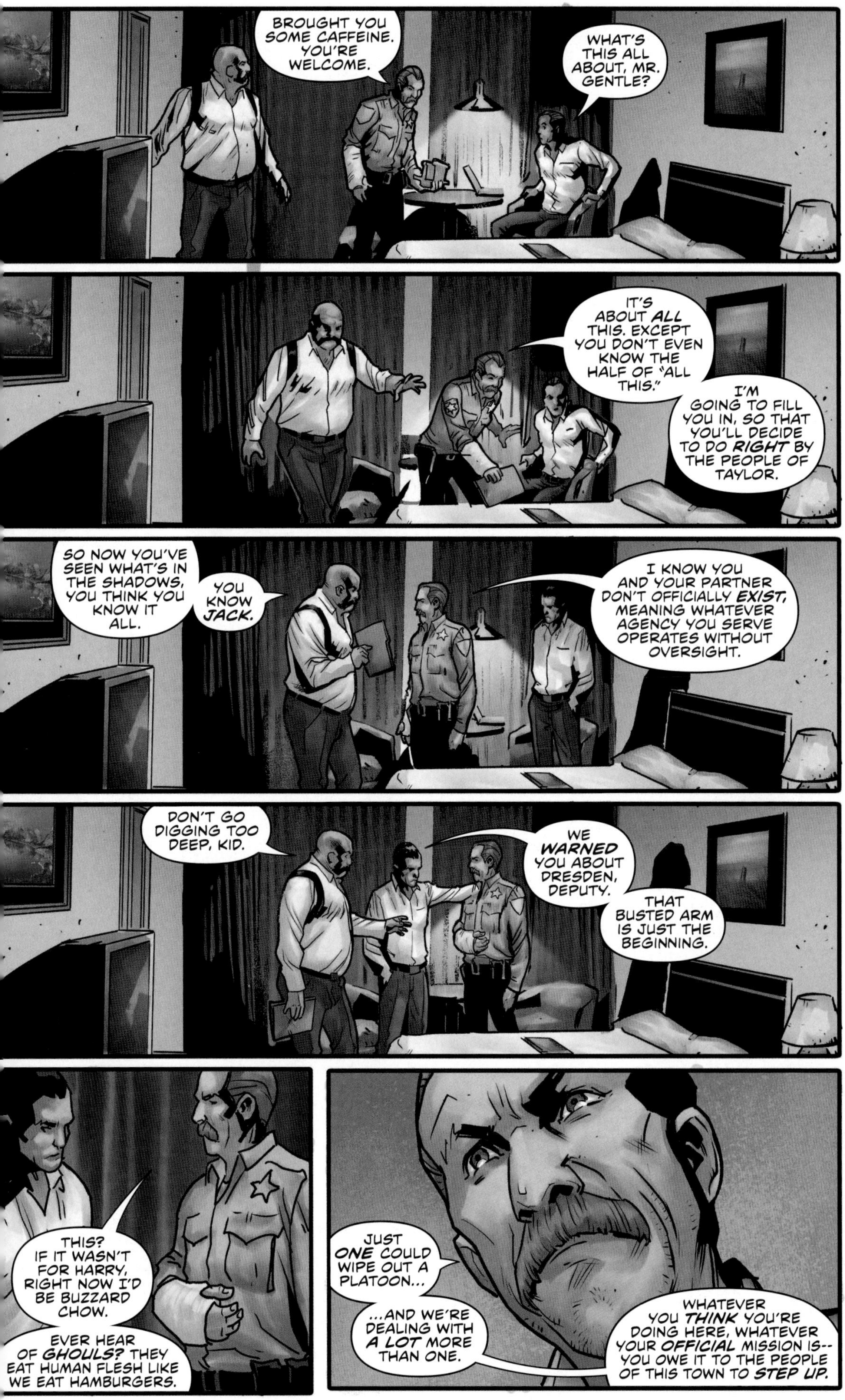
BROUGHT YOU SOME CAFFEINE. YOU'RE WELCOME.
WHAT'S THIS ALL ABOUT, MR. GENTLE?
IT'S ABOUT ALL THIS. EXCEPT YOU DON'T EVEN KNOW THE HALF OF "ALL THIS."
I'M GOING TO FILL YOU IN, SO THAT YOU'LL DECIDE TO DO RIGHT BY THE PEOPLE OF TAYLOR.
SO NOW YOU'VE SEEN WHAT'S IN THE SHADOWS, YOU THINK YOU KNOW IT ALL.
YOU KNOW JACK.
I KNOW YOU AND YOUR PARTNER DON'T OFFICIALLY EXIST, MEANING WHATEVER AGENCY YOU SERVE OPERATES WITHOUT OVERSIGHT.
DON'T GO DIGGING TOO DEEP, KID.
WE WARNED YOU ABOUT DRESDEN, DEPUTY.
THAT BUSTED ARM IS JUST THE BEGINNING.
THIS? IF IT WASN'T FOR HARRY, RIGHT NOW I'D BE BUZZARD CHOW.
EVER HEAR OF GHOULS? THEY EAT HUMAN FLESH LIKE WE EAT HAMBURGERS.
JUST ONE COULD WIPE OUT A PLATOON...
...AND WE'RE DEALING WITH A LOT MORE THAN ONE.
WHATEVER YOU THINK YOU'RE DOING HERE, WHATEVER YOUR OFFICIAL MISSION IS-- YOU OWE IT TO THE PEOPLE OF THIS TOWN TO STEP UP.

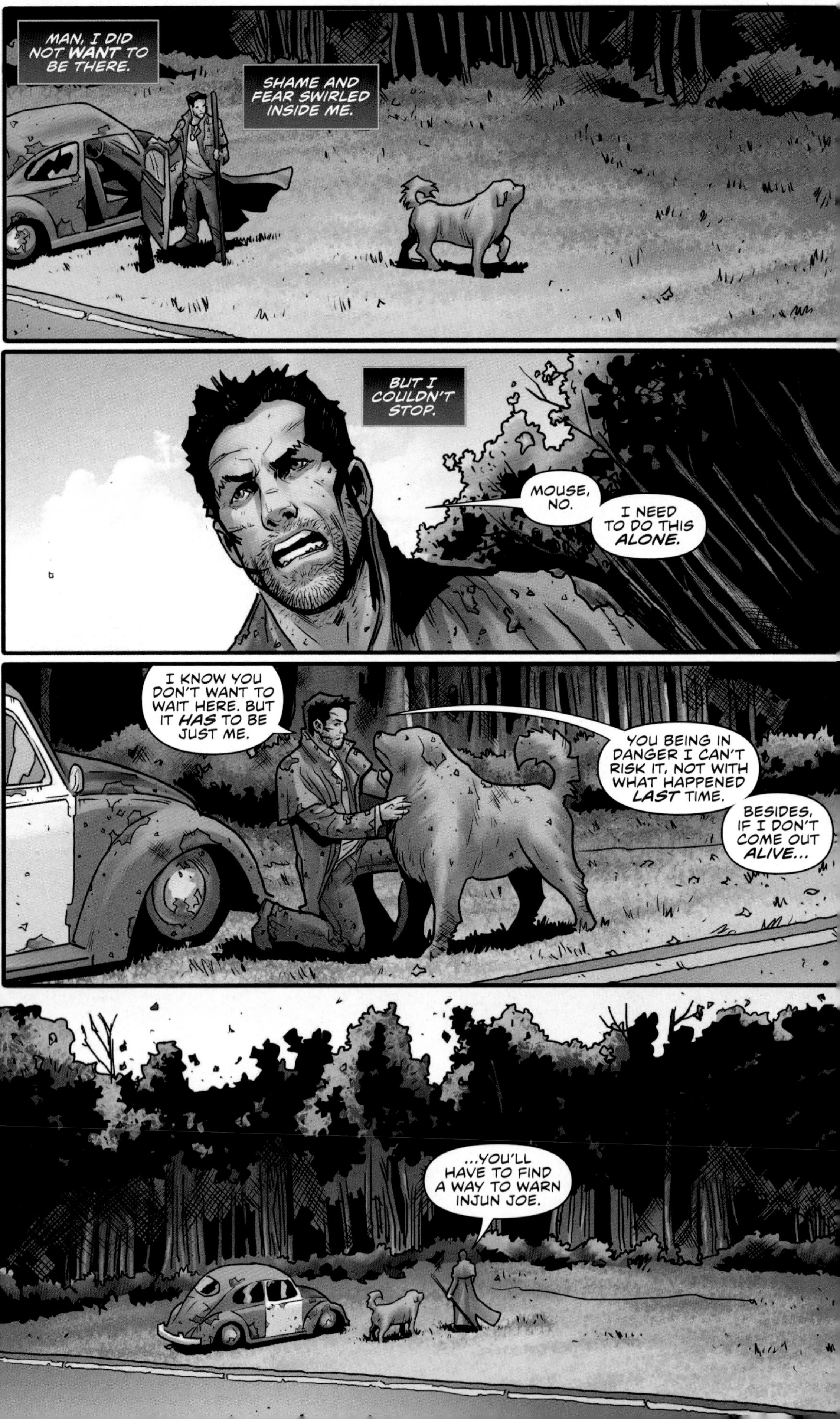
MAN, I DID NOT WANT TO BE THERE.
SHAME AND FEAR SWIRLED INSIDE ME.
BUT I COULDN'T STOP.
MOUSE, NO.
I NEED TO DO THIS ALONE.
I KNOW YOU DON'T WANT TO WAIT HERE. BUT IT HAS TO BE JUST ME.
YOU BEING IN DANGER I CAN'T RISK IT, NOT WITH WHAT HAPPENED LAST TIME.
BESIDES, IF I DON'T COME OUT ALIVE...
...YOU'LL HAVE TO FIND A WAY TO WARN INJUN JOE.

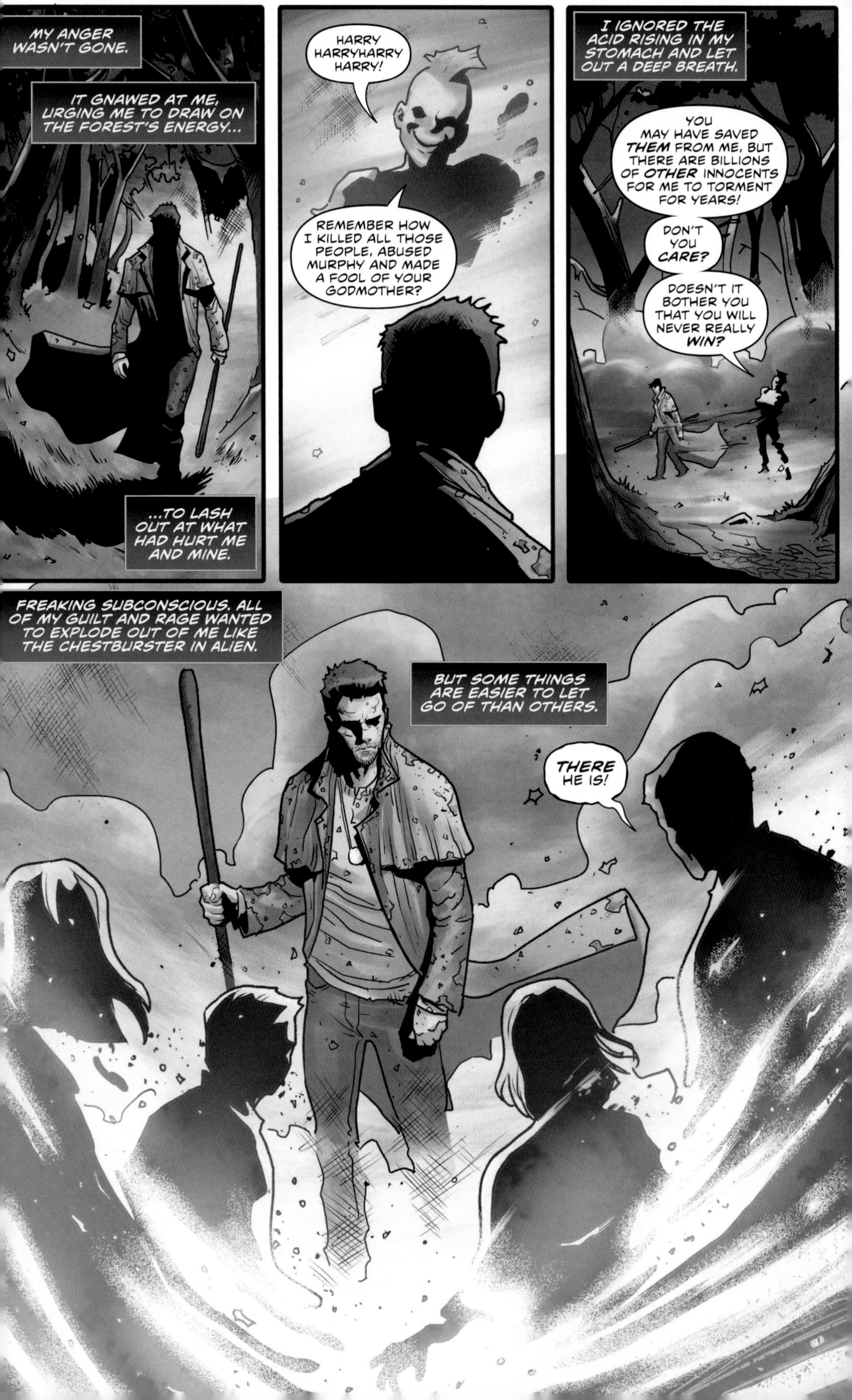
MY ANGER WASN'T GONE.
IT GNAWED AT ME, URGING ME TO DRAW ON THE FOREST'S ENERGY...
...TO LASH OUT AT WHAT HAD HURT ME AND MINE.
HARRY HARRYHARRY HARRY!
REMEMBER HOW I KILLED ALL THOSE PEOPLE, ABUSED MURPHY AND MADE A FOOL OF YOUR GODMOTHER?
I IGNORED THE ACID RISING IN MY STOMACH AND LET OUT A DEEP BREATH.
YOU MAY HAVE SAVED THEM FROM ME, BUT THERE ARE BILLIONS OF OTHER INNOCENTS FOR ME TO TORMENT FOR YEARS!
DON'T YOU CARE?
DOESN'T IT BOTHER YOU THAT YOU WILL NEVER REALLY WIN?
FREAKING SUBCONSCIOUS. ALL OF MY GUILT AND RAGE WANTED TO EXPLODE OUT OF ME LIKE THE CHESTBURSTER IN ALIEN.
BUT SOME THINGS ARE EASIER TO LET GO OF THAN OTHERS.
THERE HE IS!

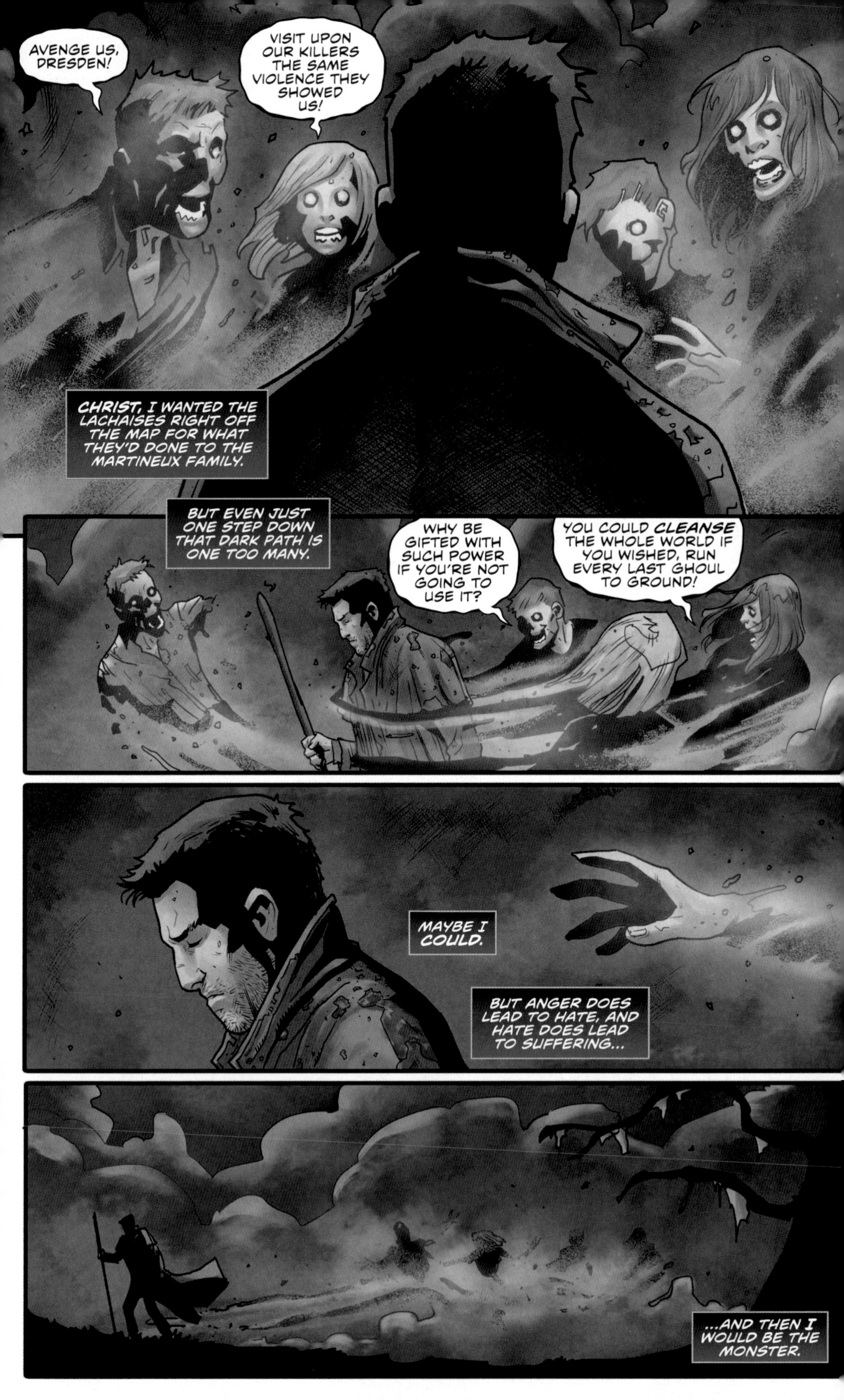
AVENGE US, DRESDEN!
VISIT UPON OUR KILLERS THE SAME VIOLENCE THEY SHOWED US!
CHRIST, I WANTED THE LACHAISES RIGHT OFF THE MAP FOR WHAT THEY'D DONE TO THE MARTINEUX FAMILY.
BUT EVEN JUST ONE STEP DOWN THAT DARK PATH IS ONE TOO MANY.
WHY BE GIFTED WITH SUCH POWER IF YOU'RE NOT GOING TO USE IT?
YOU COULD CLEANSE THE WHOLE WORLD IF YOU WISHED, RUN EVERY LAST GHOUL TO GROUND!
MAYBE I COULD.
BUT ANGER DOES LEAD TO HATE, AND HATE DOES LEAD TO SUFFERING...
...AND THEN I WOULD BE THE MONSTER.

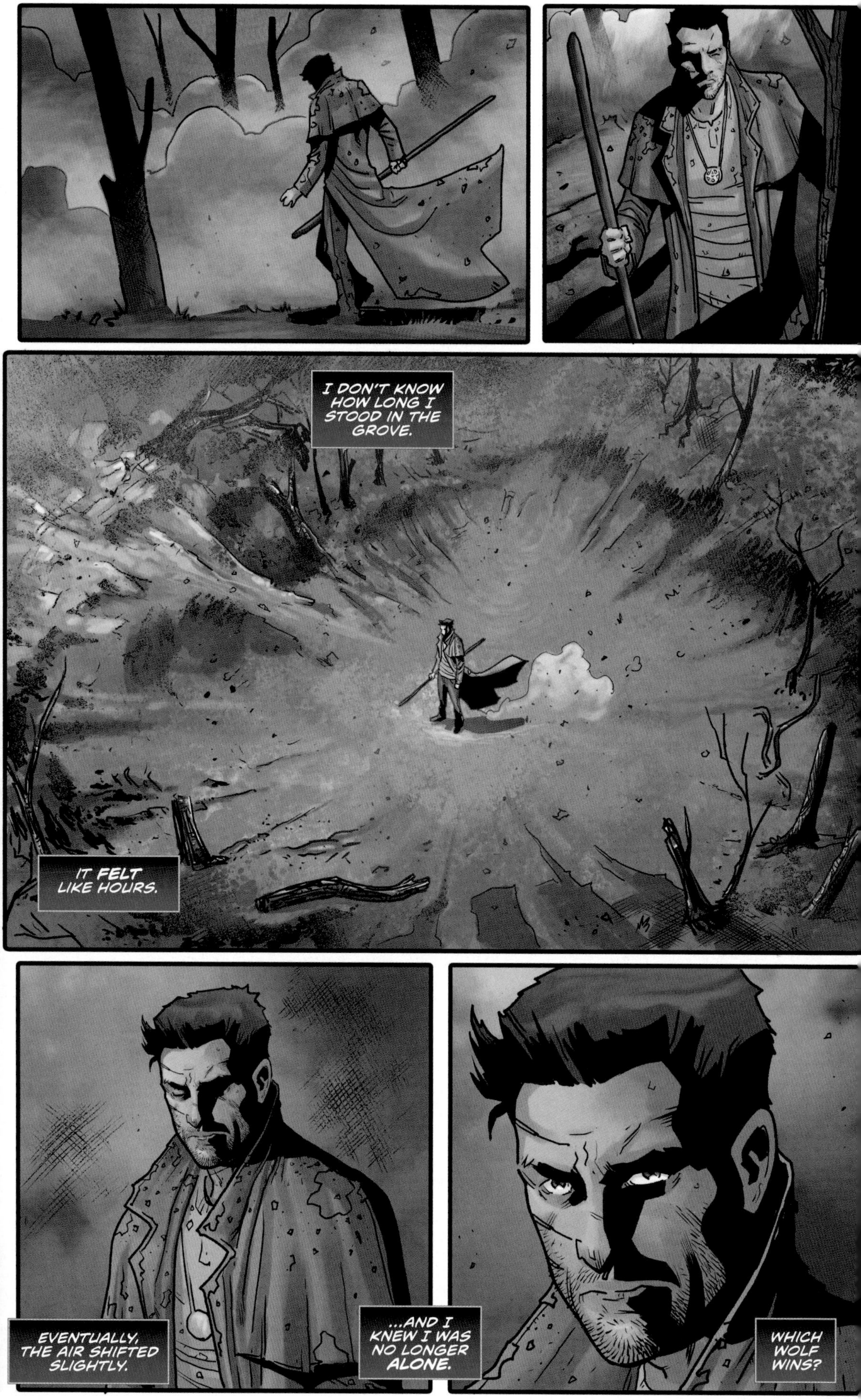
I DON'T KNOW HOW LONG I STOOD IN THE GROVE.
IT FELT LIKE HOURS.
EVENTUALLY, THE AIR SHIFTED SLIGHTLY.
...AND I KNEW I WAS NO LONGER ALONE.
WHICH WOLF WINS?

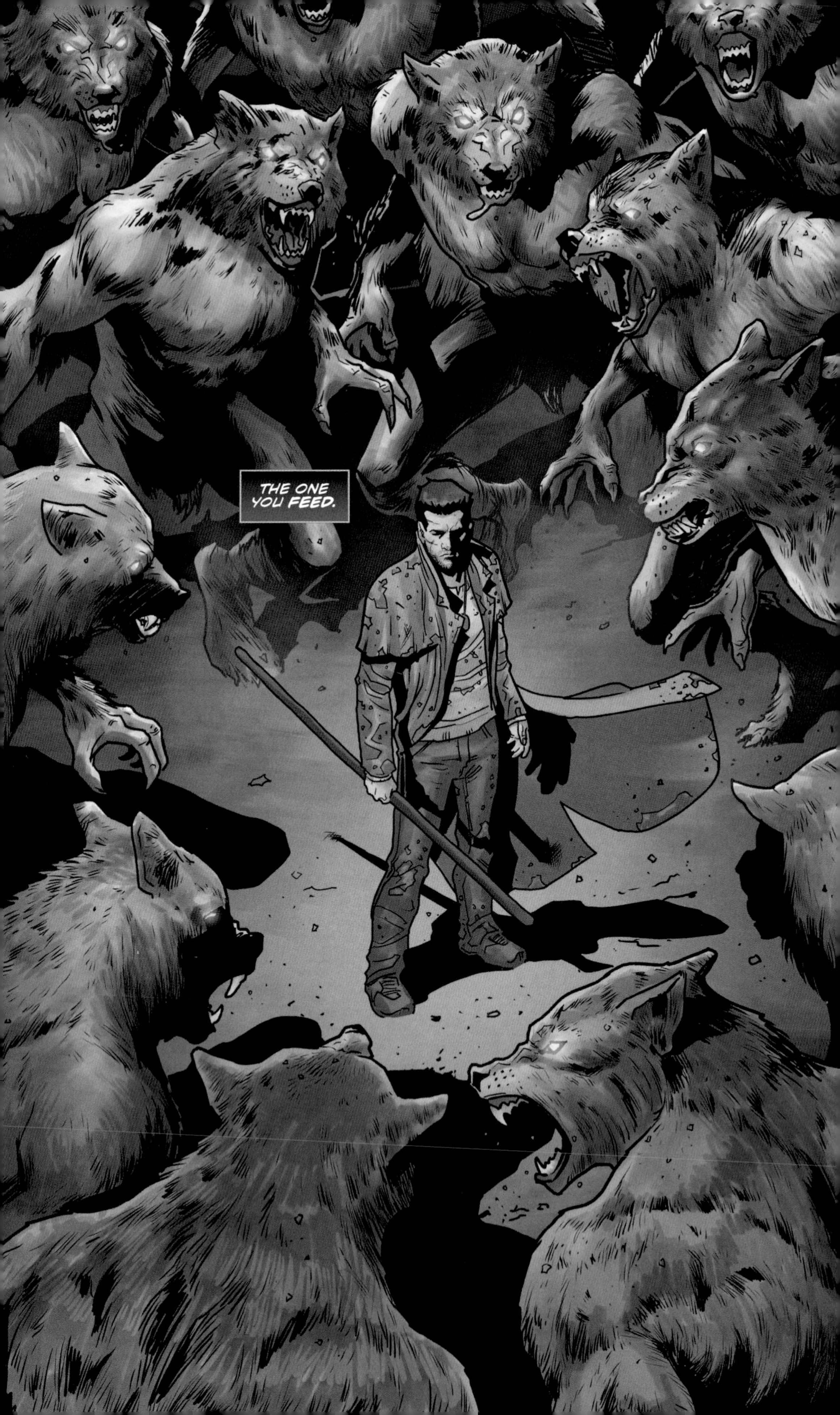
THE ONE YOU FEED.

ISSUE SIX COVER BY
DIEGO GALINDO

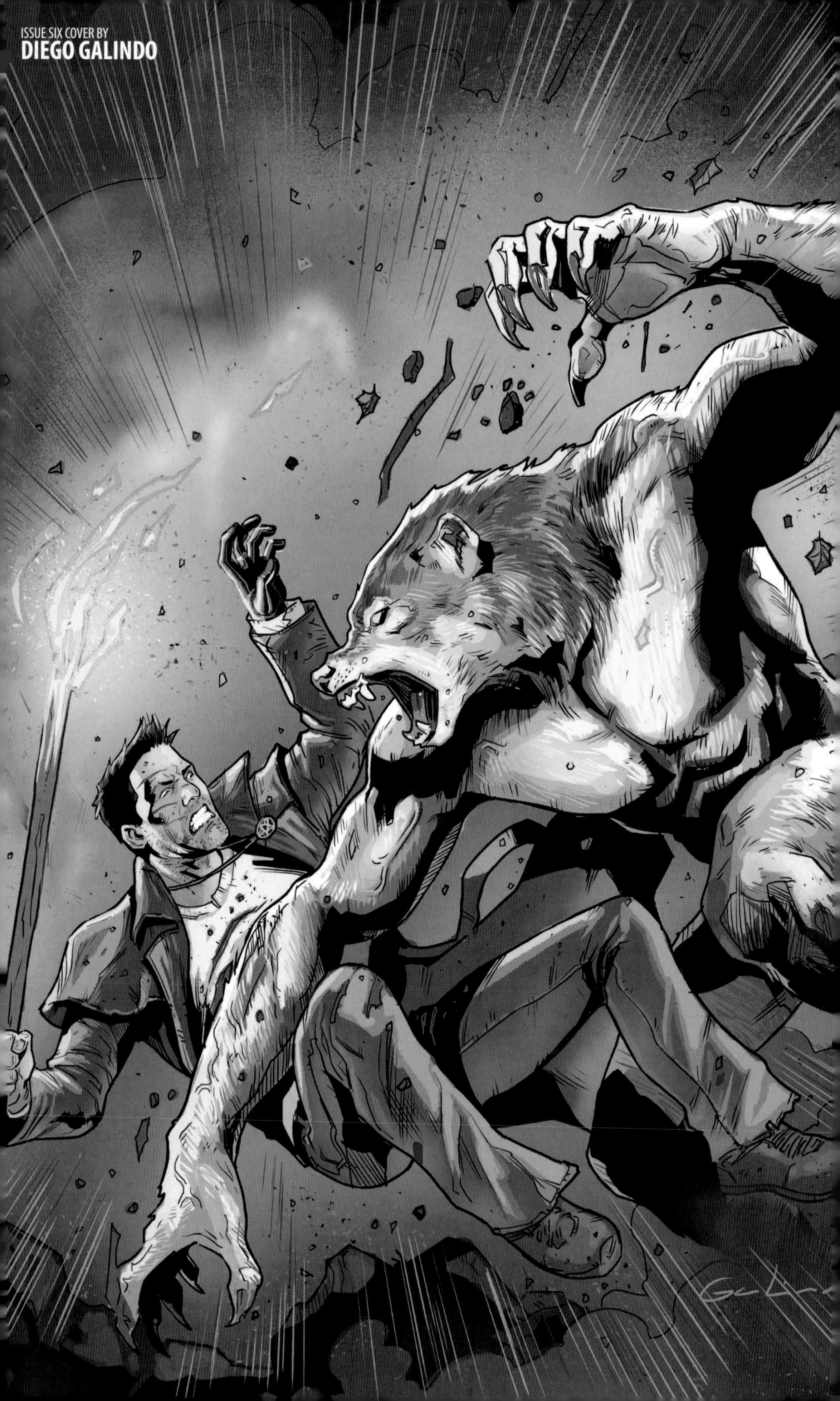

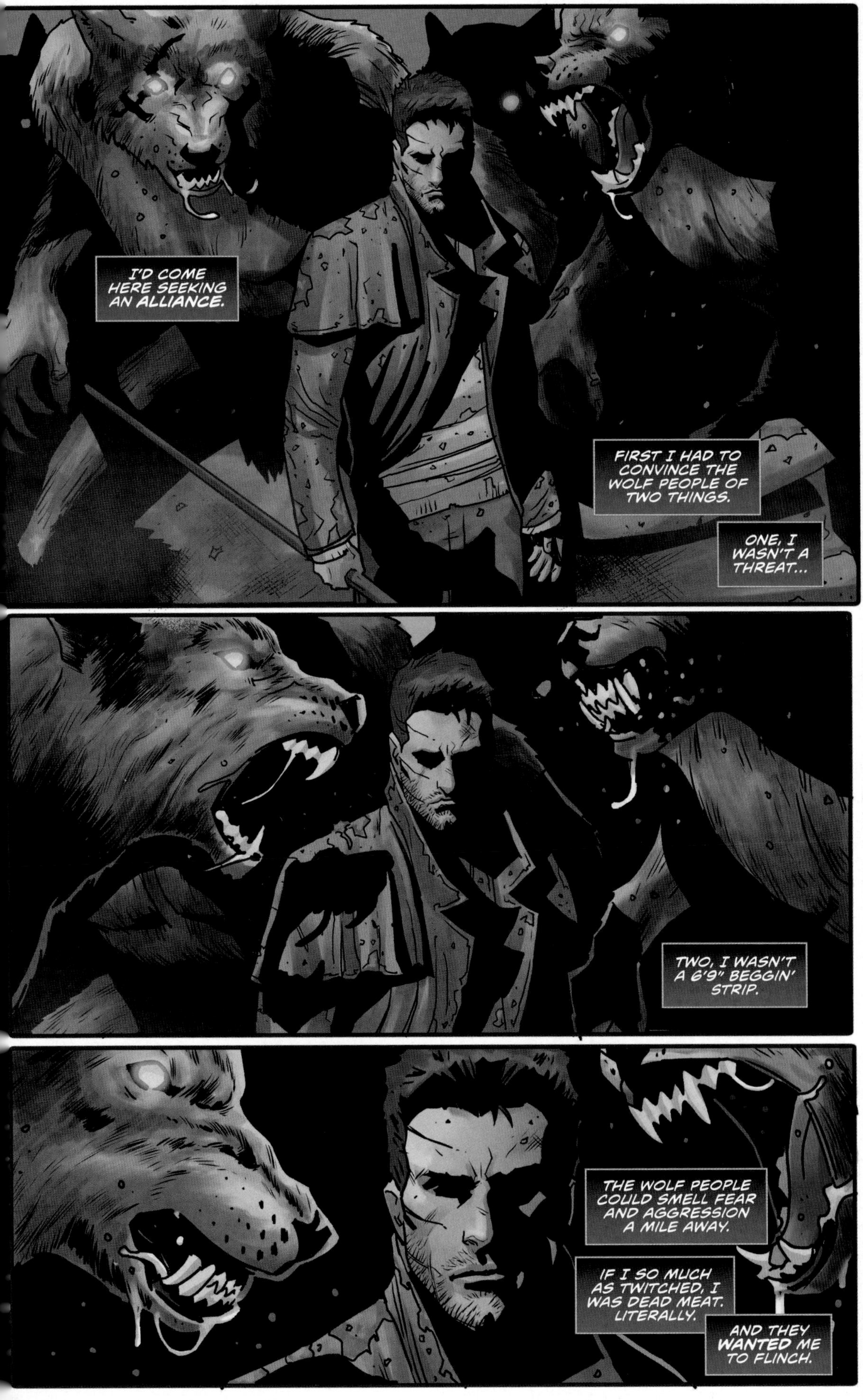
I'D COME HERE SEEKING AN ALLIANCE.
FIRST I HAD TO CONVINCE THE WOLF PEOPLE OF TWO THINGS.
ONE, I WASN'T A THREAT...
TWO, I WASN'T A 6'9" BEGGIN' STRIP.
THE WOLF PEOPLE COULD SMELL FEAR AND AGGRESSION A MILE AWAY.
IF I SO MUCH AS TWITCHED, I WAS DEAD MEAT. LITERALLY.
AND THEY WANTED ME TO FLINCH.

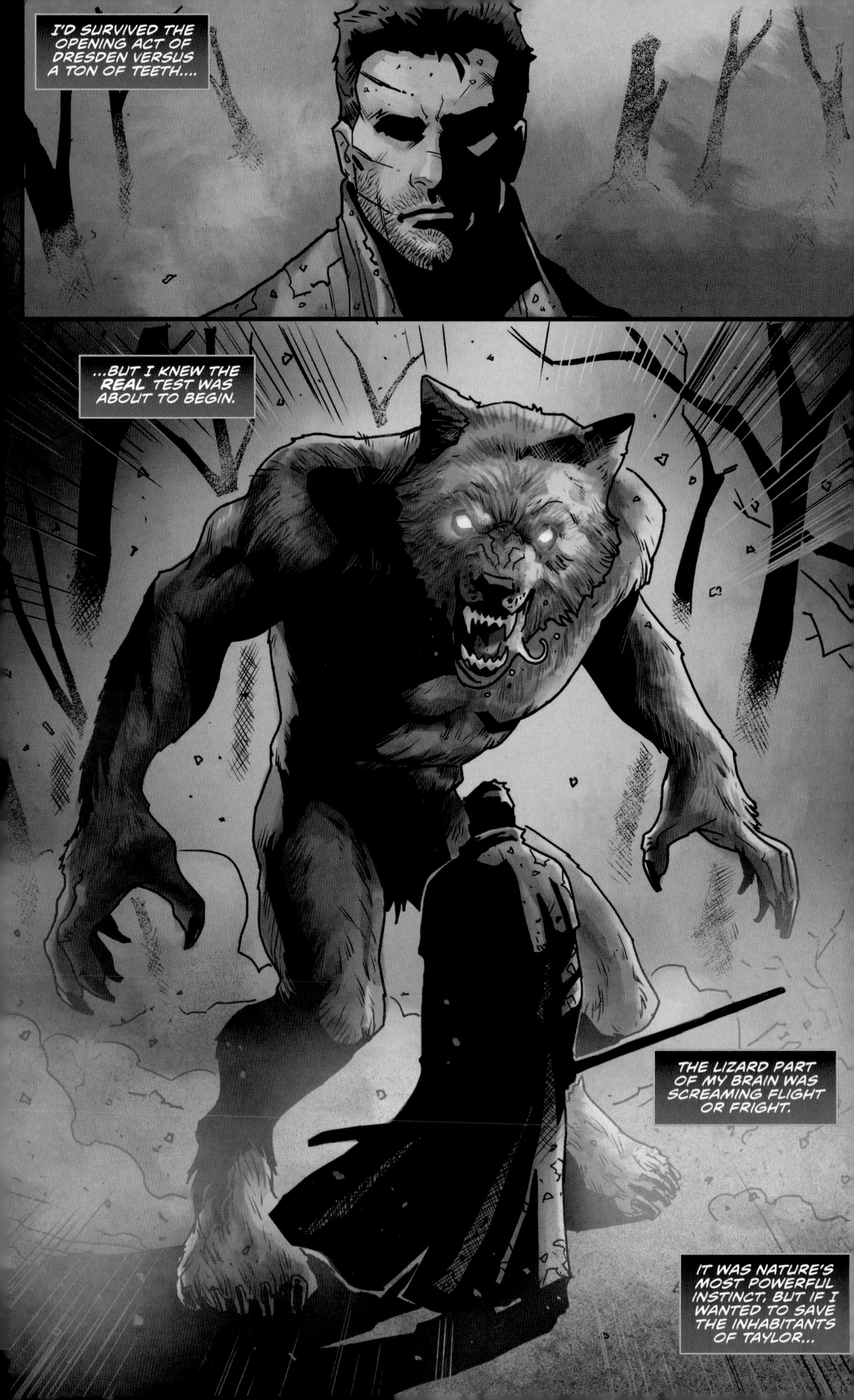
I'D SURVIVED THE OPENING ACT OF DRESDEN VERSUS A TON OF TEETH....
...BUT I KNEW THE REAL TEST WAS ABOUT TO BEGIN.
THE LIZARD PART OF MY BRAIN WAS SCREAMING FLIGHT OR FRIGHT.
IT WAS NATURE'S MOST POWERFUL INSTINCT, BUT IF I WANTED TO SAVE THE INHABITANTS OF TAYLOR...

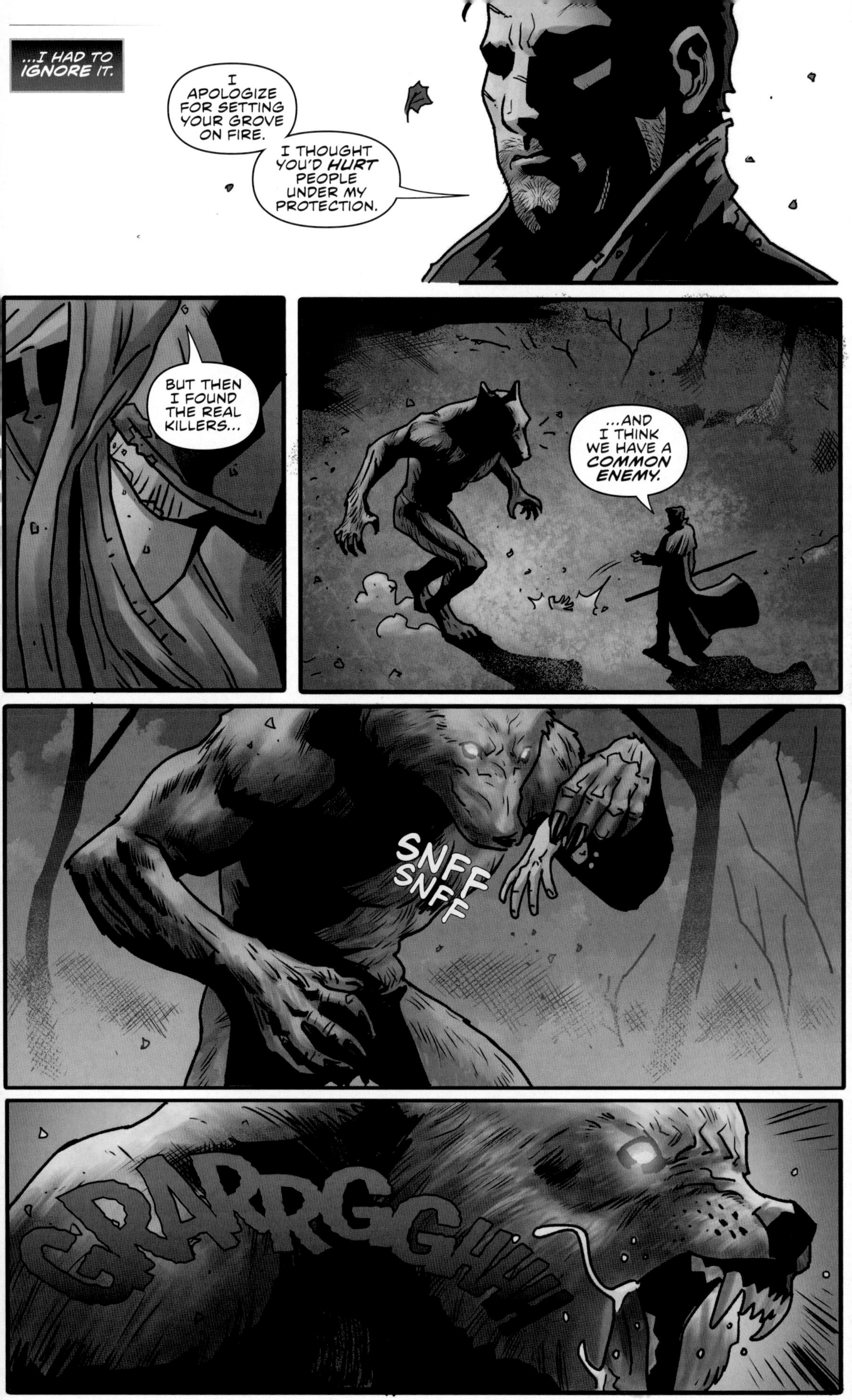
...I HAD TO IGNORE IT.
I APOLOGIZE FOR SETTING YOUR GROVE ON FIRE.
I THOUGHT YOU'D HURT PEOPLE UNDER MY PROTECTION.
BUT THEN I FOUND THE REAL KILLERS...
...AND I THINK WE HAVE A COMMON ENEMY.
SNFF SNFF
GRARRGGHH

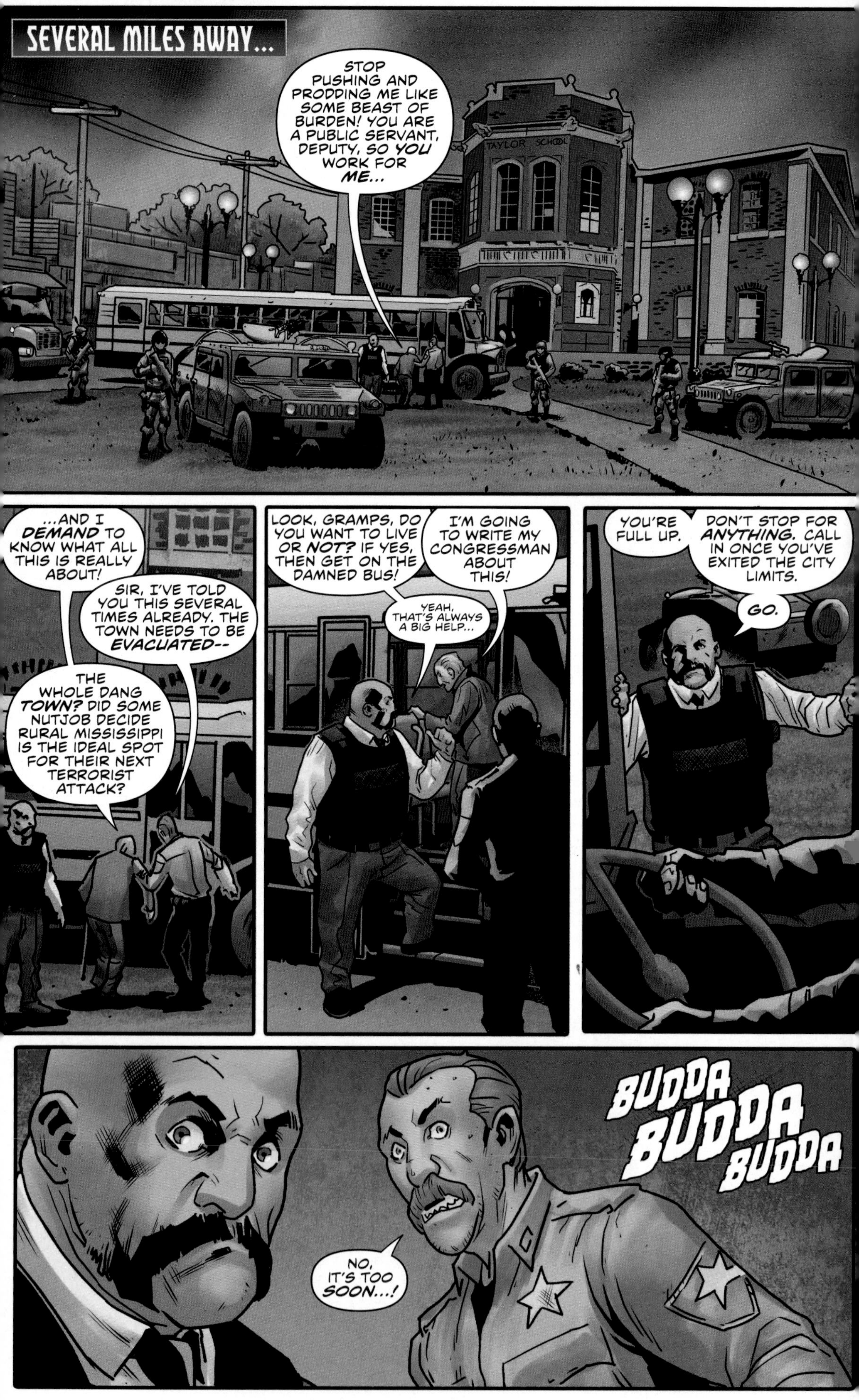
SEVERAL MILES AWAY...
STOP PUSHING AND PRODDING ME LIKE SOME BEAST OF BURDEN! YOU ARE A PUBLIC SERVANT, DEPUTY, SO YOU WORK FOR ME...
TAYLOR SCHOOL
...AND I DEMAND TO KNOW WHAT ALL THIS IS REALLY ABOUT!
SIR, I'VE TOLD YOU THIS SEVERAL TIMES ALREADY. THE TOWN NEEDS TO BE EVACUATED--
THE WHOLE DANG TOWN? DID SOME NUTJOB DECIDE RURAL MISSISSIPPI IS THE IDEAL SPOT FOR THEIR NEXT TERRORIST ATTACK?
LOOK, GRAMPS, DO YOU WANT TO LIVE OR NOT? IF YES, THEN GET ON THE DAMNED BUS!
I'M GOING TO WRITE MY CONGRESSMAN ABOUT THIS!
YEAH, THAT'S ALWAYS A BIG HELP...
YOU'RE FULL UP.
DON'T STOP FOR ANYTHING. CALL IN ONCE YOU'VE EXITED THE CITY LIMITS.
GO.
BUDDA BUDDA BUDDA
NO, IT'S TOO SOON...!

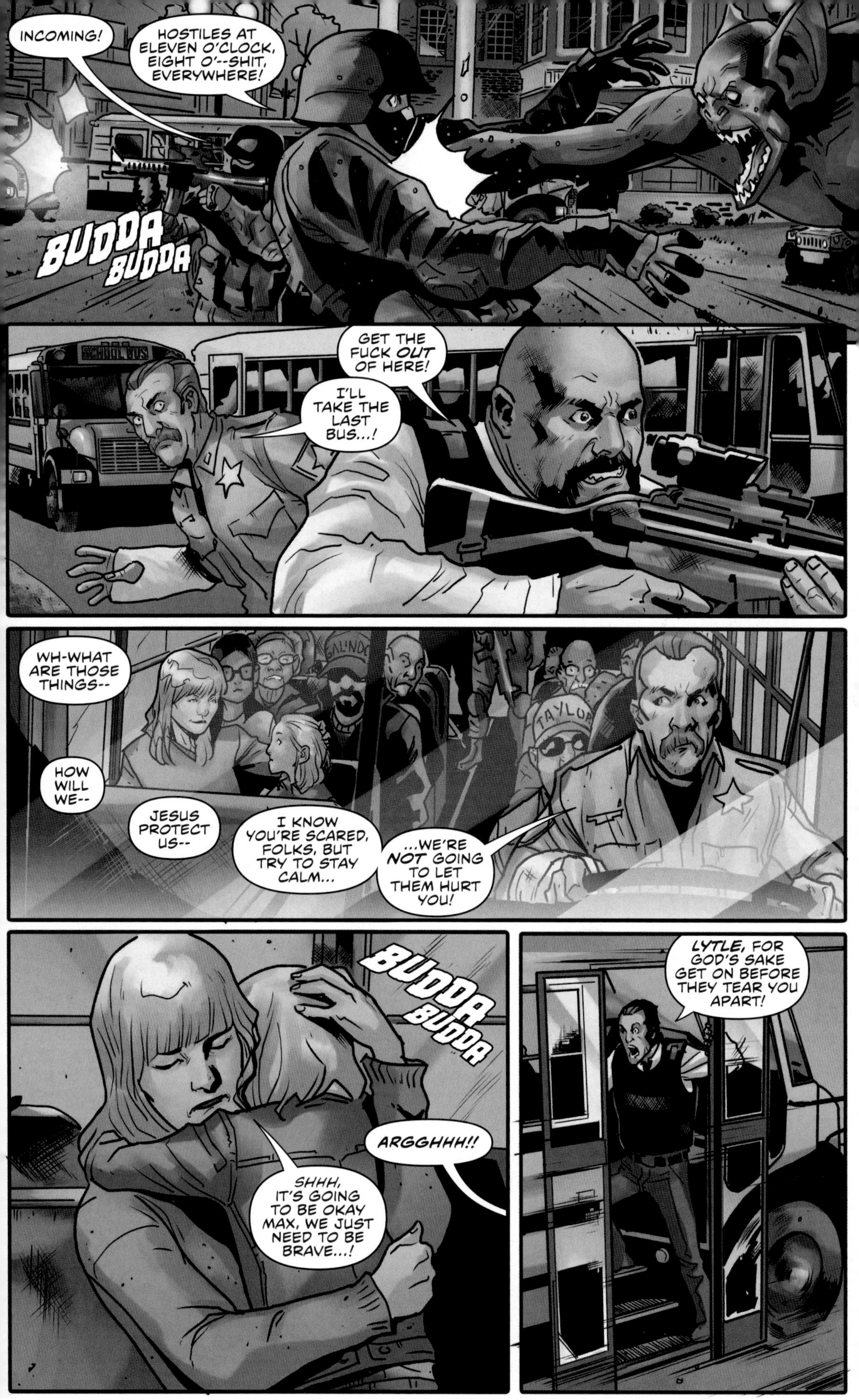
INCOMING!
HOSTILES AT ELEVEN O'CLOCK, EIGHT O'--SHIT, EVERYWHERE!
BUDDA BUDDA
GET THE FUCK OUT OF HERE!
I'LL TAKE THE LAST BUS...!
SCHOOL BUS
WH-WHAT ARE THOSE THINGS--
HOW WILL WE--
JESUS PROTECT US--
I KNOW YOU'RE SCARED, FOLKS, BUT TRY TO STAY CALM...
...WE'RE NOT GOING TO LET THEM HURT YOU!
BUDDA BUDDA
ARGGHHH!!
SHHH, IT'S GOING TO BE OKAY MAX, WE JUST NEED TO BE BRAVE...!
LYTLE, FOR GOD'S SAKE GET ON BEFORE THEY TEAR YOU APART!

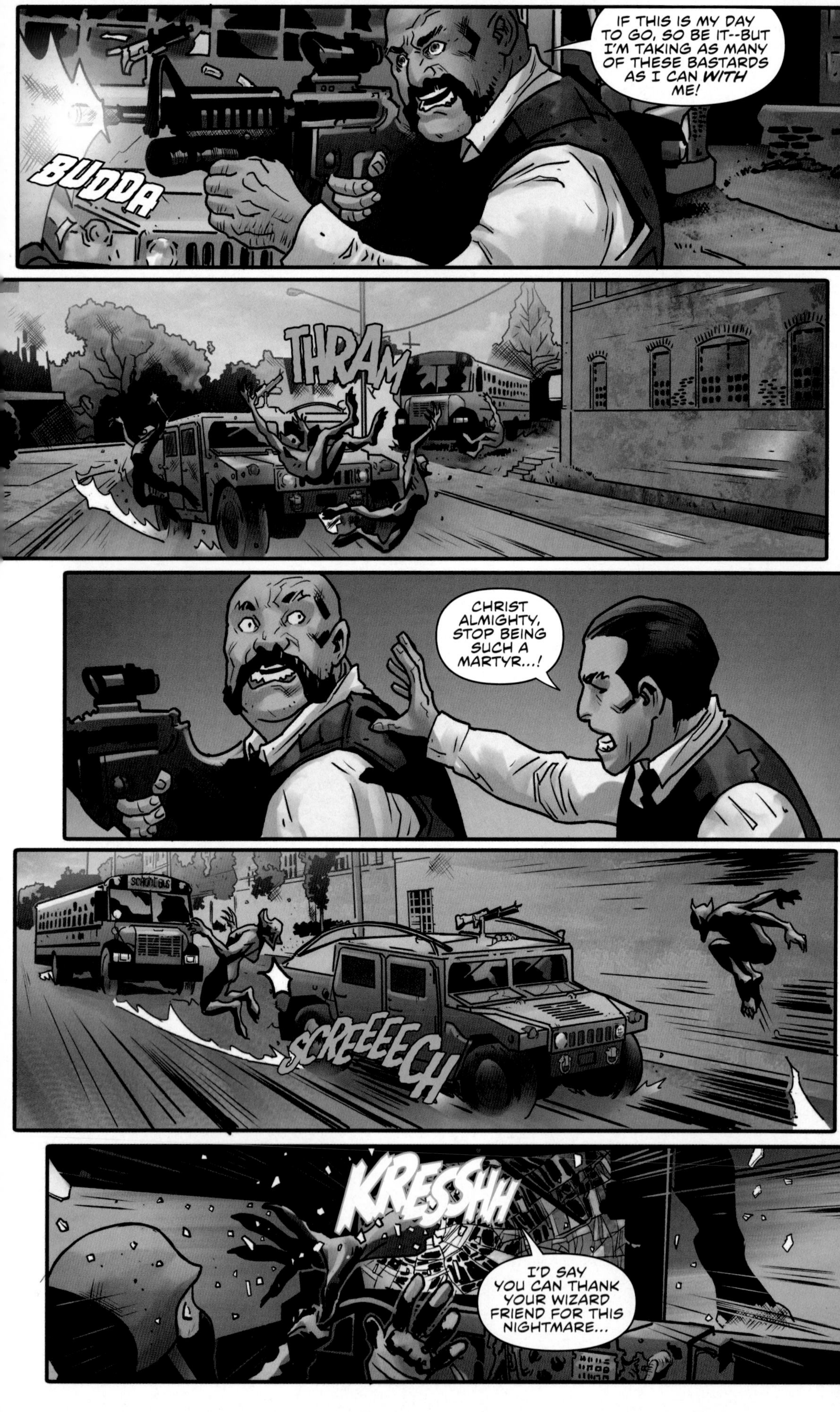

IF THIS IS MY DAY TO GO, SO BE IT--BUT I'M TAKING AS MANY OF THESE BASTARDS AS I CAN *WITH* ME!
BUDDA
THRAM
CHRIST ALMIGHTY, STOP BEING SUCH A MARTYR...!
SCHOOL BUS
SCREEEEECH
KRESSHH
I'D SAY YOU CAN THANK YOUR WIZARD FRIEND FOR THIS NIGHTMARE...

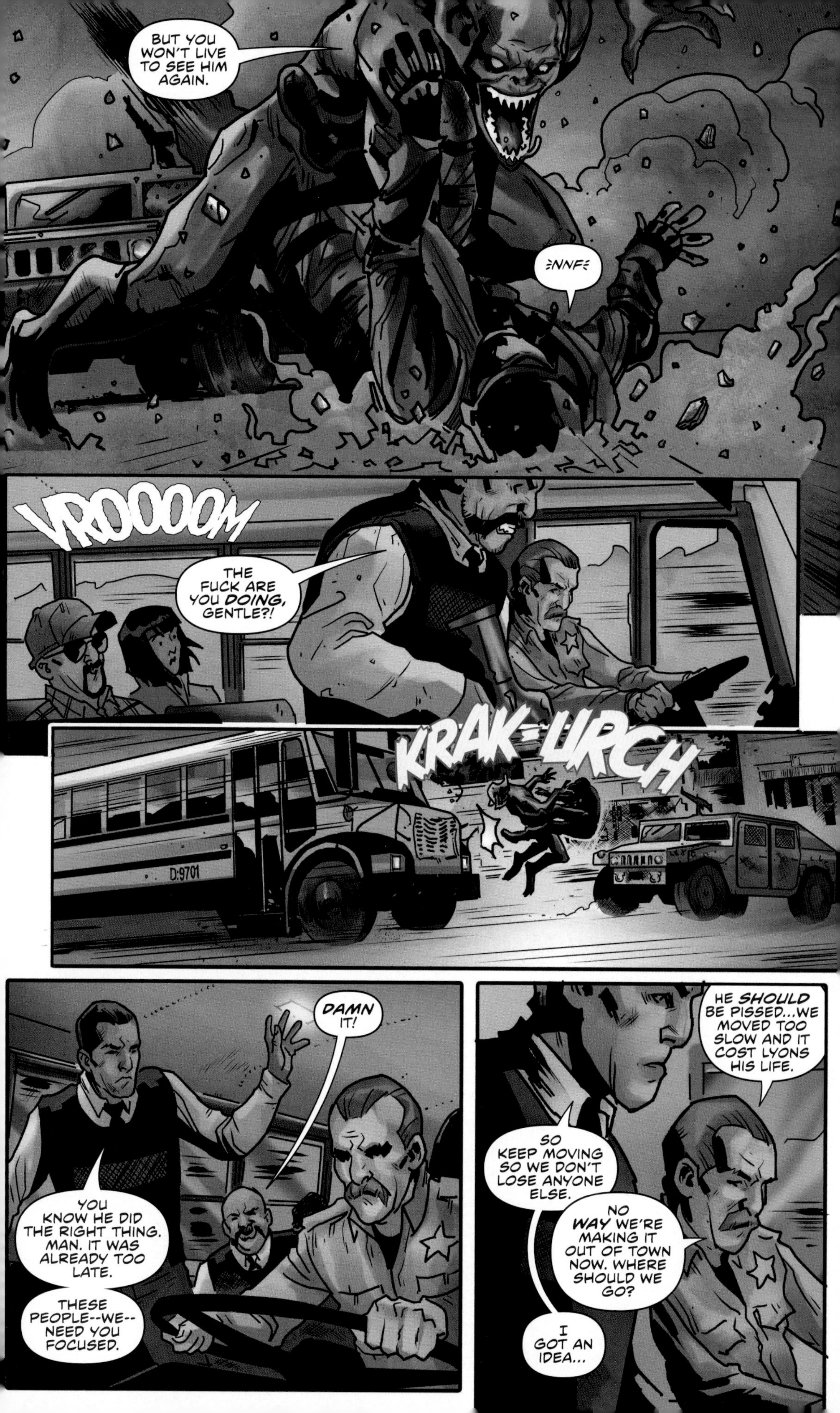
BUT YOU WON'T LIVE TO SEE HIM AGAIN.
NNF
VROOOOM
THE FUCK ARE YOU DOING, GENTLE?!
KRAK-URCH
D:9701
DAMN IT!
YOU KNOW HE DID THE RIGHT THING. MAN. IT WAS ALREADY TOO LATE.
THESE PEOPLE--WE--NEED YOU FOCUSED.
HE SHOULD BE PISSED...WE MOVED TOO SLOW AND IT COST LYONS HIS LIFE.
SO KEEP MOVING SO WE DON'T LOSE ANYONE ELSE.
NO WAY WE'RE MAKING IT OUT OF TOWN NOW. WHERE SHOULD WE GO?
I GOT AN IDEA...

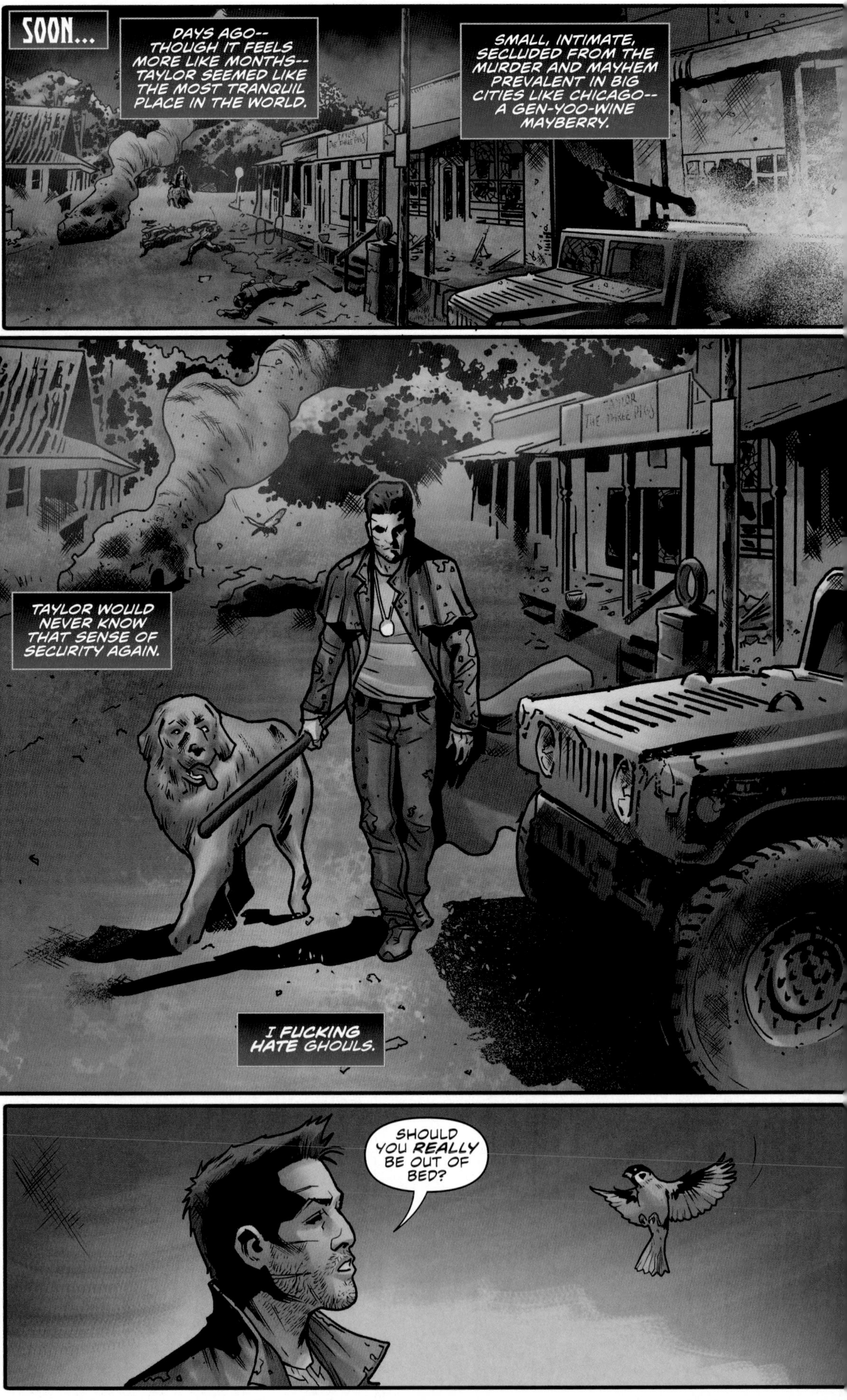
SOON...
DAYS AGO-- THOUGH IT FEELS MORE LIKE MONTHS-- TAYLOR SEEMED LIKE THE MOST TRANQUIL PLACE IN THE WORLD.
SMALL, INTIMATE, SECLUDED FROM THE MURDER AND MAYHEM PREVALENT IN BIG CITIES LIKE CHICAGO-- A GEN-YOO-WINE MAYBERRY.
TAYLOR THE THREE PIGS
TAYLOR WOULD NEVER KNOW THAT SENSE OF SECURITY AGAIN.
I FUCKING HATE GHOULS.
SHOULD YOU REALLY BE OUT OF BED?

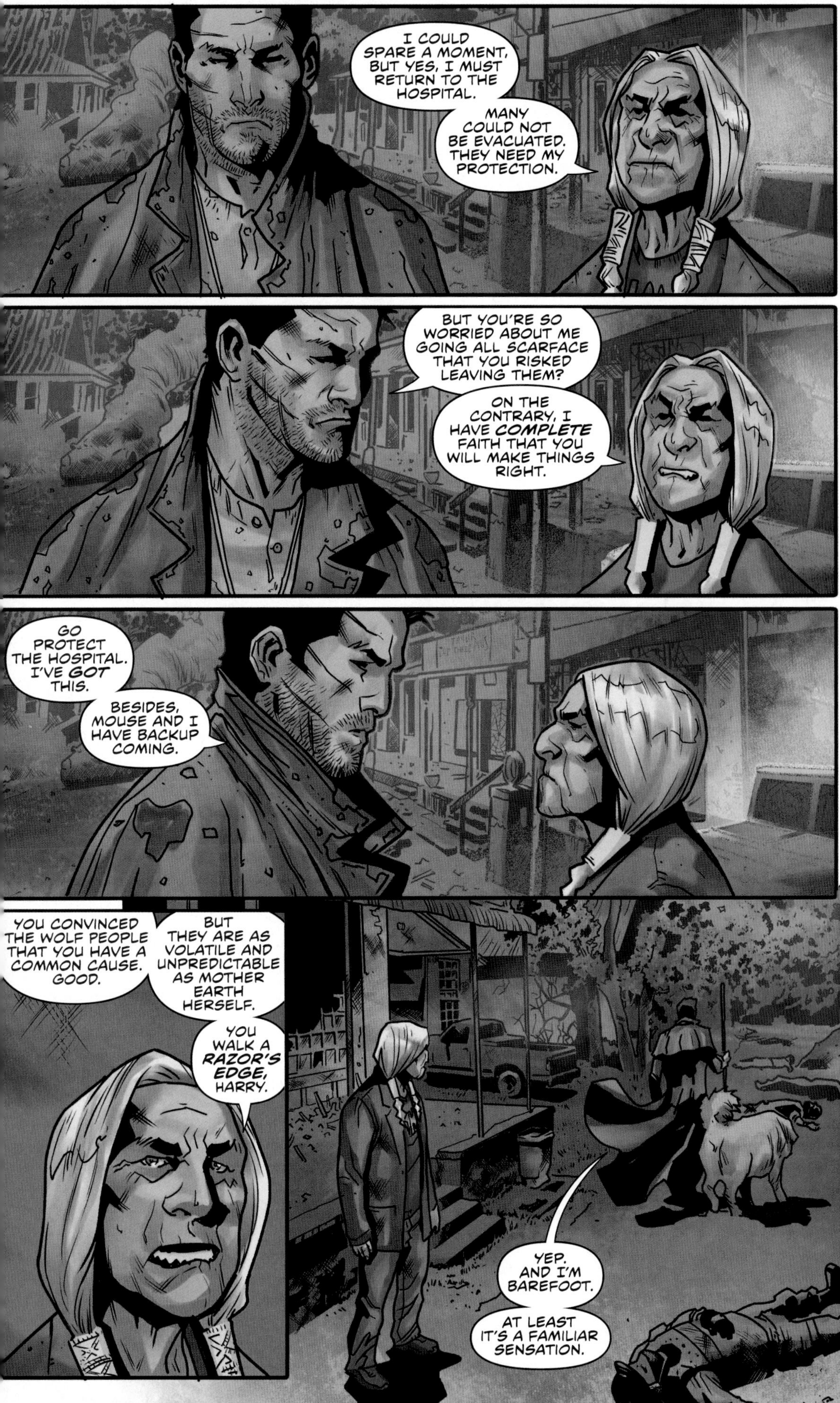
I COULD SPARE A MOMENT, BUT YES, I MUST RETURN TO THE HOSPITAL.
MANY COULD NOT BE EVACUATED. THEY NEED MY PROTECTION.
BUT YOU'RE SO WORRIED ABOUT ME GOING ALL SCARFACE THAT YOU RISKED LEAVING THEM?
ON THE CONTRARY, I HAVE *COMPLETE* FAITH THAT YOU WILL MAKE THINGS RIGHT.
GO PROTECT THE HOSPITAL. I'VE *GOT* THIS.
BESIDES, MOUSE AND I HAVE BACKUP COMING.
YOU CONVINCED THE WOLF PEOPLE THAT YOU HAVE A COMMON CAUSE. GOOD.
BUT THEY ARE AS VOLATILE AND UNPREDICTABLE AS MOTHER EARTH HERSELF.
YOU WALK A *RAZOR'S EDGE,* HARRY.
YEP. AND I'M BAREFOOT.
AT LEAST IT'S A FAMILIAR SENSATION.

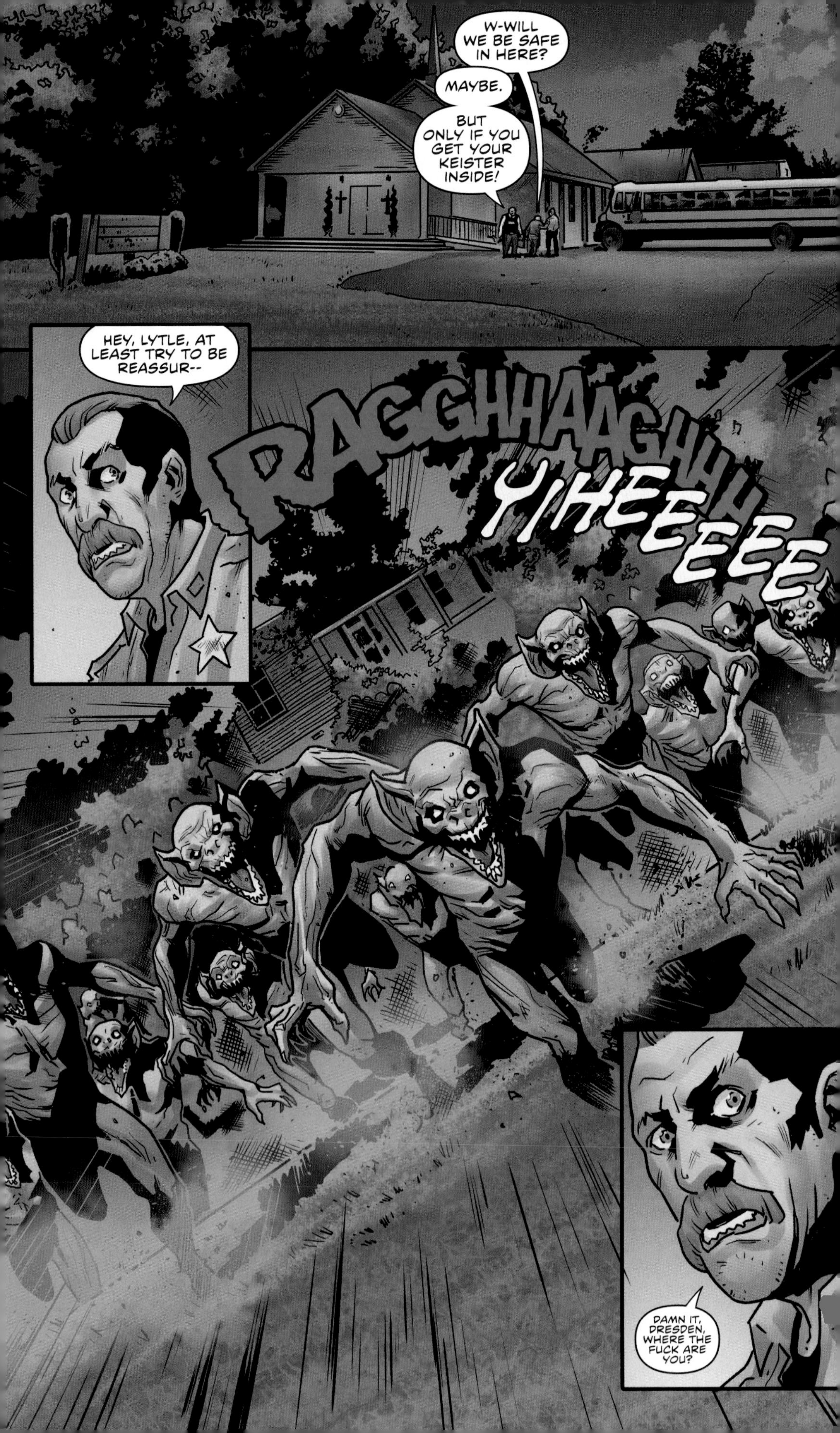

W-WILL WE BE SAFE IN HERE?
MAYBE.
BUT ONLY IF YOU GET YOUR KEISTER INSIDE!
HEY, LYTLE, AT LEAST TRY TO BE REASSUR--
RAGGHHAAGHHH
YIHEEEEEE
DAMN IT, DRESDEN, WHERE THE FUCK ARE YOU?

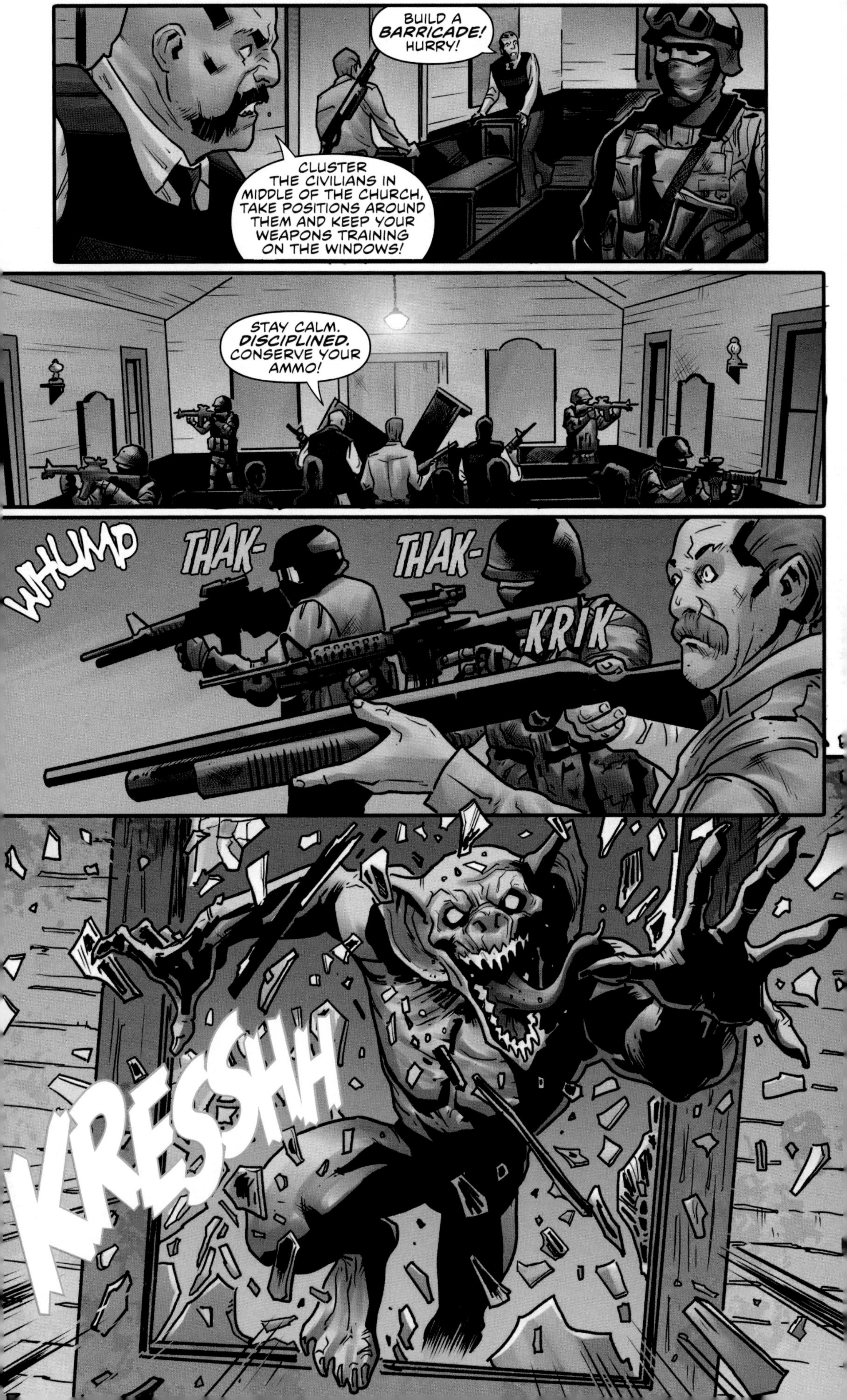
BUILD A BARRICADE! HURRY!
CLUSTER THE CIVILIANS IN MIDDLE OF THE CHURCH, TAKE POSITIONS AROUND THEM AND KEEP YOUR WEAPONS TRAINING ON THE WINDOWS!
STAY CALM. DISCIPLINED. CONSERVE YOUR AMMO!
WHUMP
THAK-
THAK-
KRIK
KRESHH

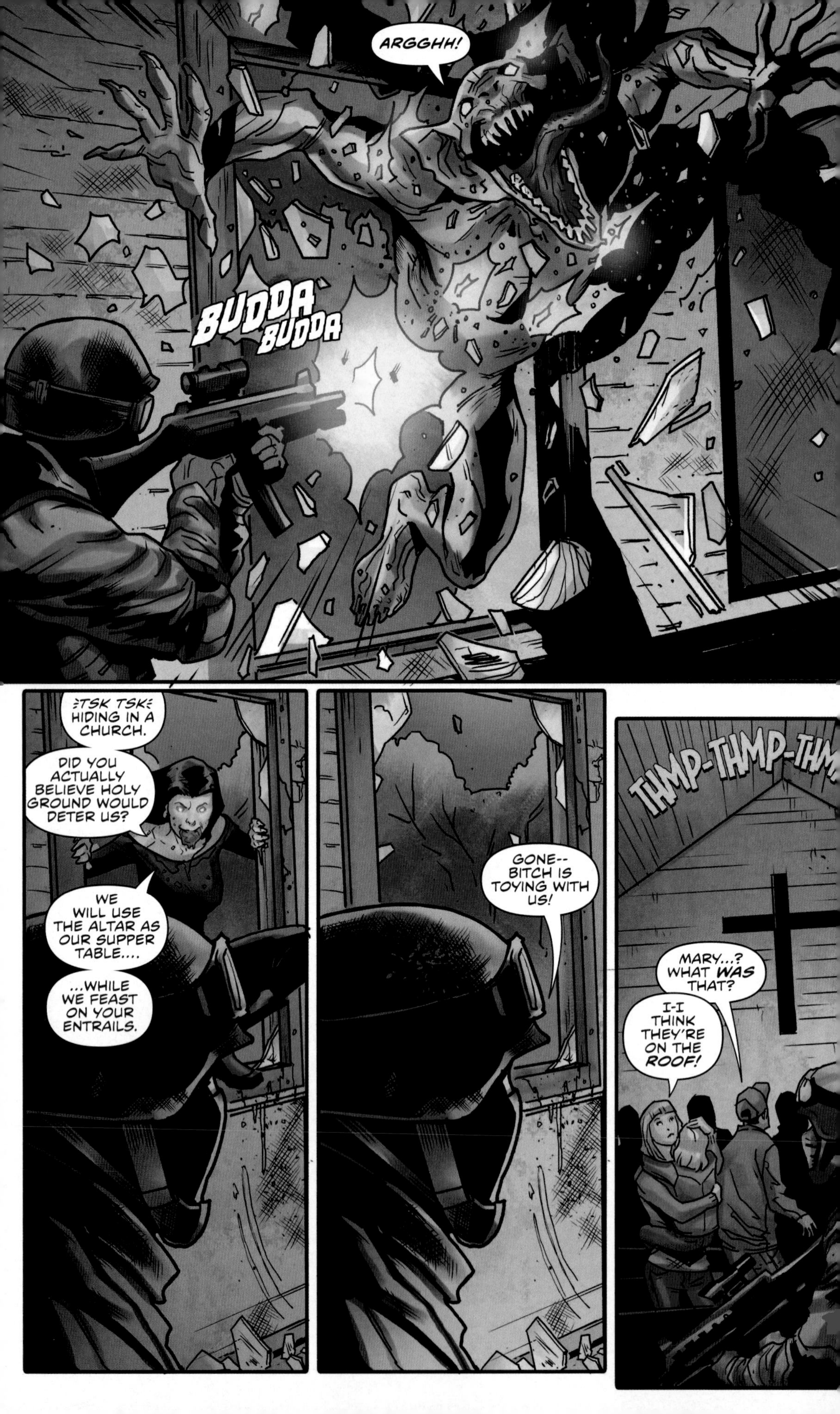
ARGGHH!
BUDDA BUDDA
=TSK TSK= HIDING IN A CHURCH.
DID YOU ACTUALLY BELIEVE HOLY GROUND WOULD DETER US?
WE WILL USE THE ALTAR AS OUR SUPPER TABLE....
...WHILE WE FEAST ON YOUR ENTRAILS.
GONE-- BITCH IS TOYING WITH US!
THMP-THMP-THM
MARY...? WHAT *WAS* THAT?
I-I THINK THEY'RE ON THE *ROOF!*

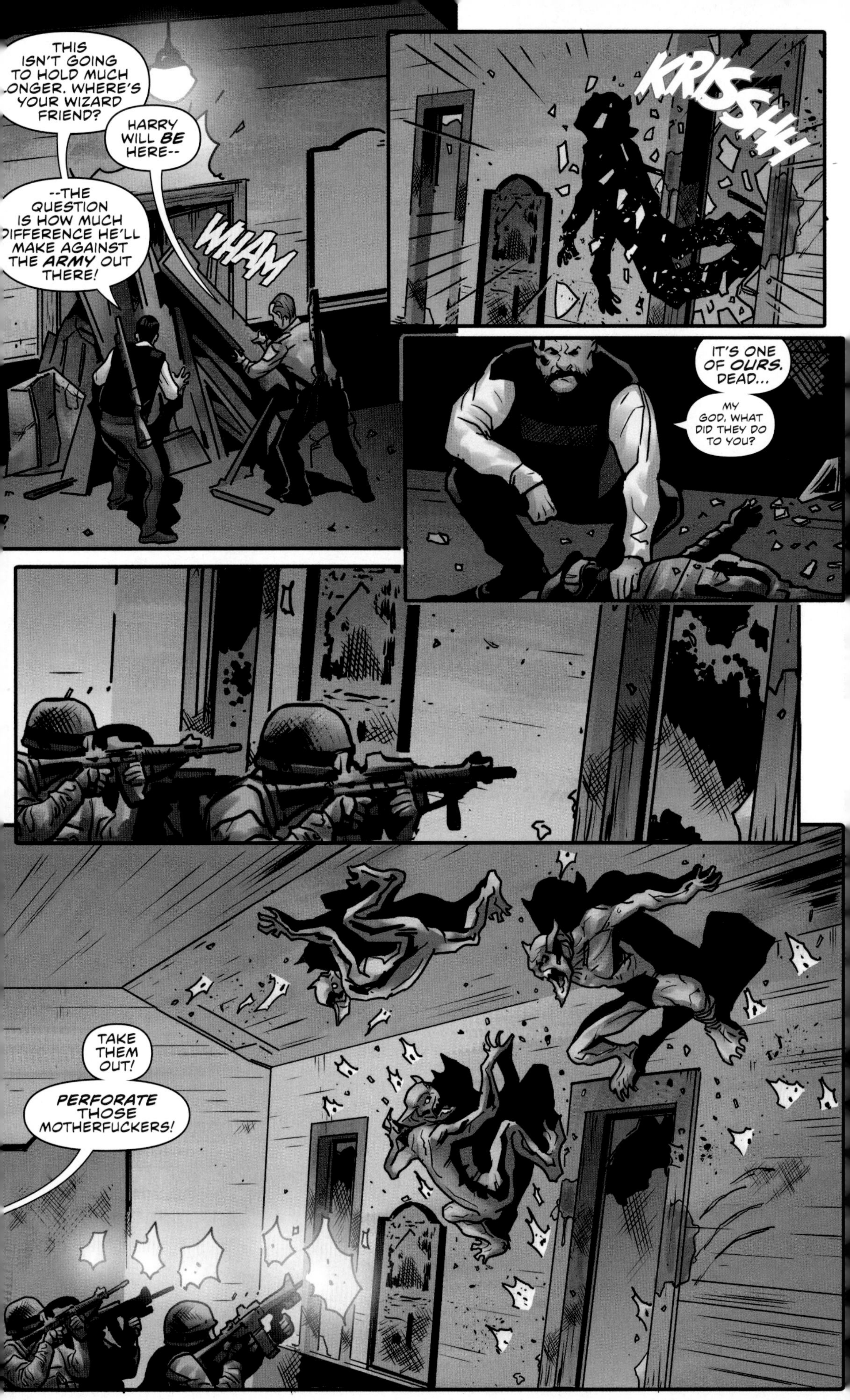

THIS ISN'T GOING TO HOLD MUCH LONGER. WHERE'S YOUR WIZARD FRIEND?
HARRY WILL BE HERE--
--THE QUESTION IS HOW MUCH DIFFERENCE HE'LL MAKE AGAINST THE ARMY OUT THERE!
WHAM
KRISSHH
IT'S ONE OF OURS. DEAD...
MY GOD, WHAT DID THEY DO TO YOU?
TAKE THEM OUT!
PERFORATE THOSE MOTHERFUCKERS!

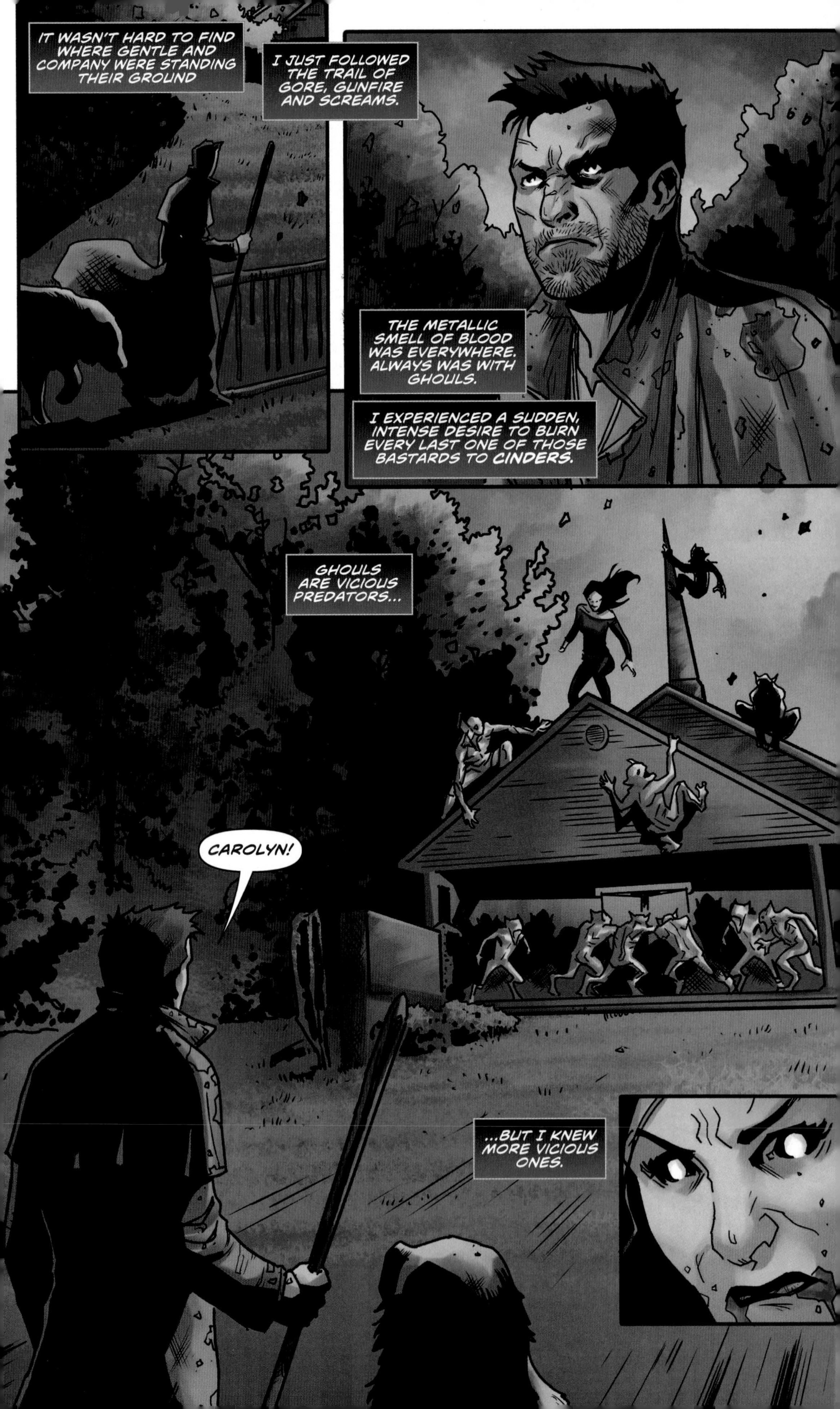
IT WASN'T HARD TO FIND WHERE GENTLE AND COMPANY WERE STANDING THEIR GROUND
I JUST FOLLOWED THE TRAIL OF GORE, GUNFIRE AND SCREAMS.
THE METALLIC SMELL OF BLOOD WAS EVERYWHERE. ALWAYS WAS WITH GHOULS.
I EXPERIENCED A SUDDEN, INTENSE DESIRE TO BURN EVERY LAST ONE OF THOSE BASTARDS TO CINDERS.
GHOULS ARE VICIOUS PREDATORS...
CAROLYN!
...BUT I KNEW MORE VICIOUS ONES.

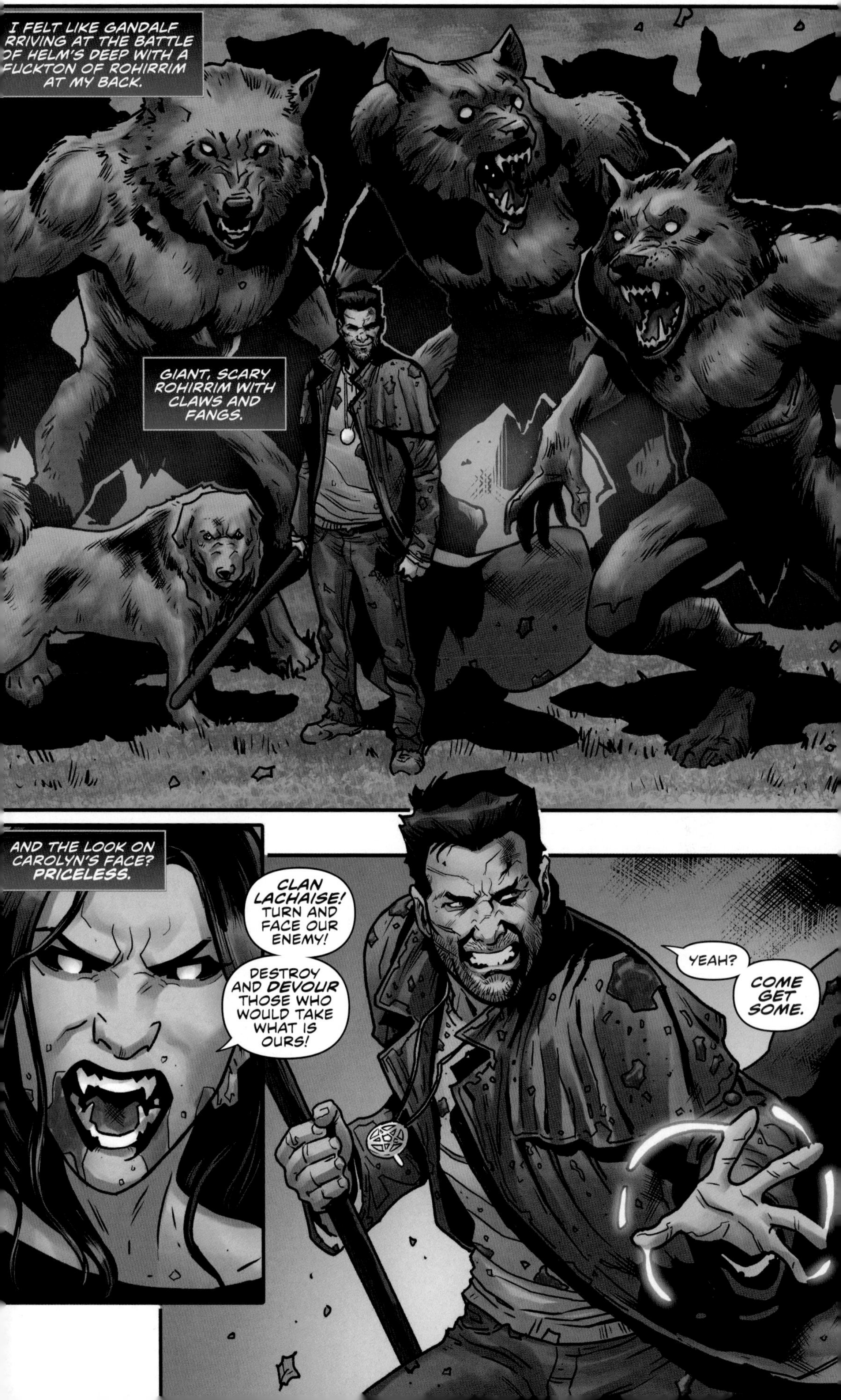
I FELT LIKE GANDALF RRIVING AT THE BATTLE OF HELM'S DEEP WITH A FUCKTON OF ROHIRRIM AT MY BACK.
GIANT, SCARY ROHIRRIM WITH CLAWS AND FANGS.
AND THE LOOK ON CAROLYN'S FACE? PRICELESS.
CLAN LACHAISE! TURN AND FACE OUR ENEMY!
DESTROY AND DEVOUR THOSE WHO WOULD TAKE WHAT IS OURS!
YEAH?
COME GET SOME.

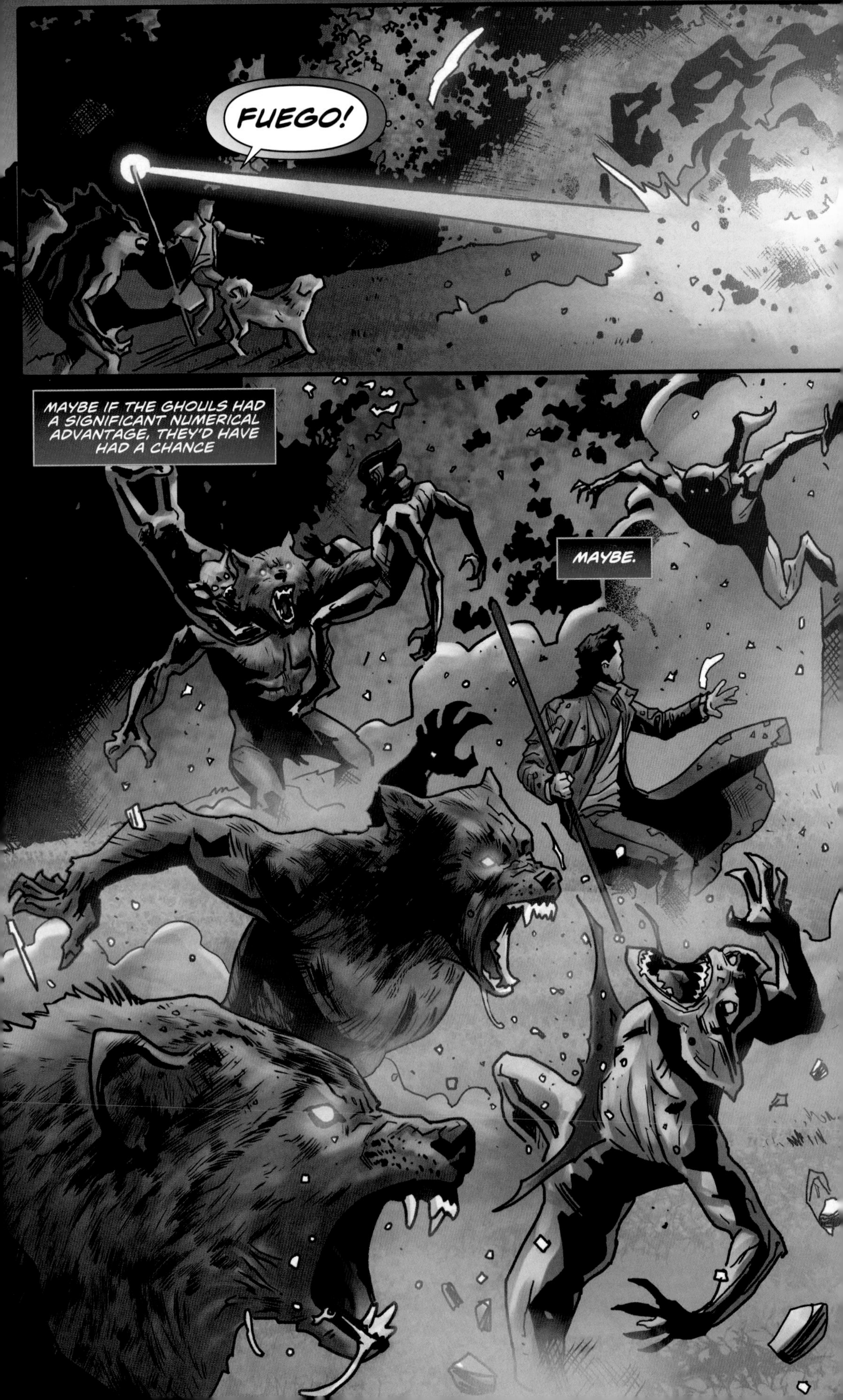
FUEGO!
MAYBE IF THE GHOULS HAD A SIGNIFICANT NUMERICAL ADVANTAGE, THEY'D HAVE HAD A CHANCE
MAYBE.

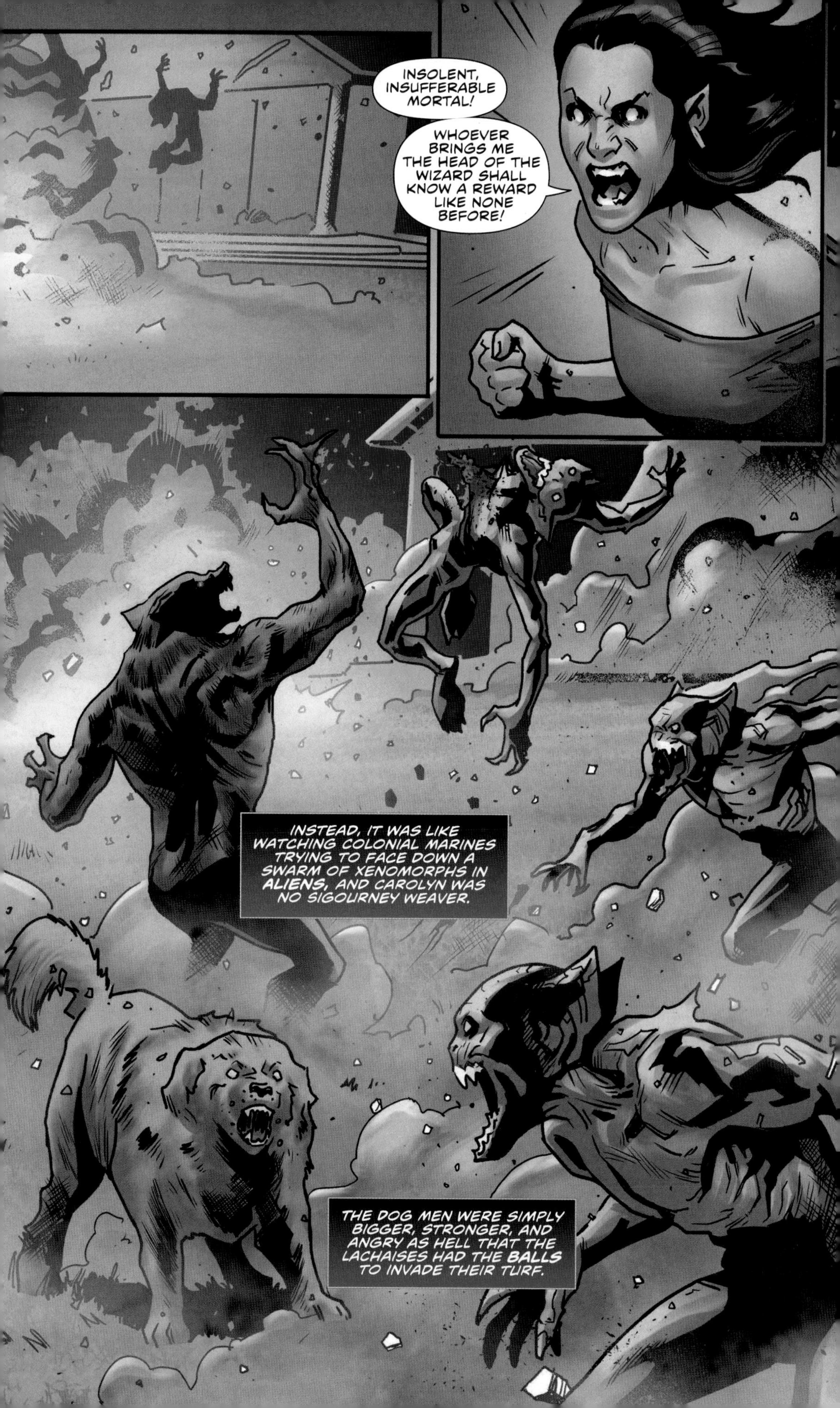
INSOLENT, INSUFFERABLE MORTAL!
WHOEVER BRINGS ME THE HEAD OF THE WIZARD SHALL KNOW A REWARD LIKE NONE BEFORE!
INSTEAD, IT WAS LIKE WATCHING COLONIAL MARINES TRYING TO FACE DOWN A SWARM OF XENOMORPHS IN ALIENS, AND CAROLYN WAS NO SIGOURNEY WEAVER.
THE DOG MEN WERE SIMPLY BIGGER, STRONGER, AND ANGRY AS HELL THAT THE LACHAISES HAD THE BALLS TO INVADE THEIR TURF.

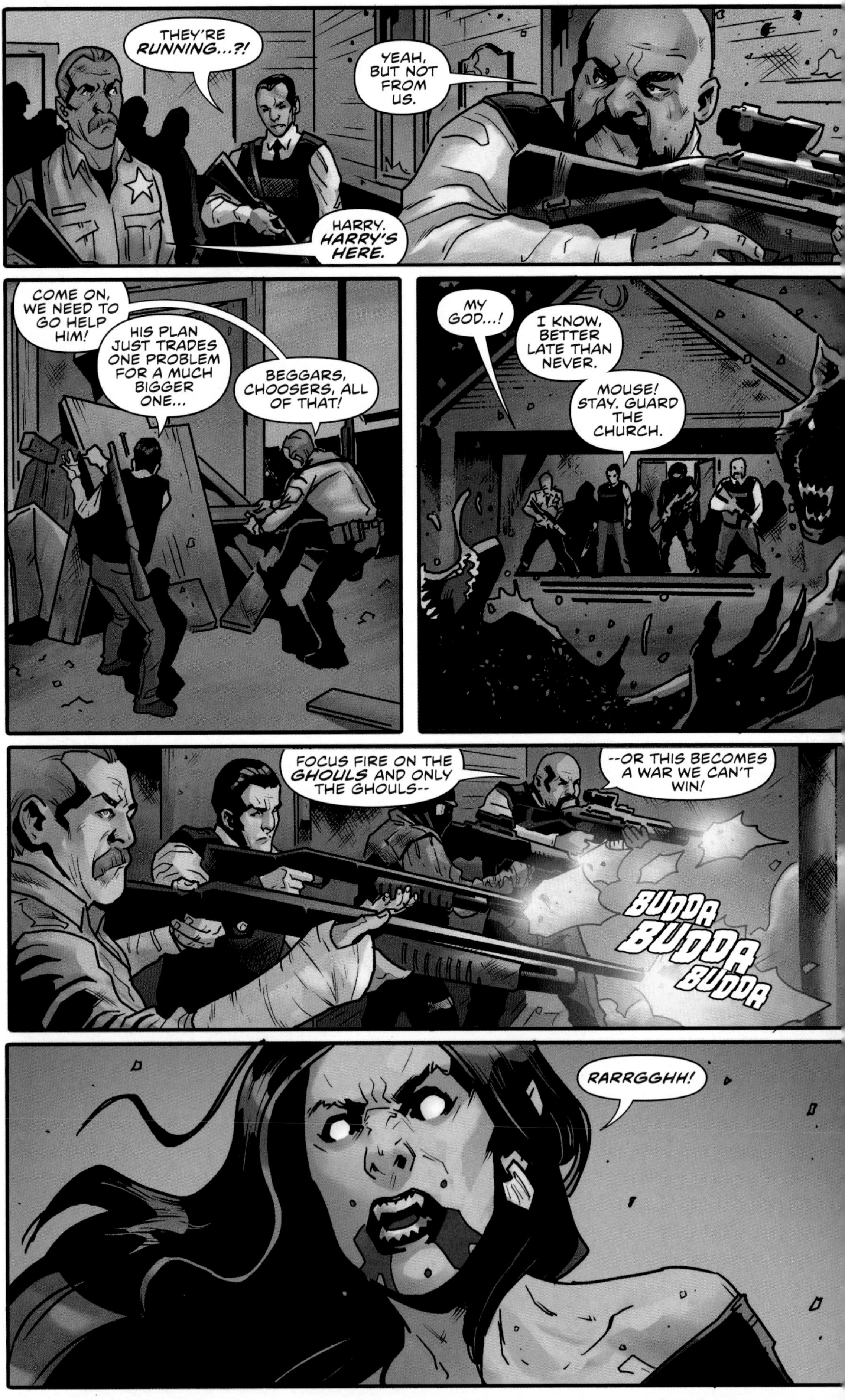
THEY'RE *RUNNING...?!*
YEAH, BUT NOT FROM US.
HARRY. *HARRY'S HERE.*
COME ON, WE NEED TO GO HELP HIM!
HIS PLAN JUST TRADES ONE PROBLEM FOR A MUCH BIGGER ONE...
BEGGARS, CHOOSERS, ALL OF THAT!
MY GOD...!
I KNOW, BETTER LATE THAN NEVER.
MOUSE! STAY. GUARD THE CHURCH.
FOCUS FIRE ON THE *GHOULS* AND ONLY THE GHOULS--
--OR THIS BECOMES A WAR WE CAN'T WIN!
BUDDA BUDDA BUDDA
RARRGGHH!

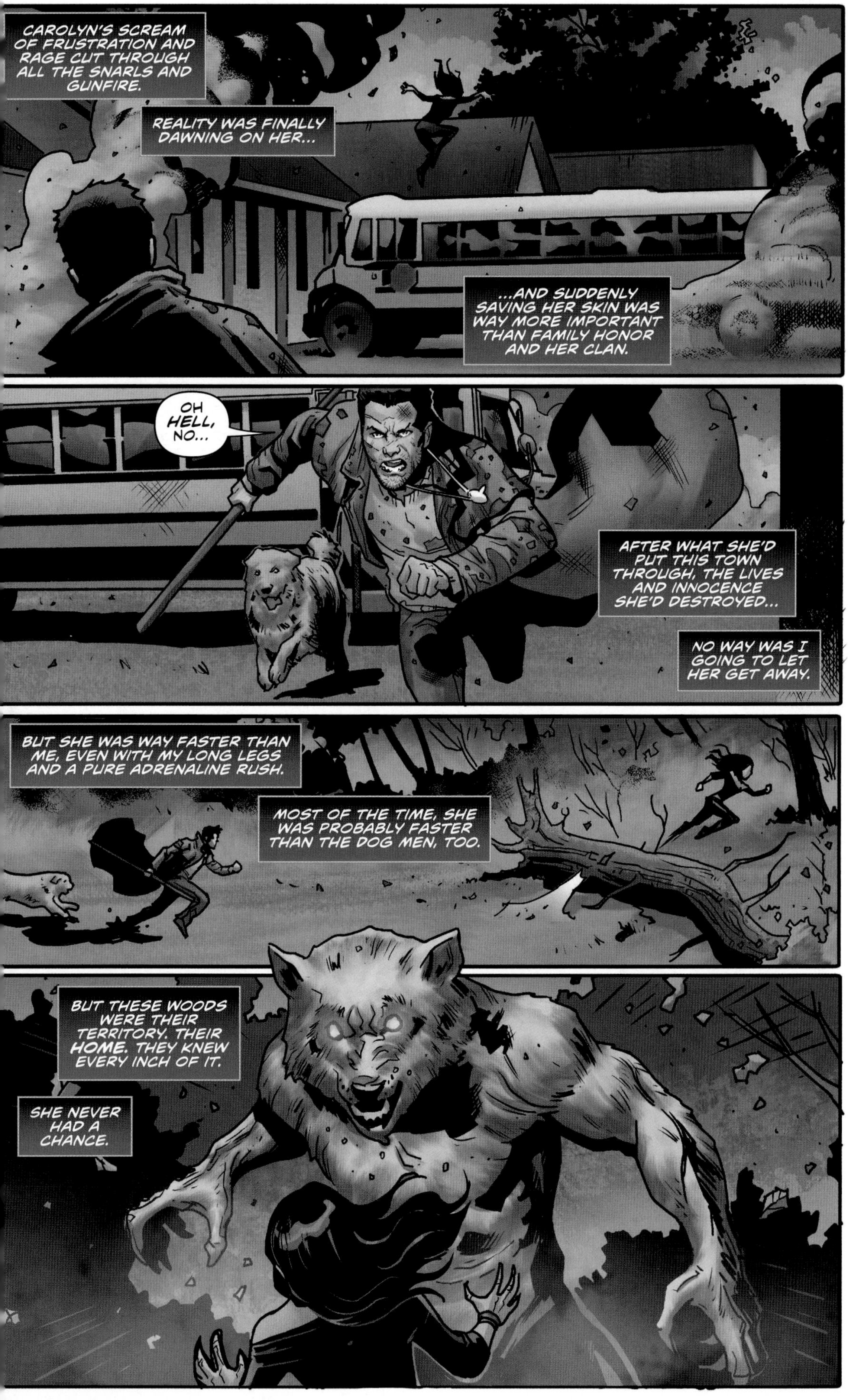

CAROLYN'S SCREAM OF FRUSTRATION AND RAGE CUT THROUGH ALL THE SNARLS AND GUNFIRE.
REALITY WAS FINALLY DAWNING ON HER...
...AND SUDDENLY SAVING HER SKIN WAS WAY MORE IMPORTANT THAN FAMILY HONOR AND HER CLAN.
OH HELL, NO...
AFTER WHAT SHE'D PUT THIS TOWN THROUGH, THE LIVES AND INNOCENCE SHE'D DESTROYED...
NO WAY WAS I GOING TO LET HER GET AWAY.
BUT SHE WAS WAY FASTER THAN ME, EVEN WITH MY LONG LEGS AND A PURE ADRENALINE RUSH.
MOST OF THE TIME, SHE WAS PROBABLY FASTER THAN THE DOG MEN, TOO.
BUT THESE WOODS WERE THEIR TERRITORY. THEIR HOME. THEY KNEW EVERY INCH OF IT.
SHE NEVER HAD A CHANCE.

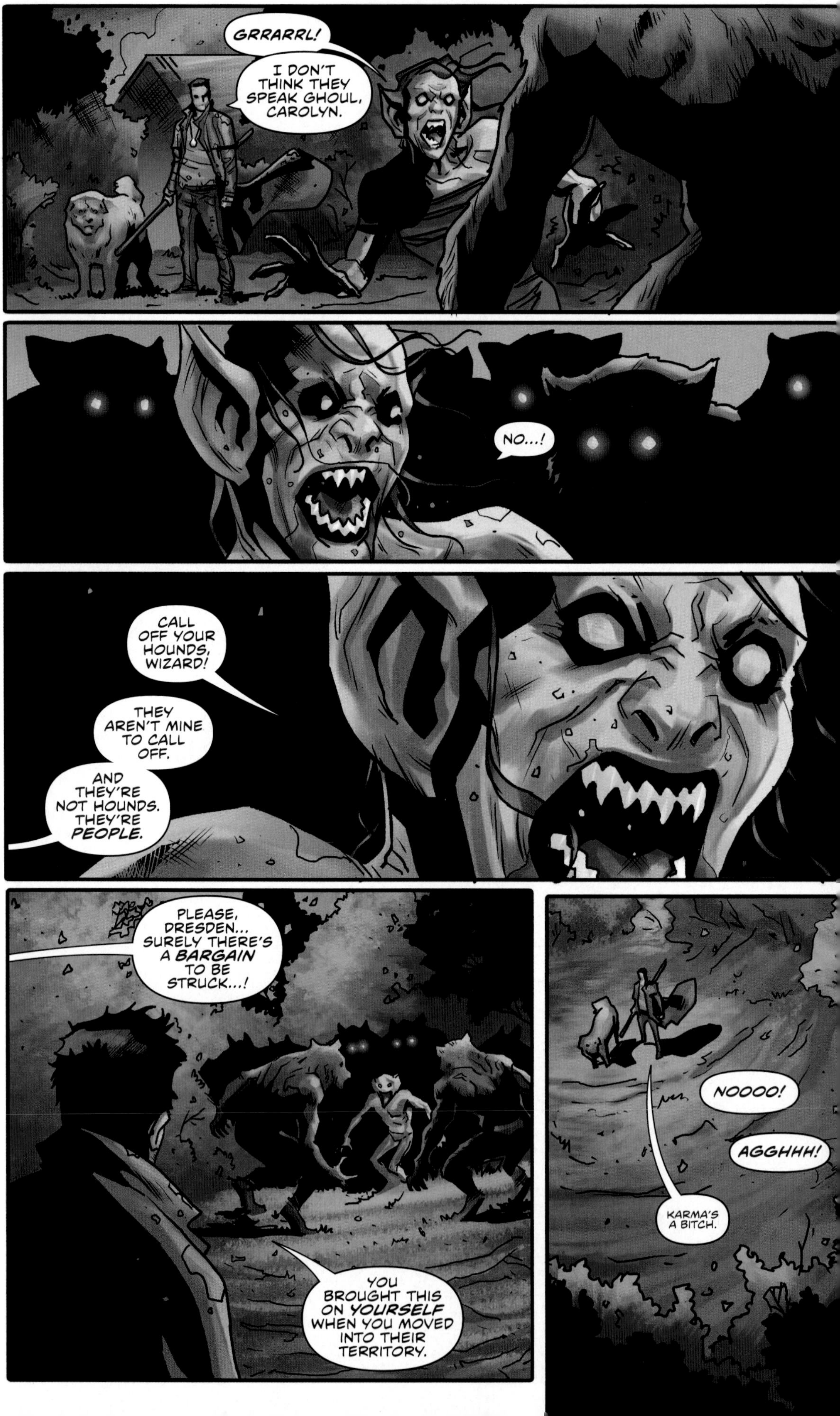
GRRARRL!
I DON'T THINK THEY SPEAK GHOUL, CAROLYN.
NO...!
CALL OFF YOUR HOUNDS, WIZARD!
THEY AREN'T MINE TO CALL OFF.
AND THEY'RE NOT HOUNDS. THEY'RE PEOPLE.
PLEASE, DRESDEN... SURELY THERE'S A BARGAIN TO BE STRUCK...!
YOU BROUGHT THIS ON YOURSELF WHEN YOU MOVED INTO THEIR TERRITORY.
NOOOO!
AGGHHH!
KARMA'S A BITCH.

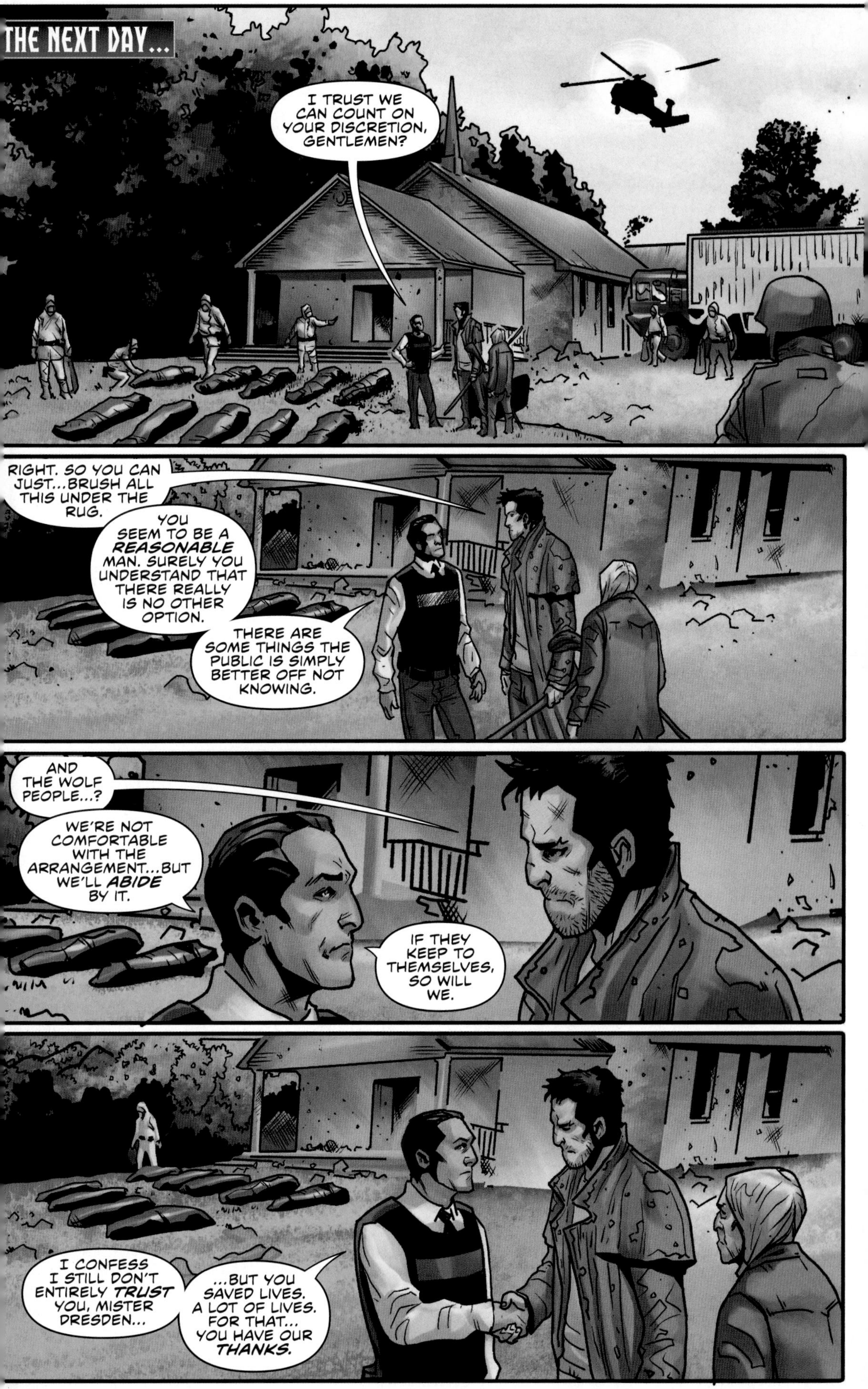
THE NEXT DAY...
I TRUST WE CAN COUNT ON YOUR DISCRETION, GENTLEMEN?
RIGHT. SO YOU CAN JUST...BRUSH ALL THIS UNDER THE RUG.
YOU SEEM TO BE A REASONABLE MAN. SURELY YOU UNDERSTAND THAT THERE REALLY IS NO OTHER OPTION.
THERE ARE SOME THINGS THE PUBLIC IS SIMPLY BETTER OFF NOT KNOWING.
AND THE WOLF PEOPLE...?
WE'RE NOT COMFORTABLE WITH THE ARRANGEMENT...BUT WE'LL ABIDE BY IT.
IF THEY KEEP TO THEMSELVES, SO WILL WE.
I CONFESS I STILL DON'T ENTIRELY TRUST YOU, MISTER DRESDEN...
...BUT YOU SAVED LIVES. A LOT OF LIVES. FOR THAT... YOU HAVE OUR THANKS.

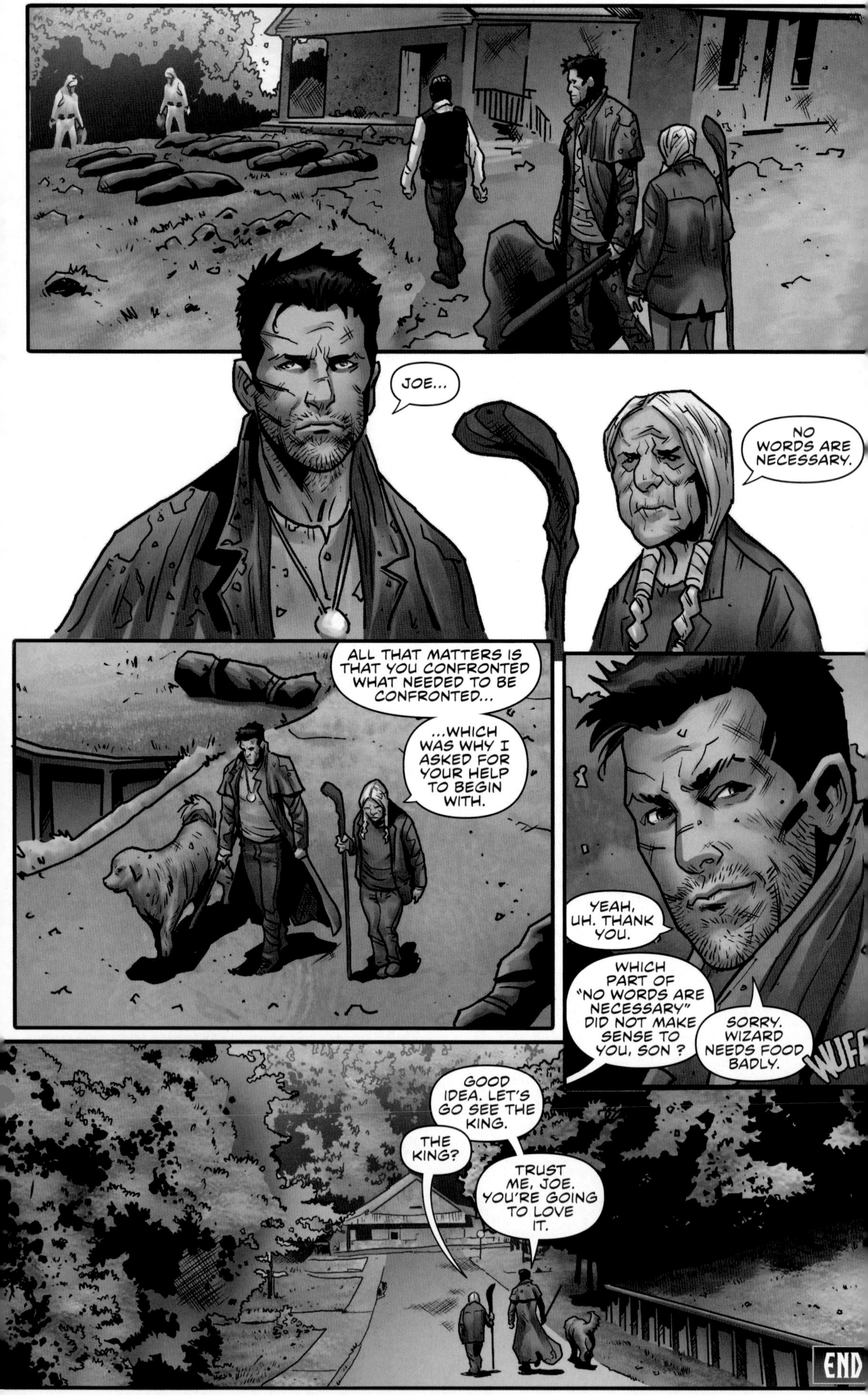
JOE...
NO WORDS ARE NECESSARY.
ALL THAT MATTERS IS THAT YOU CONFRONTED WHAT NEEDED TO BE CONFRONTED...
...WHICH WAS WHY I ASKED FOR YOUR HELP TO BEGIN WITH.
YEAH, UH. THANK YOU.
WHICH PART OF "NO WORDS ARE NECESSARY" DID NOT MAKE SENSE TO YOU, SON ?
SORRY. WIZARD NEEDS FOOD BADLY.
WUFF
GOOD IDEA. LET'S GO SEE THE KING.
THE KING?
TRUST ME, JOE. YOU'RE GOING TO LOVE IT.
END